W9-ARA-605

MORAL REASONING AND TRUTH

Moral Reasoning and Truth

AN ESSAY IN PHILOSOPHY AND JURISPRUDENCE

BY

THOMAS D. PERRY

CLARENDON PRESS · OXFORD
1976

Oxford University Press, Ely House, London W. 1

GLASGOW NEW YORK TORONTO MELBOURNE WELLINGTON
CAPE TOWN IBADAN NAIROBI DAR ES SALAAM LUSAKA ADDIS ABABA
DELHI BOMBAY CALCUTTA MADRAS KARACHI LAHORE DACCA
KUALA LUMPUR SINGAPORE HONG KONG TOKYO

ISBN 0 19 824532 7

PRINTED AND BOUND IN GREAT BRITAIN
BY RICHARD CLAY (THE CHAUCER PRESS) LTD
BUNGAY, SUFFOLK

Preface

THIS is a book about the central question of philosophical ethics: Can moral judgements or statements be justified by rational argument, and if so, how can they? In an attempt to break the deadlock which has existed on this question roughly since R. M. Hare's *Freedom and Reason* (1963), I have worked out an account of moral reasoning and truth which differs, I believe, from all the major 'types of ethical theory' familiar to students of ethics. Naturally I cannot hope that my own elucidation of these two notions will be wholly satisfactory when other people have had but limited success with them. Indeed, I have not attempted a highly rigorous or definitive statement. But I do hope to show that there is an interesting path which recent parties to this ancient debate have overlooked. May others help to explore it by criticizing and developing the ideas presented here.

The deadlock to which I refer is that between Hare's so-called prescriptivism and the attempts of various writers of the fifties and sixties to revive ethical naturalism, often in specific opposition to Hare. I think his first book, *The Language of Morals* (1952), has stood up rather well against their criticisms and counter theories. Yet the result has been a philosophical impasse and not a victory for Hare because his position in that book is, after all, a sceptical one, a position too much at odds with moral common sense for a good philosopher to remain permanently content with it. Hare recognized this when he tried, unsuccessfully in my opinion, to relieve or sweeten the extreme individualism of *The Language of Morals* in his later book. But while the neo-naturalists or 'descriptivists' have plausibly insisted that there *must* be some way to show the truth and falsity of moral claims, they seem to have run out of ideas for finding it now that their once-promising 'practice' analysis has broken down.

My own ideas cannot be usefully sketched in a preface, but I should at least indicate the main direction I plan to take. For a long time, most philosophers have held (and I agree) that one cannot establish the truth of moral statements by attempting to deduce them from true statements of non-moral fact. No such inference can be valid unless we add a premiss stating some moral principle or other moral standard. How then justify the standard? Perhaps by citing more facts and another standard which together imply it; but then we must justify the latter standard, and so on. This procedure must end somewhere, and opinion has been divided between (*a*) individualists like Hare who think one must stop with whatever basic standard or standards one personally prefers and is able to live by, and (*b*) those who hope to exhibit the self-evidence of one or more standards, either by defining moral predicates as equivalent to certain non-moral predicates—the older naturalism criticized by G. E. Moore—or by explaining in some more subtle way how certain standards are essential to morality as such. This more sophisticated naturalism is illustrated in the recent search for 'constitutive rules' of 'moral practices'. Or perhaps I should say that it is found in the *suggestion* that such rules might possibly be identified, a suggestion made plausible by some relatively successful explications of limited, quasi-moral practices like promising. Writers in this vein have not usually spoken of 'ultimate moral premisses' but of 'institutional facts' which are said to have direct 'moral import' from the rules which define the institution or institutions of morality and give sense to the descriptive terms one must use in stating such facts. But their programme, in any case, is to identify standards which are morally unchallengeable because they are constitutive of morality itself.

I intend to argue that, while ethical naturalism in either of these forms is almost certainly mistaken, we do not have to settle for the first opinion stated. We do not have to agree that one can never justify a moral judgement except in the bare and defective sense of showing its consistency with one's own principles. I shall try to explain how one can justify one's judgements in a much stronger sense, and justify them to other people, even though there are no self-evident moral standards to serve as unchallengeable premisses. My explanation will consist of a description of the existing standard of good moral reasoning, and a non-moral validation of that standard—a 'vindication' of it, in the jargon. The standard of reasoning so described will not demand the use of self-evident moral standards, or force us into a regress when we fail to produce them. It will tell us how to complete a moral argument, and no one will be able to reopen the argument by claiming that the alleged standard of good moral reasoning is itself the expression of a moral judgement which remains to be justified.

These are familiar goals in moral philosophy, and any novelty or merit in what I have to say must lie in the way I seek to attain them. A preliminary sketch of that way will be found in the Introduction which follows.

It would be impossible to sort out my debts to everyone whose thoughts have had some influence on what I have written here, but I must mention those to whom I know I am indebted. They include every writer whose work is criticized or otherwise cited, and especially the one who is criticized most extensively, R. M. Hare. I have built explicitly on one of his best known contributions to philosophy, and experienced readers will detect his influence at several places in the book. Charles Frankel, Martin Golding, James J. Walsh, and Robert Paul Wolff commented on my doctoral thesis in this subject some years ago. I benefited from lectures on ethical theory given by Charles Frankel and Sidney Morgenbesser. My colleagues James B. Brady, John Corcoran, Peter H. Hare, and Edward H. Madden commented on various parts of this essay or on papers leading up to it, as did Robert L. Martin and Rolf Sartorius. I am especially grateful to Jesse Kalin for his extensive comments on an earlier version of this book. He will find that I have often changed my mind because of them. In other cases I have included answers to his questions, and I have sometimes adapted an illustration of his to my own purposes. I have also tried to clarify matters in response to questions posed by the anonymous reader for the Clarendon Press. Some of the ideas presented here descend and depart from things I said in 'Moral Autonomy and Reasonableness' (*The Journal of Philosophy*, 1968) and 'Judicial Method and the Concept of Reasoning' (*Ethics*, 1969; reprinted in *The Buffalo Law Review*, 1969, with a response by J. D. Hyman, to whom I am indebted in other ways). I thank the editors of these journals for permission to rework certain sections of those articles. Another article, 'Moral and Judicial Reasoning: A Structural Analogy' (*The Buffalo Law Review*, 1973), uses ilustrations from an earlier draft of Section 6 and Appendix III hereof, and the editors have kindly permitted me to reprint them. Thanks are also due to the State University of New York for faculty research fellowships which enabled me to begin thinking about this project, and for a sabbatical leave during which I completed it. My friend Bob Reis generously helped with the proofreading.

Without the kindness and encouragement of my wife, Pat, I could not have become seriously occupied with philosophy or written this book. I dedicate it to her.

Contents

Introduction

THE dominant ethical theories of the middle third of this century—intuitionism, emotivism, and R. M. Hare's prescriptivism—seem to me to have been generally on the right track, while the revival of naturalism which we have witnessed in recent years is on the wrong track, although there is much to be learned from it. I think we should again reject naturalism and try to take the next step beyond Hare, just as his theory took an important step beyond emotivism, and just as the emotive theory had rightly rejected the mythical side of intuitionism. All three of these theories or tendencies cling to the fundamental insight that no one can make his own moral principles true by definition, even though it is up to each person to form his own moral opinions as best he can. But they are all weak in explaining how moral judgements can be objectively correct, or how they can be shown to be correct through reasoning. Hare's theory is the least inadequate of the three in this respect, but it is still very far from accommodating the assumption which we nearly all make, when not philosophizing, that a great many moral statements *are* true or false and often *can* be justified or refuted. My purpose is to narrow this gap between ethical theory and moral common sense as far as I can, and to do so without resorting to naturalism myself. For it is easy enough to give naturalistic demonstrations of 'moral judgements' if one will only abandon the insight to which I have just referred.

In order to identify the more specific problem with which this book is concerned, I shall begin by briefly explaining why I think Hare has not given a satisfactory account of moral reasoning and remains vulnerable at just those points where his neo-naturalist or 'descriptivist' critics have attacked him. I shall also briefly explain why I think their own theories and suggestions have not succeeded and remain unpromising. Many of these criticisms are already familiar in the literature, and I shall leave their detailed statement to the first two appendices. My purpose here is merely to say, in a reasonably concise way, how I think the main issues have evolved over the past two decades, narrowing down to questions we must now attempt to answer if we hope to move ahead.[1]

In *The Language of Morals,* Hare left himself in the position that inter-personal arguments to validate or justify moral judgements can never be successfully completed because good moral reasoning is only the consistent application of one's own principles. While he later attempted to break out of that position in ways to be noted below, it is not quite clear that he realized in his first book that he was committing himself to it. For there he gave his well known explanation of how one can 'justify a decision completely' through an appeal to principles which need not, in the last analysis, be 'arbitrary'. But he obviously left it open that two people may both non-arbitrarily (i.e. after fully informing themselves) choose different ultimate principles. If they can both give complete and sufficient justifications of their apparently conflicting decisions or judgements by appealing to conflicting ultimate principles, it must be that they are not justifying 'substantial' or 'full-fledged' moral judgements, i.e. evaluations carrying a claim to inter-personal truth or moral validity. They must only be justifying their respective claims to personal moral consistency, i.e. claims to have applied their respective principles correctly to the case at hand. This they can very well do even though their ultimate principles are diametrically opposed.

On the other hand, if Hare did mean to explain how we must reason to support substantial moral judgements, it

[1] Besides indicating how I would back up the following criticisms of Hare and the descriptivists, Appendices I and II will serve to provide a somewhat fuller exposition of the present situation in ethical theory than could be given here without too lengthy a postponement of our main business.

Bibliographical information on most writers discussed in this Introduction is given in those appendices. When a writer mentioned here is not discussed in the appendices, such information will be given in footnotes.

follows from his account that in the sort of situation just described I will be unable to justify my judgement to my interlocutor, who will also be unable to justify his to me. For, according to Hare, anyone is rationally entitled to choose whatever set of principles he likes and is able to live by. Thus, from a purely logical point of view, any self-consistent principle may serve as a moral principle, and any fact at all can be a good moral reason to offer for any judgement at all since we can always formulate a principle (a general evaluative statement) which will enable us to derive the latter from the former. Not only is inter-personal argument always liable to break down for this reason, but Hare does not explain in this book how it can justify a moral conclusion even when people do agree in their ultimate principles. After all, those principles will not have been morally justified; at best they will only have been non-arbitrarily chosen. Moral argument can thus only serve to bring our fundamental agreement to light and show that, logically, we both ought to accept a certain decision or judgement in the light of relevant facts, although perhaps morally we both ought to reject it. Imagine Hitler and Himmler thus resolving their initial disagreement about how to solve the Jewish question.

The problem of validating our moral principles without committing the naturalistic fallacy criticized by Moore,[2] Ayer,[3] and others, had been taken up two years earlier in S. E. Toulmin's book, *An Examination of the Place of Reason in Ethics*.[4] Toulmin sought to explain how a certain rule for good reasoning in morals can be identified, even if substantive principles of morality cannot be true by definition. He held that the function of morality is to regulate people's feelings and behaviour in such a way as to minimize conflict of interests, and hence frustration and pain. He argued that although 'right' does not mean 'minimizes conflict of interests', and although 'the right practice' does not mean 'the

[2] G. E. Moore, *Principia Ethica* (Cambridge Univ. Pr., 1903), Preface and Ch. 1.

[3] A. J. Ayer, *Language, Truth and Logic* (London: Victor Gollancz, 1948), Ch. 6.

[4] Cambridge Univ. Pr., 1950, esp. at p. 224.

practice which would involve the least conflict of interest attainable under the circumstances', it is always a *good reason* why such and such a practice *is* the right one that it does have that characteristic (and a sufficient reason, as the whole argument of Toulmin's book seems to require). If this were correct, it would give us our elusive method of validating moral principles, i.e. statements to the effect that certain practices are morally right. It would also give us our method of constructing complete and sound deductive arguments to certify the truth of particular moral judgements or decisions, at least if the same function of morality would also tell us how to resolve conflicts of valid principles.

There seemed to be two main troubles with Toulmin's suggestion. First, such a rule of good reasoning looks like a substantive moral principle in disguise. It seems to do the same things for us substantially, though not formally, that an ultimate moral principle would do; and it would seem to be open to challenge or exception.[5] Suppose someone wished to deny that a practice which best minimizes conflict of interests is *always* the right practice. It might seem to him that some slightly less efficient practice, among alternate practices being considered for adoption, had greater merit for some other reason. Would this not be a moral judgement on his part? And how would Toulmin refute it? It looks as though Toulmin's rule, or any rule of good reasoning which is designed to take us inescapably from non-moral facts of a certain kind to substantive moral judgements of a certain evaluative content, expresses a moral judgement on the part of the ethical theorist proposing it.[6]

Yet, Toulmin had asserted that his rule is demanded by the very function of morality (or of moral discourse, it wasn't clear). If this were true, the rule presumably would *not* be open to moral challenge or exception. But this brings us to the second trouble, namely, that he offered very little evidence that morality does have such a function. And besides

[5] Cf. R. M. Hare's review in *Phil. Quart.*, vol. 1 (1950–1).

[6] Cf. C. L. Stevenson's 'Relativism and Nonrelativism in the Theory of Value', esp. sec. 7, in his *Facts and Values* (New Haven: Yale Univ. Pr., 1963).

that, it seems a doubtfully coherent idea that the 'function' of morality even could fix its ultimate principle or reasoning rule, call it what you will.[7]

Critics of *The Language of Morals* were soon to take a more manageable, piecemeal approach to the validation of moral principles than Toulmin had taken, or so it seemed at the time. Some of the most interesting work was done by Philippa Foot, who attempted to study specific moral value concepts and show how they might have definite descriptive criteria in virtue of the institutional purpose or point of morality. But this also did not take us very far towards the intended goal of explaining why inter-personal argument in morals need not 'break down' and can accordingly justify moral judgements or statements. It was not shown that morality does have a point or purpose, much less that it has the one Mrs. Foot and other writers seemed to suggest, namely, the promotion of human good and the reduction of harm. Even if we suppose that morality has a *great deal* to do with those objectives—no doubt a safe assumption—this only leaves welfare as one important moral criterion or type of criterion. It does not exclude the possibility, which is intuitively a strong possibility or likelihood, that there are other moral criteria which are independent of welfare considerations. And it does not tell us what relative weight to give to welfare criteria and other criteria when they point to different moral conclusions.

The so-called 'practice' analysis, developed a little later in articles by Rawls, Anscombe, Searle, and others, looked at first like a refinement of Mrs. Foot's programme, just as her work had seemed to bite off smaller pieces of morality for analysis than Toulmin had bitten off. Instead of looking for conceptual ties between descriptive notions and the most general moral value predicates, which is what Mrs. Foot was

[7] Cf. R. B. Brandt, *Ethical Theory* (Englewood Cliffs, N.J.: Prentice-Hall, 1959), pp. 256–8. For another criticism, cf. sec. III and IV of my 'Moral Autonomy and Reasonableness', *Journ. of Phil.*, vol. 65 (1968). That criticism of ethical functionalism still seems correct to me, but I no longer accept the alternative to it which I offered in that paper, preferring sec. 4 of the present book.

doing after all (see Appendix II), one studies individual practices, special moral, and quasi-moral institutions. One tries to spell out clear and definite conceptual relations of the sort that Rawls was first among recent philosophers to identify. The central idea is that statements of 'institutional fact', as distinguished from 'brute fact', have immediate value import without the deductive assistance of principles. They have it because certain descriptive concepts employed in such statements already presuppose an environing practice in which the subject of evaluation occurs (e.g. the breaking of a promise), a practice which will be defined by certain 'constitutive rules' or principles (e.g. that promises are to be kept). While none of the writers just mentioned has claimed to explain the logic of moral reasoning with this device, the thought that it might be used for that purpose, and not merely to validate inferences from descriptive (non-value) facts to evaluative conclusions within separate practices, has obviously been its main attraction.

Next to nothing has been done, however, to explain how such analyses of different practices are to be assembled to give us an analysis of 'moral practice', so that we might know *what* non-moral facts are to have *what* moral significance, and *how much weight* we are to give them against opposing facts. It would seem, moreover, that in order to perform this theoretical feat we would already have to know the *whole* point of morality or moral preference. How else could we tell which practices are morally relevant, and which morally evil? How else could we know what relative weight or moral stringency to assign to 'good' practices when they conflict? It seems that we would have to know *the* supremely general criterion of morality in order to be sure that our judgements in such matters were correct. We would have to carry through the more general approach which Mrs. Foot's arguments actually suggest.[8]

[8] G. J. Warnock has set out on this route in his book, *The Object of Morality* (London: Methuen, 1971). As explained in my review in *Ethics*, vol. 83 (1973), pp. 341–6, I do not think his results are more promising than those of classical authors who tried to do much the same thing.

An interesting supplement to the practice analysis has come from an unexpected quarter in books by D. Z. Phillips and H. O. Mounce, authors of a widely read criticism of Mrs. Foot, and by their former student, R. W. Beardsmore. These writers argue persuasively that certain descriptive terms are learned in the first instance as criteria of moral value by everyone growing up in a cultural group following a given form of moral life. But I think they would admit that this still does not enable us to explain how logically complete and otherwise sound justificative arguments can be constructed. They recognize that people of different societies, or of different cultural strains within the same society, sometimes use mutually conflicting fact-value ties of this sort, even if *some* ties are used by many groups, e.g. the ties between 'lying', 'stealing', 'cheating' on the one hand, and 'wrong' on the other. They also recognize that people of similar heritage and rearing can and do disagree, and are sometimes personally torn, over the relative importance or weight of moral criteria pointing to opposite moral conclusions in a particular case. This not only *seems* to happen quite often, but logically can and does happen because, as these writers point out, we do not learn, as part of our very concepts of right and wrong, how to adjudicate all cases in which moral criteria 'seem' to conflict.

In summary, I think it can be said that the neo-naturalist or descriptivist movement of recent years has taught us many interesting things without showing any sign of reaching the main goal: that of explaining the structure of sound moral argument. It has not explained the validity of 'ultimate principles', nor (if this is anything different) has it explained and systematized the conceptual links between descriptive criteria and predicates of moral evaluation. Thus it has not shown us how to break out of the unsatisfactory position in which we were left by Hare's first book, namely, that each person must finally choose his own principles or moral criteria, and that from a purely logical point of view any principle can be a moral principle, and any fact can be a good moral reason for any judgement or decision. You may simply choose whatever principle will provide the appropriate syllogistic connection, although you must pick one that you will be able to live with, at least temporarily.

An anti-naturalist might try to break this impasse by laying down procedural restrictions on the adoption of moral principles or criteria, saying for example that we may only use principles which we are willing to allow others to use (we must 'universalize' our judgement and reasons), or that we must only judge 'from the moral point of view'. Never completely out of favour, this broadly Kantian approach has recently been emphasized in many books and articles. But if you do lay down such conditions, nothing substantive seems to follow. People can still adopt different and opposing principles even while satisfying these requirements. Moreover, we again have the objection, which emotivists are sure to press, that in imposing such restrictions one only signifies one's allegiance to moral values which other people are rationally free to reject or minimize. How does one *know* that moral principles, reasons, and judgements should only be adopted and given in such a manner?

In his second book, *Freedom and Reason*, Hare does take this approach, but in a way that is designed to avoid or overcome such difficulties, mainly by abstaining from unduly ambitious claims. He admits, or rather insists, that we cannot deduce any substantive principle of morality from the universalization requirement, and he tries to answer the emotivist's objection by showing how that requirement is part of the logic of morals, a condition of coherent moral evaluation and debate, and therefore not open to challenge. Finally and most importantly, he tries to show how the universalization test can provide a practical substitute for the general validation of principles, even though it does not entail the validity or invalidity of any principle.

Retaining the doctrines of his first book, Hare now explicitly holds that any principle can logically be a moral principle. But he plausibly insists that moral argument is not carried on from a purely logical point of view; it is normally influenced by 'inclinations' which we may rightly take into account along with logical considerations. When we point out to our interlocutor what other moral judgements his present judgement commits him to in view of its universalizability and 'prescriptivity', we shall often be able to force him to withdraw it. If he has given a descriptive reason why it is morally all right for him to take a certain action, he has committed himself to a certain principle. And in forcing him to retract such judgement we can force him to agree with us in rejecting that principle and accepting its contradictory.

Hare seems to think that his partly logical, partly psychological, device will almost always work on people who attempt to justify egregiously selfish or harmful actions, provided only (1) they are willing to accept the logical consequences of their judgements and reasons, and (2) they are sufficiently imaginative to put themselves into the shoes of other people who would be affected by their actions. He suggests, moreover, that publicly acceptable principles of a utilitarian sort might possibly be derived (for everyone but a few 'fanatics' who will be immune to the device) by considering how the device would apply in circumstances where three or more people would be affected by various proposed actions, which they would all be asked to judge. But I think there are a number of reasons why, in many moral disagreements, Hare's test would probably fail to produce its intended effect, so that it is not a satisfactory substitute for initial agreement on principles, and also cannot enable us to derive publicly acceptable principles. I shall mention two such reasons.

While satisfying Hare's test, one could always describe one's action and give reasons justifying it in such a way as to guarantee that the shoe never would be on the other foot. Hare tries to avoid this, but I think he fails for reasons noted in Appendix I. And even apart from that, many people will surely be able to accept various entailed judgements that would be disagreeable to their own interests if the shoe were on the other foot, and sometimes they will be able to act on such judgements when the shoe *is* on the other foot, although they need not be able to do the latter in order to pass Hare's test. Indeed, it is easy to think of cases in which we would nearly all be able to accept such entailed judgements, i.e. cases in which it would be *commonly* thought right to treat someone in a way which he would find painful, such as punishing him for wrongdoing, taxing him, or assigning burdensome duties to him. Hare also attempts to avoid this obvious objection, but for reasons given in Appendix I, I think his attempt is misconceived. Now, there are people with 'warped consciences' deviating from common moral opinion, and they may be able to universalize judgements which you or I or Hare would regard as inexcusably selfish or malevolent, just as I can universalize my judgement that it is all right to impose corrective penalties upon my children.

By attempting to explain more fully than in his first book what really is involved in personal moral consistency, Hare has thus tried to show how principles *can* be criticized interpersonally, at least for the purpose of piecemeal debate and perhaps for the purpose of deriving some part of a moral code, some set of principles which would be acceptable to nearly all people if they were strictly consistent in their moral judgements and reasonings. But if he has failed in this project, as I believe he has, then Hare is again left with the baldly paradoxical thesis that each person may rightly accept whatever principles he likes and is able to live by. Accordingly, he would not have managed to explain (and, of course, no one else has explained) how deductively complete and substantively sufficient arguments can be given to justify moral judgements, as distinguished from those judgements which use moral terminology but are conditioned merely on the acceptance of one's own principles.

Such is the problem we shall have to keep in mind when examining the notions of moral reasoning and truth. Our goal is to break this impasse by improving our understanding of moral statements and the type of discourse in which people seek to justify moral statements. In order to make the argument a bit easier to follow, and also to help the reader decide whether he cares to follow it, the following outline may be useful.

I believe Hare himself has enabled us to demonstrate the truth or falsity of value standards which can serve as the evaluative premisses of practical syllogisms. In the middle chapters of *The Language of Morals* he has given us all the ideas we need to construct such demonstrations. In order to show this, I shall attempt in Section 1 to work out an account of objective standards and evaluative truth, using his well known distinctions. I shall also argue that the descriptivists have been attempting to force morality into the mould of an objective standard as thus explained, and that moral evaluation almost certainly will not fit into such a mould. The reason why it will not is that an objective standard (of which there are a great many, in various fields of evaluation) depends on an indisputable purpose of choice which not only generates the criteria of value but serves to resolve all conflicts between them, giving authoritative answers concerning their proper weight and precedence in the evaluation of particular items. There is no good reason to think that one indisputable purpose determines all moral evaluation.

Such a result will deepen our problem. For it can be argued with some plausibility that all valid standards are of this type, or rather that any complete and sufficient argument for a *moral* evaluation would have to be a deductive application of such a standard, since it is not plausible that moral standards owe their truth to any legislative authority, the other obvious model. Our account of objective standards will thus furnish sceptics with a new basis for claiming that moral arguments never are substantively completable, and hence that the evaluations for which we offer them are not rational evaluations. But I think it will also yield an important lesson, and give us an analytical device which can be put to anti-sceptical use later on.

The lesson is that we should now firmly reject reasoning from objective standards as our model or ideal pattern for moral reasoning. The descriptivists, and indeed many earlier ethicists of various teleological persuasions, have had so little success with this model that we are well advised to try something else. In Section 2, I shall therefore attempt to describe moral reasoning as people commonly engage in it, including in the description various commonly recognized requirements of good moral reflection and argument, without succumbing to the temptation to force moral reasoning into that same pattern once again.

Our theory of objective standards and evaluative truth will then be put to a different, constructive use in Sections 3 through 5. I shall attempt to show how evaluations of moral reasoning performances, as distinguished from moral evaluations of actions, motives, persons, etc., can be made and certified as true, even if it be admitted that there are no substantive moral standards which are objective in the sense required, and hence no such thing as moral truth. That is, I shall try to explain how the commonly accepted criteria of reasonableness in moral reflection and argument, spelled out in Section 2, can be explicated and validated as an objective standard, or in other words, how they can be given a non-moral vindication. A person who has satisfied this standard would thus have been morally reasonable, and the moral evaluation which he has thus arrived at and argued for could be said to be a reasonable evaluation for him to make. That his argument satisfying the standard would be a piece of 'rational justification' rather than non-rational 'persuasion', even though it could not certify the truth of his moral judgement, will then be argued at length with the aid of a legal analogy. It will be explained how reasoning which satisfies this standard is similar in many ways to good judicial reasoning in difficult cases. And I shall maintain that the notion of rational justification does properly apply to discourse conforming to this common form or pattern, contrary to certain objections reminiscent of Hume.

If the discussion up to that point is substantially correct, it will have shown how an argument seeking to justify a moral statement can be successfully completed, for it will have explained how the standard of good moral reasoning can be validated in non-moral terms. The emotivist's objection noted above will thus have been overcome, and the other main obstacle apparent in the foregoing discussion will also have been circumvented. That is, we will have rejected the model of deduction from facts and objective standards as our form for justificative argument in morals, and therefore we will not have to assume that moral principles occurring as the general premisses in such deductions must themselves be shown to be true or valid in order to assure a sound argument. How else moral principles will be conceived to function in moral arguments cannot be usefully explained here except to say that they behave somewhat as legal principles behave in legal arguments.

It is an important piece of common sense, however, that moral statements are often true or false, not merely reasonable or unreasonable. Sections 6 and 7 will therefore attempt to explicate the notion of moral truth, preserving it against the doctrine of evaluative truth presented in the first section and provisionally accepted as applicable to morals in the intervening sections. The thesis that the truth of an evaluative statement consists in its entailment by true statements of fact and an objective standard will be rejected as inapplicable to substantive moral evaluation, even though it is applicable to the evaluation of moral reasoning performances and a great many other things. Following a discussion of various moral judgements which would be commonly regarded as true beyond question, we shall present a quite different conception of the basis of moral truth. This conception will be developed and defended by answering a number of objections, and also by pointing out (in Appendix III) an important disanalogy between law and morals regarding the basis of evaluative truth. Again, it is not possible to explain our results in advance. Let it suffice here that in our discussion of moral truth we shall make a number of points similar to those which recent ethical naturalists have made, but we shall not attach the same significance to them because we shall not succumb to naturalism ourselves.

Finally, in Section 8, we shall briefly compare our own account of moral reasoning and truth with several well known ethical theories and types of theory, arguing that it has definite advantages over each of them. I hope it will be clear, in particular, that we have built on the solid parts of Hare's theory and have taken an important step beyond it, somewhat as he improved upon the emotive theory while still agreeing with it on some basic points.

PART I
Moral Reasoning

1. Objective Standards

OFTEN we can determine the truth or falsity of an evaluative statement simply by applying a valid standard to the item which is being evaluated. Philosophers continue to discuss the question whether evaluative statements are ever true or false, possibly because they are still in doubt whether a standard can ever be quite safely valid or indisputable. But there seem to be at least two types of demonstrably valid standards. Let us begin by identifying them, so that we can go on to consider whether moral standards fall into either of these types.

The first type consists of standards laid down by an authoritative lawmaker. Let us suppose that I am a member of the breeders' association and have entered my Airedale in this year's competition. Let us also suppose that the duly selected standards committee has authority under the by-laws to prescribe any criteria they wish for good Airedales, and that they have prescribed such and such criteria. Then, as far as the goodness or badness of my dog is concerned, I shall not be able to challenge the standard thus prescribed. I shall not be able to deny that it is the appropriate standard to use in evaluating my dog in this competition, and I shall not be able to contest the judges' refusal of a ribbon if my dog, by its pertinent characteristics, is neither good nor borderline but clearly a poor specimen according to that standard. True, I may criticize the standard as a poor one, possibly citing facts from the tradition of dog-showing which argue that this committee and its standard ought to be rejected for next year's competition. But while such facts will therefore be germane to various evaluative questions, they will be irrelevant to the proper evaluation of my dog today. For the fact is that this was to be an official evaluation under the association's auspices, and I must admit that the associations's committee did have unrestricted discretion to prescribe the standard it did prescribe.[1]

By using this kind of illustration rather than laws of the state, I mean to by-pass such troublesome questions as whether political legislatures ever have unrestricted discretion, and whether a law which is grossly immoral or unfair can be a valid law in this or that legal system. Of course, it may be that officials who set standards in dog shows and other competitions do not normally have complete discretion either; but those in my illustration do have it. The point is that here we see one way in which it is logically possible for standards to be demonstrably valid. Once certain facts about the institutional origin and use of a standard have been established, facts like those recited in the preceding paragraph, one can no longer rationally challenge its validity and applicability to the particular item being evaluated. The synthetic but mysteriously necessary connection between descriptive and evaluative predicates is not mysterious in this case; it has been effectively provided by legislative fiat.

For that very reason, however, this type of valid standard will not be very helpful in our attempt to understand the validity of moral standards. I suppose a parent or, at least until recently, a Pope, could validly and bindingly prescribe moral standards to children or to the faithful. But we might still wish to ask, and logically could ask, whether the standards prescribed were morally binding in content, not merely whether they had been duly prescribed according to the institutions of the family or the church.[2] After all, a father's declaration that it is wrong to lie or bully smaller children is not what makes it wrong. And it was thought that the Pope could not err in faith and morals because God saved him from error, not because he was the source of moral and re-

[1] Such 'competition examples' come in for brief mention in P. Foot's 'Goodness and Choice', *Proc. Arist. Soc.*, supp. vol. 35 (1961).

[2] Cf. G. J. Warnock in *The Object of Morality* (London: Methuen, 1971), p. 51 f.

ligious truth. Can God himself create moral standards by fiat? Can a theistic moralist use a legislative model to understand the validity of moral standards? It seems that even he will have serious trouble with it, as did Euthyphro in Plato's dialogue. On reflection, even the pious will hesitate to admit that something is right merely because God approves of it, rather than conversely, or that God even could—though he would not—make something right which we all regard as horribly wrong.

The second type of demonstrably valid standard is one which can be placed beyond challenge by showing that the purpose or interest which people have in choosing among items of a certain kind is indisputably so and so, and that this requires such and such good-making or right-making characteristics, as philosophers have sometimes called the criteria for correctly preferring some members of a kind to others. In the most obvious sort of case, the controlling purpose or interest will appear in the functional name of the thing being evaluated: chronometer, glass cutter, family car. This is commonly contrasted in the literature with cases in which there is no definite purpose to be served in preferring one thing of the kind to another, so that criteria can only be set up arbitrarily or whimsically and are binding on no one, as in the case of Hare's cacti.[3] But between these two extremes there are a great many cases in which standards of the present type can also be identified. The controlling purpose or interest in choice may often be sufficiently obvious, even if not from a functional name. Let us consider such a case and use it to underscore the point that a standard may very well be immune to challenge when we have to answer particular value questions, and may yield true answers to those questions, even though for other purposes it is subject to criticism, change, or abolishment. This will be worth doing because the point never comes through clearly in the *locus classicus*, probably because Hare is so concerned to emphasize that standards may be freely adopted and revised to suit our needs.

Consider American football and the question whether

[3] *The Language of Morals*, p. 96 f.

Jones is a good player of that game. The characteristics of a good football player are known intuitively to anyone much interested in the sport, and if occasion demands they can be spelled out fairly clearly and justified by reference to the rules, the methods of play, and of course the purpose of winning games played by those methods and according to those rules. It is definitely decidable whether someone is a good player or not, certainly in clear cases. To take a very clear case, consider a man who tackles and blocks hard and reliably, frequently breaks into the opposing backfield, quickly sees through enemy plays, kicks long punts and field goals, is a fast and elusive ball carrier and pass receiver, and never seems to get injured or too tired to play. Such a man is obviously an extremely good player at many positions, even though he may pass badly and be unimaginative in calling plays, so that he is a poor quarterback. (Hare of course explains how the value terms appearing in such a standard or list of good-making characteristics can be explicated in turn.) Having such a player on one's team will certainly improve one's chances of scoring more points than the opposition. Now, when we are discussing the question whether Jones is a good player, it will be irrelevant for anyone to object to these criteria by appealing to some 'higher' standard under which they might be subject to criticism. Whether there should even be such a game as American football, whether it should be on the calendar of sports for schoolboys, whether the joint-cracking professional games should be carried on television, etc., are all debatable questions. But however we must answer them, it is still a fact that Jones is a good player (or a bad one, or an indifferent one) of that game.

In order to make sure of this, let us try to construct a counter-example using a narrower standard: that of a good quarterback. Suppose our friend Bill at the neighbourhood tavern maintains that quarterback *X*, who does not win many games, is nevertheless better than quarterback *Y*, who usually wins. (They play for the same team against the same opposition, start the same number of games, etc.) In defending this surprising judgement, Bill shows that he is still in love with football as it was played fifty years ago. He tells us that he greatly admires *X* for his deceptive hand-offs, the variety and unpredictability of his plays, his agility and speed as a broken-field runner, his power to inspire team-mates to greater effort. X is indeed superior to Y in all of these respects, and the fact that he passes very weakly and inaccurately doesn't much bother this elder sportsman even though it costs *X*'s team dearly under the present rules and style of play. *X* really is (or would have been) a great quarterback in the ancient mould, and that is the sort of quarterback our friend enjoys watching. It is clear, then, that Bill is not using the criteria that are now commonly used. But who is to say he must? Can't he choose whatever standard he likes in such a matter? And if so, doesn't this show that the statement, '*Y* is the better quarterback', which most people would subscribe to, is neither true nor false?

No, it does not. Once we are all aware that Bill *is* using different criteria, and why, there is nothing left to argue about; or so it would seem. He and we have been using different 'comparison classes', each with its own appropriate criteria. We can all now agree that X would have made the better quarterback fifty years ago, and that *Y* is better in today's game. Both evaluations are perfectly true. It is time to order another round and change the subject.

But now suppose that Bill objects to this solution, and insists that *X* really is the better quarterback because the old rules and style of play were 'better football'. Then we will wonder whether he has understood what was just said. We will ask him politely what he means by 'better football', although this may not be of much help. For, even in the unlikely event that he should succeed in establishing the criteria of good athletic games, and then the criteria of good 'football' games, and then demonstrate to us that football really was better fifty years ago, this won't in the least affect our statement that *Y* is the better quarterback. For what *we* meant to say is that *Y* is the better player at that position in the game played today. It seems that what Bill should go shouting from the housetops after his unexpected demonstration is not that

X is a better quarterback than *Y*, but that the old game was a better game. It would be a poor joke, or perhaps an unhappy sign of age, if he were now to insist that there is an absolute standard for quarterbacking which retains its validity through shifting rules and styles of play, and that X satisfies that standard better than *Y*. There is no such standard, and the proper standard is always ascertainable, in principle, when we are rating players according to their probable success in playing whatever game it is we are talking about. What characteristics are most conducive to success in that game will be a straightforward question of fact, although not an *easy* question when rough criteria must be refined to help us choose among players of established reputation.

There is one thing more that Bill might say in defence of his claim that X is the better quarterback. This final rejoinder may very well be correct, and we should be clear on the point that it cannot affect the truth of the value statement we wish to make, even if it is correct. Suppose that Bill *has* shown, and we all now agree, that old football was better. Are we not then committed to prefer old football, and hence old-style quarterbacks, since old quarterbacking was an integral part of old football? Is it not rational, other things being equal, to prefer old-style quarterbacks and therefore to proclaim that *X* really is better? Of course, we may be forced to admit that other things are not equal in view of the way the leagues are now constituted and managed, and the great difficulty of getting the old game restored. If so, it may be that *Y* is regretfully to be preferred. But is there not a sense in which *X* is the better quarterback, nevertheless, and not just the sense of 'better quarterback in the game as it was played fifty years ago'?

Possibly so. But '*Y* is the better quarterback in the game played today' is still unshakably true. This is because we can identify the criteria of a good quarterback in the game played today and put them beyond challenge by showing that they are in fact demanded by the purpose we have in choosing among quarterbacks as quarterbacks, namely winning, And *Y* clearly satisfies those criteria better than *X* does.

Throughout this book, I shall always refer to standards of this type as objective standards, and I shall reserve the term for them. Not that I wish to suggest that this is the only kind of standard which can be the basis of evaluative truth; indeed, I have already described one other which can be. I merely wish to have a way of referring uniquely to this type, which also does rate such a name since standards of this type *are* demonstrably valid and thus a basis of evaluative truth.

Are moral standards objective in this sense, and therefore valid, even if they are not legislatively valid? The question is important because here we have a decently clear model of evaluative truth which is not immediately or obviously inappropriate to morals. And it gains further interest from the fact that descriptivism, sketched in the Introduction and examined in Appendix II, does tend to interpret morality as if it were one grand objective standard. It begins by looking for fact-value connections or moral criteria, based on purposes of moral preference. But it needs to systematize these criteria, to marshal them under a controlling purpose—some simple objective or closely coherent (rarely inconsistent) set of objectives—if the standard which they together constitute is to be capable of yielding definitely true answers to all or nearly all moral questions. This becomes clear in the way Mrs. Foot must attempt to subordinate 'non-welfare' criteria to 'the' point of morality which she has in mind. It must also be her device for avoiding an uncritical conventionalism in morals (see Appendix II). She must deny that the ties between descriptive and evaluative notions prescribed in, or constituted by various commonly accepted principles are logically sacrosanct. She must hold that they are subject to re-evaluation and restatement in light of the fundamental purpose of moral preference. Similarly, it has been noted in the Introduction and explained in Appendix II how the 'practice' analysis must also suppose that there is a controlling purpose or value underlying all moral institutions if it promises to give us an account of moral reasoning. The several 'practices' would have to be composed into a unified normative system, and it is hard to imagine how else this might plausibly be done except teleologically. In his recent book, Mr. Warnock also recognizes such a need when he joins the perennial quest for 'the' object of morality.

If this quest should finally be successful, it would turn out, as I have suggested, that all of morality (or rather, all sound morality) constitutes one objective standard. But we could still conveniently speak of several objective moral standards; e.g. the standard (the several derived criteria) applicable to actions, and the standard (the several derived criteria) applicable to character traits or habits; similarly, the standards for motives, intentions, persons, and other subjects of moral evaluation—all such criteria and special standards being determined by the fundamental point or object of morality, in the light of relevant non-evaluative matters of fact.

To begin to consider the question whether morality is an objective standard, or consists of objective standards in this way, I shall first mention some reasons why *prima facie* it is not. These are far from conclusive reasons, but I hope they will serve to fix the concept of an objective standard more firmly in our minds and indicate more definitely what sort of considerations will be pertinent in deciding whether morality as we know it will fit into this mould.

The evaluation of people's actions, intentions, character, etc., in moral terms is similar to the evaluation of football players and many other things at least on the point that there are common criteria to which we intuitively appeal in making moral evaluations. But it may well appear that the similarity ends there because moral criteria are open to challenge and debate in a way that well-established criteria in many other types of evaluation are not. That is, one can question their validity even as one attempts to decide particular value questions to which they apply or seem to apply. In debating whether someone has acted as he morally ought to have acted in a certain situation, it would not be irrelevant or a sign of confusion to reject or seek to revise some common moral principle which applies by its terms to that sort of action in that sort of situation. Consider the principle, by now rather commonly accepted, that abortion during the first weeks of pregnancy is morally permissible. In denouncing abortion at any time, or in arguing for abortion on demand even in the final week of pregnancy, the moral eccentric would not be in the logical position of our eccentric football fan. We hear such challenges to common opinion fairly often, and usually with no feeling that the challenger is arguing incoherently or changing the subject, or attacking 'morality itself'. Quite the contrary, it seems that moral evaluation is just the sort of affair in which well accepted principles *may* be disputed. Surely one can make a moral argument in the very attempt to reform popular morality, and there is nothing logically amiss in doing this even while debating particular cases.[4]

In response to this last point, it may be asked whether there cannot also be criticism of *non-moral* standards which are objective or determined by an indisputable purpose. And cannot this criticism occur as part of the immediate evaluative activity, not merely in some external context of evaluation, as when the whole game of football came in for criticism? We may want to question whether the recognized criteria really are justified by that purpose. Is their use or observance really well calculated to achieve that purpose, or do some of them actually conflict with it? An example would be criticism pointing out a lag of 'good medical practice' behind physiological knowledge and newly available techniques. Or it might be desirable to sharpen rather than substantially change the recognized criteria. To rework one of Hare's examples, the rough criteria of good sewage effluent might be obvious enough from well known chemical and epidemiological facts, but the purpose we have in mind in deciding when effluent shall be discharged into public streams and when it shall not might be better served by telling a board of experts to write a detailed standard and inspection procedure. Or, to make a slightly different point,

[4] Granted, it is well to be explicit about it if one means to do both. Cf. S. E. Toulmin, *An Examination of the Place of Reason in Ethics*, (Cambridge Univ. Pr., 1950), pp. 150–2.

varying circumstances will require subtle adjustments in the standard to be applied, and it will be an occasion for criticism that these adjustments have not been properly made. For example, when we are choosing new players for our team the relative importance of the several criteria of a good player may depend in part on what sorts of talent we are now strong or weak in, what style of offence or defence we use, and so on. So it might be argued that although we sometimes do criticize well-recognized *moral* standards when deciding whether and how to apply them to particular cases, this is no proof that such standards are not objective, for we do the same thing with objective non-moral standards.

The point is no doubt correct, but it does not take us very far. In defining an objective standard, I said that such a standard can be placed beyond challenge in the work of evaluating items of a certain kind by showing that it is in fact required by the governing purpose or interest in choosing among items of that kind. The sorts of challenges and criticisms just referred to all pertain to that factual showing, do they not? They may help us determine more reliably or more precisely what standard *is* thus required, but once that question has been answered the standard thereby identified will be immune to challenge. And it would appear, at least superficially, that this point can never be reached in morals. Even if the moral standards commonly recognized by a certain group of people were actually designed and intended by the great majority to further a certain purpose, and were well designed, how would this place any logical shackles on sincere eccentrics or radical critics of popular morality? It seems off-hand that such persons would be well within their rights, logically speaking, to take exception to that purpose and propose others more to their liking. They might even say that the commonly agreed purpose is morally wrong. Most other people would think them arrogant, but they would not be misusing moral language. Indeed, one can easily imagine oneself saying such a thing if one were a member of an exploited minority in a society regulated by standards which coherently and efficiently served the greater happiness of the majority. This verbal intuition is *some* evidence that any purpose which may be alleged to determine all moral principles may itself become the subject of moral evaluation. If it may, then morality is not an objective standard.

But doesn't the criticism of non-moral standards extend at times even to the examination of basic purposes or interests in choice? This might be appropriate, for example, where people have begun to use criteria of value which do follow from certain purposes they seek to further in the choosing activity in question, but where such purposes 'really' are extraneous to that activity. Suppose it became the fashion to seek only giant-like men for our team, or to have only superior students as players, so much the fashion that these criteria became as important to us as the criteria of athletic excellence. (We want to glorify sheer size and strength, or get rid of our reputation as a football university.) Then cases would arise in which a candidate of prodigious size or intellect but slow physical reactions or other athletic deficiencies would be chosen over someone of indifferent size or brains who could actually be of more help to us on the field. A critic of these goings-on could then rightly ask what mere bulk or academic performance have to do with winning, which is after all the purpose to be served in choosing players. True, winning games may not be our only purpose in fielding a team. Other purposes will restrict the class of persons eligible to try out, e.g. to students of our school who are in good standing academically, who have passed a physical examination, and who have released us from personal injury claims. But these other purposes do not include the two just mentioned in parentheses, at least not as fundamental purposes if we intend to retain athletic competition more or less as we have known it. So the critic might well dispute the appropriateness of those purposes and the criteria they generate, even while debating whether a certain candidate should be chosen. And so, it might be objected, the moral debatability of any 'basic purpose' that may be proposed for morality does not show that moral standards cannot be objective in our sense.

Such an argument would be wide of the mark, although

this new variation on our football example will prove useful in a moment. I said at the beginning that we have an objective standard when there is an *indisputable* purpose or interest in choice which the standard appropriately serves. The sort of criticism just referred to would not be directed against such a standard or such a purpose. Rather, it would have the function of identifying one purpose as indisputable while rejecting certain others. In order for the same sort of criticism to occur in morals, it would have to be similarly possible to identify *the* indisputable purpose of moral preference, which *would* then be logically immune to moral evaluation. And any non-moral criticism of that purpose would be irrelevant to the consideration of particular moral questions we may have to answer.

Well, so much for skirmishing. Even if moral preference does not have a dominant purpose which is obvious to everyone, does it nevertheless present us with a logical situation similar to the last variation of our example? Can the essential purpose of morality be revealed by peeling away extraneous and sometimes conflicting purposes which have come to overlay that essential purpose in popular moral thought? Perhaps these extraneous purposes obscure the real point of moral preference more effectively than the imagined fads of giantism or high-gradism might obscure the true purpose of preferring one player to another, so that they create a more difficult problem of explication. Once that point were revealed, criticism of moral principles might properly be made in light of it. This might then explain the intuition that there is nothing logically odd about such criticism.

One possibility to keep in mind, however, is that morality might once have consisted of an objective standard (or a unified set of objective standards) but does so no longer. More exactly, morality as we now have it may not be an objective standard, although it may descend from a partly similar and partly different institution which was. To illustrate the thought, imagine *per impossibile* that the fashion of high-gradism were really to catch on in college football. Then its devotees might soon be unmoved by the plea that it conflicts with 'the very point' of choosing players; and they might be right, depending on how well their own point had become entrenched. Let us suppose that their point is to encourage male students to work hard academically, knowing that practically all of them would like to be on the team. If this purpose became as firmly established as the purpose of winning, many cases could arise in which a candidate would be good by one criterion or set of criteria and poor by another, with no court of appeal. This would not be like the situation we now have, in which conflicts of criteria can in principle be resolved in light of the purpose of winning. We would not have an objective standard then unless we *agreed to eliminate or definitely subordinate* one of these purposes, thus changing the activity from what it was—from what it had actually become—into some quite different activity.

There are several indications that morality may similarly lack a coherent immanent purpose, a single basic objective or rarely inconsistent set of basic objectives, whatever may have been the case with its earlier forms, or with the diverse social norms which have come together from various cultural sources to form morality as we now have it. And here I think we begin to build up a *strong* presumptive case, as lawyers say, even though it may turn out that we can never prove that case conclusively. One such indication is the perennial problem of justice in teleological moral theories. Justice and utility seem to conflict often enough, and a whole line of philosophers have tried without success to show that they do not really conflict because justice derives from utility. Even if we could confidently say that moral preference always serves some ulterior purpose or other, and we cannot even say that (see below), it would not appear that morality has purposive *unity* since it often seems to be morally wrong to sacrifice justice to utility, the most favoured candidate for 'the' purpose.

Another indication is that many other moral principles besides that of justice or fairness do not seem to depend on the purpose of maximizing welfare (though many do), or on any other single purpose. Here one thinks of various religious duties which people also consider moral duties; also duties to one's family, friends, and country; also many special duties attaching to social roles; also certain ideals of personal life and work which give rise to feelings of moral duty; also various standards of sexual behaviour, and notions of obscenity and public decency; and we must not forget the most common example, the duty to keep one's promises. In many of these classifications, no doubt, there are specific rules which promote the welfare of the individual or group in fairly obvious ways. But of other rules this could hardly be said; for example, many dietary laws and other religious taboos, sacred duties of a ceremonial kind, the proscription of deviant sex acts even when harmlessly performed by consenting adults in private, rules against contraception, guilt attaching to masturbation, and so on through a familiar catalogue of sins and crimes which many utilitarians would say cannot be rationally forbidden or blamed.

It is easier to guess than to show that moral principles of this latter group derive from now-forgotten beliefs in the helpfulness or harmfulness of various types of behaviour—helpfulness for hygiene, say, or harmfulness for maintenance of the population against a high death-rate. But even if this were proved to be the case, it of course would not follow that such principles or criteria of right and wrong ought now to serve utilitarian ends or be dropped. To think it does follow is to beg two different questions: whether all moral preference now has one controlling purpose, and what that purpose is.

It not only seems unlikely that we could bring all such common moral notions under one objective or coherent set of objectives, but many of them are widely held to be intrinsically valid, in need of no validation by ulterior purposes, a point to which I alluded a moment ago. This may seem irrational to some philosophers, but then why is it rational to recognize the intrinsic goods which these philosophers recognize, be it pleasure, friendship, aesthetic experience, or whatever? In any case, our business as philosophers is to explicate the purposive structure of morality as we find it, not to reform it to coincide with our own ideals. Or at least that is the only business presently relevant. I do not deny that we are all free to criticize or reject moral principles which seem pointless or harmful if we have adopted utility as the basic purpose of our own normative ethic. But to say that they conflict with, or fail to serve, *the* purpose of morality seems little more than rhetoric in our present state of philosophical knowledge.

Still another indication that morality lacks purpose unity is the fact that anyone is free to propose an ideal to compete with or supersede the objective which moral preference might now be thought to have, or which it might actually have in the minds of the majority. It does not seem to be a linguistic or logical offence to disagree with any *summum bonum* that others may care to embrace or propose. Nietzsche provides a handy illustration in his criticism of utilitarianism and the popular ideal of happiness. It is sometimes suggested that he had his own conception of human nature and human flourishing which merely differed from the English philosophers, so that he was himself a special kind of utilitarian. But even if we accept this, it only illustrates my point in another way. If competing purposes in moral preference are all to be lumped together as the purpose of making life better, then we must acknowledge that men have had irreconcilable notions of what a better life would be like, notions that determine irreconcilable moral criteria.

Finally, there is a more general consideration which seems to underlie and explain many of those already mentioned, if not all of them. The idea that morality is an objective standard in our sense, or consists of several of such standards, seems to be inconsistent with the fundamental claim of personal autonomy in moral judgement. If there were a coherent basic purpose in all moral choice, a purpose which is unchallengeable in the course of moral evaluation and debate, then it would be possible to prove to a person, by a moral argument, that his own most careful and sincere moral opinion about something was wrong. No matter how completely and firmly he had his facts in hand, no matter how impeccably he had applied his principles in the light of those facts, no matter how careful and morally disinterested he had been in selecting those principles or deriving them from the purpose which *he* thinks morality ought to serve, and no matter how outraged he might be by the judgement *we* have derived from 'the' purpose and 'the' principles of morality, he would nevertheless be wrong in disagreeing with us.

Such a result seems offensive and incorrect. If a principle requires a particular judgement or action which strikes us on due reflection as morally wrong, then perhaps we should qualify the principle so as to avoid that result. Or at least we are entitled to ask for an explanation of why this qualification should be disallowed. And we are entitled to judge whether that explanation is morally sufficient or not, even if it purports to invoke 'the' very purpose of morality itself. In short, it seems that each person has the right finally to decide general moral issues for himself, and to answer particular moral questions for himself. An indisputable purpose determining all moral preferences would be an 'infringement' of that 'right'.

This right or claim seems to be of a very special kind. It does not seem to be based on any rule or principle which needs, or could have, a moral justification of its own. Rather, personal autonomy seems to be a moral 'principle' in the sense that it is a presupposition of moral evaluation and discourse—or at least of that type of evaluation which philosophers since Kant and Rousseau have found to be characteristic of modern moral thought and highly puzzling. Of course, personal autonomy would not be presupposed in the moral thinking of people who accept moral rules as valid merely on the ground that they have been laid down by an authority, or passed down from earlier generations. And in some philosophical inquiries it would no doubt beg the question against theological ethics, or perhaps against ethical naturalism, to admit such a presupposition. I am thinking of inquiries which proceed on the assumption that we can hope to demonstrate that there is one supremely general moral principle which is binding on all human individuals and groups, or of inquiries which more intelligibly, if less interestingly, *propose* some such principle for adoption, perhaps through a stipulative definition of basic moral terms. But the present inquiry is one in which we are merely trying to make clearer sense of various features of moral discourse and reasoning as we find people actually engaging in them. In such an inquiry, the presupposition of autonomy will receive whatever philosophical justification it needs if we eventually find (i) that it is indeed a prominent feature of common moral thought, at least when that thought is carried beyond the most simple-minded conventionalism, and (ii) that its recognition does help us understand various other features of moral thought.

I think we have already begun to see the first of those two things. But before proceeding with our inquiry through a 'description' of moral reasoning in Section 2, it may be helpful to point out very briefly how twentieth-century moral philosophy can be seen, in large part, as a reaction to this same basic assumption or structural feature of moral evaluation. I especially have in mind G. E. Moore's famous doctrine of the 'naturalistic fallacy' which has been accepted in principle by three of the four major tendencies in analytical ethics: intuitionism, emotivism, prescriptivism, but not by naturalism. This is the doctrine that we may reject any definition of a value predicate which has been taken as basic to ethics (intrinsic 'good' in Moore's own theory), where the definiens is non-evaluative or 'naturalistic'. We may do so, it is plausibly asserted, without any sense of logical oddness or linguistic error; and this is illustrated in Moore's 'open question'. For any such definiens 'D' which has been offered as the meaning of 'good', it will always be intelligible (not pointless) to ask whether everything whatsoever that is D is also good. This would not be the case if some such definiens really were equivalent in meaning to 'good'. For then the question would mean the same thing as the question, 'Is everything good also good?', and it would be so understood by anyone who already knows both the meaning of 'good' and the meaning of 'D'. Moore suggests that we try this out for all definientia that may have some initial plausibility. And he predicts that the question thus formulated will never seem pointless or self-answering, but will make good sense. Without entering into the exegetical and critical debate on Moore's doctrine which has continued intermittently since he published it in 1903,[5] I only wish to make the following point to those who believe, as I do, that Moore was driving at something true and important. I suggest that the reason why all such naturalistic definitions can be properly rejected is that they are all incompatible with the principle of autonomy. They all seek to generate moral principles which are at once substantial and rationally unchallengeable, and which serve as the basis of all other moral principles. The verbal intuition that all such definitions are incorrect may reflect the fact that the autonomy assumption is so common and basic in the moral thought of many people as to have shaped the meanings of words.

To all appearances then, morality—or at least the morality of autonomous persons—does not consist of an objective standard or a unified set of objective standards. And I think we are entitled to conclude that things probably are as they appear to be, until someone shows otherwise. In light of the foregoing discussions, the burden of proof surely rests with anyone who claims that there *is* a basic, indisputable purpose underlying and determining all moral preferences. The descriptivists would seem to be committed to maintain such a thesis for reasons which we have noted, but they have done very little to substantiate it. So I think we should conclude that, in all probability, the sort of moral theory which they have been driving at is really beyond reach.

Now, someone may wish to object that, although it may seem unlikely that morality is an objective standard or consists of such, this *must* be so if we are to escape the counter-intuitive thesis that each person may choose whatever moral criteria he likes. But which of these two implausible theses are we to accept? A sceptic will say that morality is basically

[5] *Principia Ethica* (Cambridge Univ. Pr.).

incoherent. Thus, we believe that some moral judgements are true and others are false, and this seems to demand that morality be an objective standard or consist of such, because we can safely reject the notion that moral standards and criteria are *legislatively* valid. But we also insist on personal autonomy, which seems to lead to an irreducible variety of moral criteria that people sincerely embrace and use. If morality is to be coherent, the sceptic will say, we must either eliminate personal autonomy in any strong sense, or drop the notion of moral objectivity. And the result of this radical surgery will not be morality as we know it, but something quite different.

I think we should reject this conclusion and continue to look for *some* objective basis for moral principles and judgements, even if not in the model of objective standards of moral value. But it will be salutary not to underestimate the strength of the sceptic's position. Let us pause for a moment to develop it.

It will be said against the sceptic that even if there are no objective standards in morality, this shows at most that it is impossible to *demonstrate* moral statements. How would it follow that they can never be true? Surely it will not be maintained that proofs are possible in every field of thought in which we comfortably speak of truth, as we do, for example, when referring to highly confirmed scientific theories. Scientific theories are commonly said to *be* true or false, and the process of reasoning by which some of them have been shown overwhelmingly to be true is not that of deducing them from established truths. Why should such an extreme requirement be laid down for the truth of moral statements?

The sceptic's answer will be that moral statements are a species of evaluative statements, and that our discussion has made it highly plausible that the truth of evaluative statements, at all events, *does* consist in their entailment by certain other true statements, namely, statements of non-evaluative facts and valid standards. There is no need for the implausible assumption that truth is *always* a function of deductive entailment; nor is the sceptic merely *assuming* that moral truth is. The theory of objective standards, spelled out above as a theorem of the value theory developed by R. M. Hare and other recent philosophers, *seems* to be the one decently clear account of evaluative truth which has even an outside chance of explaining the notion of moral truth. What it apparently means for a particular evaluation to be correct against all contrary evaluations is that it is entailed by the facts of the case in conjunction with a self-consistent standard which is assuredly the correct standard to apply to that sort of case. So if we have a type of evaluative statement for which those conditions never are fulfilled, statements of this type cannot be true. Neither can they be false, i.e. contrary to some statement which is thus entailed.

While I am not going to surrender either moral objectivity or personal autonomy, I think the sceptic's argument and the discussion which preceded it do make it rather clear that the model of objective standards must now be firmly rejected as we continue to look for an acceptable account of moral reasoning. For the remainder of Part 1, I shall assume that there is no way to show that moral statements are true, since neither model of evaluative truth which we have identified is suitable for morals. I shall look for a means by which interpersonal arguments to *justify* moral statements can be successfully completed even if their truth or falsity cannot be shown.

2. A Description of Moral Reasoning

LET us now attempt to describe moral reasoning in a way that does not force it into the mould of the deductive application of demonstrably valid principles or standards. Let us resist the tendency to do so, and hence the tendency to assume that a moral argument can never be complete until the principles it invokes *have* been demonstrated. Our description will cover *reflection* on moral questions as well as *argument* in support of one's answers to such questions. We may begin by noticing several criteria of reasonable reflection which are commonly recognized by people who know how to engage in moral reflection and discourse—not, of course, that they always manage to satisfy these criteria.

Several procedural requirements for making up one's mind reasonably on a moral question have often been collected under the philosophers' rubric, 'the moral point of view'. Thus, we ought to take full account of the facts that are relevant to the question; and we should form our judgement or make our decision when we are in a psychologically normal state; and that judgement or decision should be disinterested, i.e. impartial and universalizable. Whether an ideal satisfaction of these requirements would be a sufficient sign of the *truth* of the resulting judgement is of course doubtful; but that is not our present concern. It is widely recognized, in any case, that this is the morally responsible way to make up one's mind. Now, the statement of these requirements bristles with ideas that philosophers have found problematic: *relevant* facts, a *full* account, a *normal* state, an *impartial* and *universalizable* judgement. But let us try to understand these several requirements in as simple and direct a way as we can, assuming as we go along that it is possible to satisfy them, and therefore always preferring that interpretation of moral reflection which would permit their satisfaction.

TAKING FULL ACCOUNT OF RELEVANT FACTS

What facts are relevant to a moral problem? And how does one know when one has covered all of them? Let us discuss these two questions in that order. It seems clear that the relevance of a non-moral fact to a moral judgement depends at least in part on some rule or principle. The fact that a particular action, say, has a certain non-moral characteristic will be logically independent of the statement 'That action is wrong' except in connection with some principle which, together with the facts, entails the quoted statement or some contrary statement.[1] Hence, moral reflection constantly involves an appeal to principles, although often enough in vague or ambiguous ways. A certain fact may seem worth considering because it is connected by one or more readily imaginable principles to the moral question before us. Not, of course, that just *any* principle providing the logical connection will do. The moral relevance of a fact will depend on the *plausibility* of the principle invoked. A bit of dialogue reported or imagined by Stevenson[2] can be used to illustrate how principles are tacitly invoked and may be defended as plausible. (It is obviously an example of moral reflection rather than justificative argument.)

A: The proposed tax bill is on the whole very bad.

B: I know little about it, but have been inclined to favour it on the ground that higher taxes are preferable to further borrowing.

[1] In such an entailment, the principle is of course stated in general form, rather than as one criterion among others, i.e. with a *ceteris paribus* reservation. It is not suggested that such an entailment is the basic form of justificative argument, but only one necessary condition of the relevance of a fact for moral reflection.

[2] *Ethics and Language* (New Haven: Yale Univ. Pr., 1944), p. 118.

A: It provides for a sales-tax on a number of necessities, and reduces income-tax exemption to an incredibly low figure.

B: I had not realized that. I must study the bill, and perhaps I shall agree with you in opposing it.

B first suggests (not very strongly) that it is a good bill, and he is appealing rather explicitly to some such principles as that lesser evils are to be preferred to greater, and that in fiscal and economic circumstances like the present ones higher taxes are a lesser evil than borrowing. Such principles are of course challengeable. At least the second one is; the first is perhaps tautologous. In order to defend the second principle, one presumably would try to show that although higher taxes are unpleasant and would sacrifice certain interests, they would have less undesirable consequences of this or that sort, in view of the present conditions of taxation and public debt, than further borrowing would have. This in turn could be disputed. Is a certain consequence bad or not? Is it worse than some other one? And so on. But there is little doubt that this principle which has been appealed to by *B* is worth considering.

Similarly, *A*'s second statement probably appeals to some such principle as that a tax placing a great burden on the poor is a bad tax, and it relies on the tacit factual premiss that a tax containing the provisions mentioned would place such a burden on the poor. This principle might be defended by showing that it is a special case of some other, more widely accepted principle, such as the principle that giving burdens to those least able to bear them is undesirable, unfair. The latter principle could also be controverted, at least in its present application; and so on. But again, there can be little doubt that the principle appealed to by *A* is plausible or worth considering. If we were asked to say in general terms what this plausibility consists in, I suppose we could only answer that these are principles which have to be paid attention to in moral thought because many people are known to accept them, or because they reflect interests which various people do have, whether they realize it or not. This would seem to be enough to show their relevance for moral reflection, without having to demonstrate their 'validity' in some manner.

Notice that we have a two-way street here. Principles determine the relevance of facts, but facts also help to pick out relevant principles. If a fact strikes us as plainly relevant to the evaluation of an action or course of conduct, we may stop and reflect on how it is relevant, to what evaluative result it tends. In answering and generalizing our answer, as we apparently must, we will spell out a principle. This principle will probably seem plausible, the fact having seemed plainly relevant, but it may happen that in spelling it out we will come to realize that it is not plausible as a *moral* principle. Hence, the fact will no longer seem relevant, at least not in the same way. For example, the fact that Jones often tries to humiliate people he thinks are unable to retaliate is morally relevant to a judgement of his character because it is wrong to make others suffer merely for our own amusement or ego-inflation. Is it also relevant to the question whether his victim would be morally right in trying to make *him* suffer? Plainly yes; but how? Unless we accept the principle that vengeance is morally right, it would not be relevant to the justification of the latter action but only to its mitigation.

It is worth noticing here that the practice analysis which is discussed in the Introduction and Appendix II would seem to account for a good deal of this plausibility phenomenon, but not all of it. Descriptions which are unique to certain practices, and are obviously value-laden therein, will seem relevant to anyone who knows of such practices. They will strike one as something one may have to consider even if one does not take part in those practices, or even approve of them. And many descriptions connected with evaluations even in a less obvious way within practices one is intimately acquainted with will also have intuitive significance. But if we may judge from the foregoing examples, not every intuitively relevant fact or description can be placed within some definite practice where it has necessary evaluative force.

To turn now to our second question, is there any way to

identify all plausible principles relevant to a given subject of moral evaluation, so that a review of all the relevant facts can be made? It seems very doubtful that this can be done. In a great many cases at least, there could hardly be an exhaustive survey of principles relevant to the action, motive, person, institution, law, or whatever it is we are judging in moral terms. The principles which are relevant to the subject may not be only those which easily come to mind. A large number of other principles could sometimes be generated by many interests, needs, customs, maxims, feelings, and so on, touching the subject. Nevertheless, it seems that 'taking full account of the relevant facts', understood as a major requirement of reasonable moral reflection, would mean 'taking a reasonably complete account'. It would not require an examination of every fact relevant under any principle that could possibly be regarded as plausible after a perfectly exhaustive inquiry, whatever that might mean. A reasonably complete account would no doubt include all kinds of facts which informed people know are commonly regarded as relevant to the sort of moral question that is being considered. And it would also include other facts the relevance of which reasonable inquiry would reveal, especially facts that would be relevant under principles suggested by the needs and interests of people affected by the subject of judgement. What sort of inquiry, and how much of it, is 'reasonable' inquiry will no doubt depend on the difficulty and importance of the evaluation which we have to make. 'Reasonable' is here a value term which seems to be connected to a vague but commonly recognized standard. It seems that people often know how to apply this standard in clear cases, and perhaps they can apply it well enough for most practical purposes.

Granted that we are well informed or have made reasonable inquiry, how are we to tell which plausible principles are to be accepted and applied, and which are to be rejected? And what is to be the correct priority for applying them when they conflict? First of all, it seems obvious that there is no correct list and strict hierarchy of principles—none, certainly, which careful moral reflection will inevitably reveal or settle upon. Nor is there any need to try to work out such a hierarchy if our business in reflecting on a particular problem is to judge that case as carefully as we can, rather than to produce a conclusive demonstration. And that does seem to be our usual purpose when reflecting on real moral problems. We may believe that many or most problems do have a true solution, but I think most morally reflective people will have scant faith in their ability to construct such demonstrations in matters of any real difficulty, even if they should happen to be philosophers with a favourite moral theory ready to hand. So I think the extensive and perhaps endless inquiries which loom when we think of constructing a valid system of valid moral principles may safely be neglected. Nevertheless, in reflecting on a moral problem one does have to decide for oneself and for that problem what the most salient facts and principles are, and how they determine its solution. Here are one or two ideas on how this seems to be done.

A principle which is relevant in the minimal sense that it picks out facts which have to be considered might not *finally* be accepted as relevant in making up one's mind. We might find that we are unable to accept that principle on due reflection, although we had to consider it. Or it may be that we do regard it as morally sound but find it to be outweighed by other fact-principle combinations in the circumstances of the particular problem. In other words, in arriving at our judgement we may not accept the evaluative tendency which some initially relevant fact has from its principle; or we may allow it that tendency but feel that its effect is overcome by other facts in the case. The latter sort of decision or 'intuition' has been much discussed in ethics, but the former is also common enough, as the following statement will serve to illustrate: 'I admit that the proposed school district would promote greater intimacy between the races. But it would help to lessen the educational disadvantages now borne by the minority race. Moreover, the whole ideal of racial exclusiveness is bad for the very reason, among others, that it perpetuates these disadvantages.' In judging the proposed school district, both principle 1 (that intimacy between the races should be avoided) and principle 2 (that a minority race should not be placed at an educational disadvantage, and any existing disadvantages should be removed) are initially taken into account. But then facts the relevance of which depends on principle 2 are cited for the rejection of principle 1. With the rejection of principle 1, we deny the relevance of facts which depend on it for their relevance.

JUDGING DISINTERESTEDLY, IN A NORMAL STATE OF MIND

How one makes the sort of decisions we have just been discussing can obviously be affected by the psychological state one happens to be in, so it is a requirement of good moral decision making that our condition be a normal one. This means, among other things, that one must not be very tired, depressed, or mentally ill; one must not be drunk, overcome with grief, or wildly excited. This list of abnormal states could no doubt be extended to considerable length, and a complete list or sufficient negative test of psychological normality could hardly be given. But we seem to know well enough for practical purposes what we mean by a psychological condition that would be an abnormal one for judging responsibly in morals.

As I said before, I am using the phrase 'a disinterested judgement' to mean a judgement which is impartial and capable of being universalized. An impartial judgement is one which does not 'respect persons'; that is, the author of the judgement must be prepared to make the same judgement concerning the subject of evaluation no matter what person or persons it might involve, relevant facts remaining unchanged. And a judgement is universalizable if its author believes that it is the proper judgement for anyone on any occasion to make concerning the same subject, or other subjects similar to it in all relevant respects. As so many writers on ethics have pointed out, these seem to be essential features of a moral judgement. A person who expresses an evaluation in characteristically moral terms takes responsibility for judging in this way. If he does not intend to be impartial or to make a judgement that others might equally well make in similar circumstances, he misuses language and deceives others by expressing himself in this way—although, as we shall illustrate shortly, it is perfectly possible to *attempt* to make a disinterested judgement and fail.

These requirements have proved troublesome to philosophers because it is difficult to say when two cases or situations or objects are 'the same in all relevant respects'. No two cases are ever the same in all respects, and which respects are the relevant ones may be thought to present a moral problem in itself. But the foregoing account of moral reflection seems to provide a solution to this. Those facts about the subject of our judgement which seem to us to have significant weight under principles which we have finally regarded as morally sound would constitute the 'relevant respects' referred to in the impartiality and universalizability requirements. We must be prepared to make the same judgement in all cases having *such* general features, and no *other* features sincerely judged to be of sufficient countervailing weight. And we must be prepared to concede that anyone else may and should make the same judgement in other such cases even though we ourselves would be adversely affected by such a judgement in such cases.

This reading of the universalization test differs from R. M. Hare's easily trivialized requirement (see Appendix I) since the relevant characterizations of one's act and circumstances are simply those which one sincerely regards as morally significant. If we were to amend his universalization argument to incorporate our test, I think that argument would become roughly equivalent to the standard of reasonableness which we are here describing. More precisely, Hare's argument would become a special application of that standard, using it to test evaluations which someone suspects are self-serving and not universalizable. This can be seen from the fact that, along with his own formal, non-intuitive criterion of relevance in description, Hare requires that we be well informed of the facts about the action which we have said is morally right, especially about its probable consequences, and that we be imaginatively attentive to its impact on others, as seen from their point of view.[3] It should be noticed here that, in accepting a purely intuitive test of relevance, we might be accused of relapsing into a form of emotivism. The accusation would be that the universalization requirement merely attempts to 'redirect attitudes' through such questions as 'How would you like it if that were done to you?' and 'Wouldn't you think it wrong if someone did that to you?'—there being no *logical* requirement that anyone should attend to such an appeal, especially in view of the fact that no one need accept any particular description of 'that' action. But by the end of Part I, I hope to show that there *is* a logical requirement that one attend to such appeals, and attend to them under a particular description of the action, namely, a statement of its qualities and relations which one would admit are morally relevant if one were sincere. Or at least I hope to show that an interesting argument to this effect can be mounted.

Let us now consider how the requirements which we have mentioned would operate in one fairly detailed illustration. The illustration concerns a kind of moral problem which readers of this book are likely to encounter more than once during their professional lives. For easy reference, I shall list and number various aspects of the subject of evaluation (a certain action) and of the circumstances in which someone is called upon to evaluate it.

(1) Mr. Smith is serving as admissions officer of a college which has many more qualified applicants for next year's freshman class than it can accept.

(2) In reviewing young Jones's application, Smith finds that while (*a*) Jones could probably succeed at most colleges (*b*) his academic record falls somewhat below the ordinary minimum standard for admission to Smith's college, and (*c*) there is nothing in the available information

[3] In the concluding section, I shall return to this point and the one immediately following.

about Jones to suggest that his grades in school are not a reliable index of his ability and promise.

(3) Smith has the discretion to admit a small number of students whose previous academic achievement falls below the standard, if he thinks there is good reason to do so in the individual case.

(4) Smith knows that Jones will probably not be able to attend any college next year if he is not admitted to Smith's college. This is because it is the only college in the town where Jones lives, and Jones lacks the funds to go away to other colleges where he would be accepted.

(5) Jones happens to be the son of Smith's friend.

(6) Smith believes that it is improper for a college admissions officer to be influenced in his decisions by considerations of friendship.

(7) Smith admits Jones on the basis of reasons 2(*a*) and 4.

(8) It is also a fact (which could be confirmed by reviewing Smith's written dispositions of many previous cases) that if Jones had been a complete stranger to Smith, Smith would not have admitted him but would have evaluated his application somewhat as follows: 'It's too bad that Jones cannot afford to go away, and it is just possible that he would be successful here. But his grades really are too low considering the reputation of the school he comes from, and he doesn't seem to have any of the other promising qualities one looks for in a doubtful applicant. Perhaps he could work and save money next year and go away the following year; or he might even contrive to go away and support himself at college next year with a part-time job. All in all, it is better not to exclude some fully qualified applicant by accepting Jones.'

(9) Smith is not aware of (8).

We see that Smith's judgement is not impartial because he would not have been prepared to make the same judgement regardless of the identity of the applicant, even though the facts which he regards as relevant, namely (1) through (4), were unchanged. But Smith's judgement is presumbly universalizable in view of (6) and (9). He apparently does believe that it is the proper judgement for anyone to make in a situation where facts like (1) through (4) obtain. We should notice that Smith's partiality consists in allowing the relative weight of relevant principles and facts to vary with the identity of the applicant. When the applicant is the son of his friend, facts 2 (*a*) and (4) are dominant in conjunction with a plausible principle, viz. that young people willing and able to pursue higher education should have the chance to do so. Otherwise, he subordinates them to facts 1, 2(*b*), 2(*c*), and plausible principles indicating *their* relevance, e.g. that one should not undermine academic standards when deciding hard cases, and that one should be fair to all applicants. Either way, Jones can make out an apparently good case for his biased decisions, whether to his colleagues or to himself.

MORAL ARGUMENT

Can we learn something about justificative reasoning from the foregoing description of reasonable reflection? If we hold on to the conviction that it is somehow possible to justify a moral judgement, what pattern of justification will be suggested (I do not say proved or established) by our account of moral reflection? It seems to me that there are lessons to be drawn concerning (1) the moral acceptability and priority of principles, (2) the proper way to argue for a moral judgement, and (3) the sense in which we will sometimes be able to 'justify' our judgements.

First, it seems to be impossible to *demonstrate* the validity of our principles and their relative weight or priority. But are we not *justified* in accepting and applying certain principles when answering a particular moral question, namely, those principles which *seem* valid to us for answering that question when we have really satisfied the foregoing requirements of reasonableness? And may the same not be said for the priority we assign to them? Seeing that there are no demonstrably correct priorities, we would surely be justified in giving principles such relative weight as seems right to us when reflecting as one ought to reflect on a moral question.

Second, what argument should we offer to others in support of our answer, our moral judgement? Should it not be that very dialectic of facts and principles which has determined our judgement? In relatively easy questions, a mere statement of the salient facts would no doubt suffice as the reasons for our judgement. But in more complex cases we should probably add our reasons for thinking that such and such facts and related principles are more important than others, and for rejecting certain facts as irrelevant which some people might regard as relevant. The further considerations thus appealed to might consist of more facts and principles, or they might simply record our own sense of the relative 'importance' of various facts, or of what 'fairness' or 'good sense' seem to require.

It seems that we should always give that argument which we really regard as the correct one, not just any argument that arranges relevant facts and principles in such a way as to entail the judgement we want to defend. Otherwise we could construct such an argument to 'justify' a judgement we privately regard as morally incorrect. And even if we did defend our sincere judgement but offered an *argument* other than the one we sincerely regard as correct (motives for doing so are easily imagined), it seems that, strictly speaking, we would be violating the rules of *moral* reasoning. To be sure, if we are convinced that a certain moral judgement is correct and are anxious that our interlocutor should agree with it, we may wish to deploy all plausible arguments we can think of, hoping that he will be convinced by at least one of them. But to do this without telling him which argument we regard as best is not to adhere strictly to the standard of good moral reasoning, although it could be a morally defensible thing to do in some circumstances. The circumstances may make it more important that we get him to agree than that we engage in moral reasoning with him, just as it is sometimes better not to engage in rational discourse at all but to employ emotional appeals, or to stop talking altogether and act.

Third, if we reflect and argue in the ways described, will we not succeed in justifying our judgement? It should be noticed (1) that *we* will be justified in *holding* that judgement, at least if we have made no errors of fact or deductive reasoning. Could anyone be *more* justified in holding a moral opinion than one who has formed his opinion and is prepared to defend it in this way? It would seem not, at least if demonstrations from demonstrably valid principles are out of the question. And (2), our judgement itself may also be said to be justified in a derivative sense, namely, that it is a particular judgement of a particular person who is justified in making it, whether or not other people who reflect in the moral way on the same question would arrive at this same judgement. (Presumably they will tend to do so.) Then (3), there is a closely related sense in which our judgement will have been justified when we have *argued* for it in the manner described above. We will have given an objective justification for it by offering factual reasons and principles arranged in an argument that has been constructed in what seems to be the most objective way in which a moral argument could possibly be constructed. Of course, our argument will in no sense be a proof which our interlocutor must accept on pain of being morally irrational.[4] It will simply be an invitation to him to consider the question under discussion in the moral way himself and see whether he will find such an argument convincing, and so accept the moral statement which stands as its conclusion.

EXPLANATION AND ILLUSTRATION

Such a conception of moral reasoning is a good deal more promising than may appear at first glance if one is addicted to the model of deduction from demonstrably valid principles.

[4] This is as good a place as any to underscore the point that I am concerned throughout with the requirements of moral reasoning and rationality, not with the ancient question whether we ought, rationally, to be moral at all or to engage in moral reasoning.

To show this, I shall briefly consider a number of objections which will probably be made to it, saving the most fundamental objection for last.

1. My recital of the requirements of good reflection and argument may have given the impression that every moral question requires extensive research and prolonged reflection. This would be a serious defect; for while some moral questions do demand patient study, many others do not. Our account matches up just as easily, however, with common modes of reflection and talk on simpler matters, as I think the following illustrations will show.

Suppose a man makes a promise to do something and then fails or refuses to do it. If that were a description of all the relevant facts, anyone would say that the man ought to keep his promise, or that it is wrong of him not to keep it. Obviously, this is because we accept the principle that it is wrong to break one's promises; and it would normally be superfluous to mention this principle. But suppose the man is ill, and that it would cause him distress or risk aggravating his illness if he were to do what he promised, let us say to read a paper to some academic group. Then almost anyone would hold that it is all right for him to break his promise, because we recognize the exception that one may break one's promise (or at least promises of that sort) in order to protect one's health. Indeed, one ought to protect one's health. Thus we have one plausible fact-and-principle combination outweighing another. But how are we to know that these are all the facts which need to be considered? A little familiarity with the man and his circumstances, and with the promisee and his circumstances, might well give us practical assurance that no other facts will be salient or of important weight. For instance, we may learn that the promisee, the chairman of the group, is having trouble getting another speaker on short notice. Or it may be pointed out to us that the promisor will now be able to spend the day at home with his family. If only facts of this 'order of weight' can be adduced, we may well conclude that they will not affect our judgement either way. All we will need to say is that the man's failure is not wrong because, although he promised to read a paper, he cannot, for medical reasons. Here we have an acknowledgement of a countervailing fact, both relevant principles remaining tacit. On the basis of all the factual inquiry which the question could be held to require if we were to be reasonably well informed of the facts, our judgement would be eminently reasonable and justified. Obviously it would be no less reasonable if, by some unlikely series of coincidences which no one could have been expected to anticipate or inquire into, his going to read the paper would have resulted in some great good to many other people and only small discomfort to himself. Thus a limit to inquiry is possible under our account, just as one would ordinarily assume.

Let us add a few more facts that might influence one's judgement in view of other principles. Suppose the man decides that it is his duty to speak to the group, a science convention, in spite of a very grave illness. He thinks he has made an important discovery, but he is now too weak to prepare an adequate report of it. He fears that this may be his only chance to disclose it informally to competent people. Then one might well agree with him that he ought to do what he promised, although now it is not the promise itself but something else which is the basis of his duty. At least such a judgement on *his* part would be justified, given his dedication to science. But his wife, although fully aware of these circumstances, concludes that it is by no means his duty. She feels that he should try to prolong his life by avoiding this severe tax on his strength, hoping to make his disclosure at a later date. Assuming that she is as disinterested as she is well informed about her husband's problem, her judgement is justified. Thus contrary judgements may both be justified.

2. The last point reminds us again that there is no way to demonstrate the truth of a moral judgement according to this account. But is it not common sense that very often there is only one moral judgement which could possibly be correct or acceptable in answer to a given question? Yes it is, but one

can see fairly easily how our account is compatible with this and even helps to explain it. First of all, there are various reasons why people *typically* will be in substantive moral agreement if they faithfully observe the procedural requirements of moral rationality which I have described. The common moral tradition in which they have been raised will have given them a similar sense of what is relevant and important, while the two greatest sources of disagreement will have been eliminated: ignorance and selfishness.

Secondly, while there are subjects of moral judgement (as in the foregoing example) on which equally informed and disinterested people may disagree, there are many others on which this is practically impossible psychologically, even though it is not logically excluded. On the question of whether Hitler's slaughter of Jews and Gipsies was wrong, it is scarcely imaginable that *anyone* could actually satisfy the above requirements of good reflection and judgement making but fail to conclude that it was wrong. And in many everyday judgements people will automatically and tacitly agree on the controlling proximate principle, so that agreement is assured once the facts are ascertained. Citing such facts and principle will then constitute justification in our sense, provided the salient facts are few and obvious, and the parties to the discussion are considering the matter disinterestedly. Thus, if Jones and Smith both think a certain principle is morally valid and wouldn't dream of challenging it (e.g. that it is wrong, *ceteris paribus*, to torture stray cats), it would be silly to maintain that, having once proved that it *was* Mary who mistreated the cat and intentionally made it suffer, Jones had not fully justified his judgement (that Mary acted wickedly today) because he had not justified the principle. But this is because we can safely assume in this case that both parties *are* looking at things in the morally reasonable way. That Jones has justified his judgement of Mary's action does *not* follow from the mere fact that a principle which requires his judgement when applied to such facts has been *left unchallenged*. Nor does it follow from the mere fact that Jones and Smith both *subscribe* (in any way at all or for any motives at all) to a principle which requires such a judgement in the absence of countervailing facts.

While our interpretation of moral reasoning can save the phenomena of moral common sense on the point discussed by referring to the 'psychological necessities' obtaining in many cases, I had better give equal emphasis to the logical situation if I am not to be misunderstood. While the parties to an ethical debate who follow our method of reflection and argument may ordinarily be expected to reach agreement, there is nothing in the method itself which obliges them to do so, or guarantees that they will in fact do so. Thus, to take an extreme sort of case for illustration, suppose two parties to a moral debate are responding, in effect, to exactly the same array of facts and principles (it would be extreme to say that they will necessarily do so if they are both judging reasonably). And suppose further that they accept and reject just the same principles (which is certainly not required). Even so, their resulting judgements could conflict because of their differing assignments of weight or priority to the principles accepted.

3. Let us turn to the last and most important objection. Cannot someone's judgement be justified according to this account and still be wholly objectionable in content? The logical situation just noted would seem to show that this is entirely possible. But how could a moral judgement which is obviously wrong be 'justified'? Doesn't this show that our interpretation of this notion is inappropriate for moral discourse?

My answer is that if we find someone making a moral judgement which is 'obviously wrong', there are two points that we ought to bear in mind. (1) We are not really entitled to say that he is wrong unless *we* could satisfy requirements at least roughly similar to those which I have set forth. This seems to follow from the meaning and normal use of 'morally wrong'. We would not be justified in using this phrase to make a snap judgement in disagreement with that person, even if we could deduce our judgement from known facts and principles which we have clung to all our lives (say, in a selfishly belligerent way). We would need to have considered the subject of his judgement in the morally reasonable way before we would be justified in rejecting his judgement in such terms, and this in itself is a strong point in favour of the foregoing interpretation. (2) It may be that the person has not considered the matter that way himself. It might be possible to determine whether he has, and he poses no theoretical problem if he has not. But if he has, and if we have also, then we will certainly regard him as a very eccentric person—unless we happen to be the eccentric ones, and know it! To say that his judgement is 'obviously' wrong, however, only seems to assume that our own opinion is the absolute standard. Or at least it assumes that there exists some method of certifying moral judgements as uniquely correct, and that its results are, or would be, the opinion which we prefer. But there is no warrant for the first assumption, and the second is guesswork. If a person had formed his moral opinion in the morally reasonable way, it would be quite unreasonable for anyone who knew this to say that it was an absurd or outrageous opinion. Indeed, the latter person would have a new reason to reconsider his rejection of it. The more we use this method, the more likely it is that our substantive evaluations will tend towards agreement, and no other method of forming and testing our moral judgements would seem quite so likely to have such a tendency. Moreover, when people do arrive at contrary results there is a very good chance that they will retain some degree of mutual respect and understanding if each knows that the other has made up his mind in this way. Indeed, there will probably be a better chance of that occurring than in almost any other situation one could imagine.

Let us consider a difficult example, one involving a moral judgement which 'we' (the writer and readers of this book) would no doubt consider definitely wrong if we reflected on it properly, but which some other people might adopt after *they* had satisfied the criteria of reasonableness. It seems quite possible that some people born and raised in the United

States, especially in the South, could disinterestedly and in full awareness of relevant facts and the interests of everyone concerned, judge that racial segregation ought to be preserved, and that it is morally wrong to require or permit desegregation. (Of course I do not believe that the *millions* who still favour segregation have reached, or could have reached, this position via our method.) Now, much as one might regret that anyone should hold such a view, especially a disinterested and informed person, I think it would be quite unreasonable to say that he is substantively wrong and 'obviously' so. It would be unreasonable because there does not seem to be a single fact or inference of any kind that one could advance to show that he is wrong. All we could say is that a careful examination of the salient facts and principles leads us to make a judgement contrary to his. We might well be amazed that he could persist in his attitude while actually viewing the question disinterestedly and in full awareness of the interests and desires of everyone concerned, and of the effects of racial segregation as they are now estimated by competent students, and of all other plainly relevant facts. But notice that even in such a case ethical disagreement does not necessarily end in a blank wall of mutual hostility. For despite one's amazement and disappointment, one could not have utter contempt for someone who was willing to test his moral opinions in the way I have described. One might regret that our civilization has been such as to produce this kind of civilized person (one with such opinions), but civilized he would be in an important and desirable way.

If anyone should insist that such a person's judgement is reasonably held but nevertheless incorrect, I can only ask him to produce a way of showing that it is incorrect. Until such a method is given, the best we might hope to show (and I think it would be a slim hope) is that in fact no one *could* arrive at or retain that judgement if he satisfied the standard of reasonableness which I have described. But we shall return to the notion of moral truth in Part II.

3. The Point of Moral Reasoning

I SAID in the Introduction that I intended to argue that the standard which has now been described is an objective standard and therefore valid and immune to challenge when we are engaged in evaluating the things to which it applies, i.e. pieces of moral reflection and justificative argument, or in short, moral reasoning performances. If I manage to establish this, it will then be clear that anyone who has satisfied this standard can safely and conclusively appeal to it in order to show that he has reasoned well in justifying a moral statement. By proceeding in this way, I shall attempt to overcome the following major objection.

'One may choose to accept the standard just described if one wishes, and one may recommend it to others or remonstrate with them for failing to satisfy it in their moral reasoning. But they are equally free to reject it. They are free not merely in the sense that they are able psychologically to reject it, or in the sense that they are rationally free to abstain from moral discourse altogether. They are also free in the sense that they are not obliged to accept this standard for moral reasoning itself. From the fact that people who engage in moral reasoning *do* commonly pay lip service to this standard, or even attempt to satisfy it, we cannot infer that they *ought* to do so. To prescribe the standard which has been described in Section 2 is to announce a moral judgement. This is made doubly obvious by the peculiarly moral character of the standard itself. It does not merely lay down norms of rationality like logical consistency and respect for evidence; it goes on to express moral ideals that everyone does not hold. To use a handy if overworked phrase, they are the special ideals of Western liberal morality. Liberals may think it desirable that moral evaluations should be made calmly, on the basis of full information, universalizably, etc., and that only reasons tested in this kind of reflection should be presented in moral argument. Perhaps they are as well entitled to hold this opinion as anyone else might be to reject it. But it *is* a moral opinion, as debatable as any other, and supportable in the end by persuasion merely, not by logically sound arguments. It also seems to have a boot-strap illogic all its own. For, in order to justify this moral prescription, it seems that liberals would have to invoke the very standard which they are thus prescribing to us.'

In addressing ourselves to this objection, the first question we have to consider is whether there is some basic, unchallengeable purpose in choosing among moral reasoning performances—saying that some are good and others are bad—and whether that purpose requires the commonly recognized standard, i.e. the several criteria described in the preceding section. It should be noticed that this question is clearly different from the one I have already answered in the negative, i.e. the question whether there is a basic, unchallengeable purpose in choosing among actions, intentions, persons, etc., saying that some are morally right and others morally wrong, etc. To put this another way, the question (A) whether there is some fundamental objective which we necessarily seek to achieve in evaluating moral reasoning performances, is different from the question (B) whether there is some fundamental objective which we necessarily seek to achieve in our substantive moral preferences.

The present section will be mainly occupied with question (A), but I should point out at once that it will not take us all the way to our goal even if we show that there is such an objective and hence that the standard described in the preceding section is an objective standard. For it still may be asked whether the reasoning performances, so-called, which satisfy that standard and are accordingly good, may rightly be said to *justify* the moral statements for which they are made or given. Reasons for doubting that this is so will be noted at the end of this section and dealt with in Sections 4 and 5.

If we glance back at the discussion of objective standards in Section 1 and consider the arguments given there, I think we can see that it is at least logically possible that there should be such a definitive purpose in choosing among moral reasoning performances (other than the obvious purpose of 'justifying' moral statements, the very notion we are attempting to elucidate throughout Part I.)[1] For if our purpose in choosing among items of this kind were well understood by practically everyone who has occasion to make such choices, then it would not make sense to challenge or object to that purpose while considering whether a certain specimen is good or bad. We might object to it in some other context, e.g. while considering whether moral reasoning as we know it should be radically changed or abolished, but not in the context of judging whether a certain piece of reasoning is good. For good moral reasoning would be, precisely, reasoning which furthers that purpose. A good family car is one that would enable us to get our family about safely, comfortably, and economically; whether a car is likely to do this will depend on whether it has certain physical characteristics, which we accordingly take as the criteria of a good family car. Similarly, a good moral reasoning performance would be one that would enable us to achieve a certain purpose, and whether a piece of reasoning would be likely to do so would depend on whether it had certain characteristics, which would accordingly be the criteria of good moral reasoning.

Before proceeding, let us add two points in clarification of the above, and stipulate two points of verbal usage. (1) We can say that a new Chevrolet Bel Air (the type) is a good family car, and also that *this* new Chevrolet Bel Air is a good family car. Can we say, similarly, that a certain type of reflection-plus-argument is good, and that *this* performance by Jones of that type is good? Yes, but we must be careful to avoid an equivocation. It might be objected that here the

[1] See the next to last paragraph of this section.

'type' is really the standard, but this is not what is meant. We can say that a certain type of reflection and argument about some moral question is good because it satisfies the standard, and also that *this* performance of that type (this piece of reflection and argument by Jones on that question on this occasion) is good for the same reason. (2) A particular car can be a good family car even if it does not enable Jones to get his family about safely, comfortably, and economically, because of something peculiar to Jones and his family. Similarly, a particular moral reasoning performance can be a good one even though it does not enable Jones on that occasion to accomplish the normal purpose we have in choosing among moral reasoning performances, because of something peculiar to Jones or his interlocutor, or their relationship. (3) The word 'objective', used as a substantive, can mean both the purpose of bringing about some state of affairs, and the state of affairs itself. I shall use it in the latter sense only, reserving the word 'purpose' to express the former. Thus I frequently speak of the purpose (singular) of jointly achieving two or more objectives. (4) I also use the phrase 'purpose in choice' as a useful bit of jargon to refer to the normal purpose or interest which determines the criteria of an objective standard. The more natural sounding phrase 'purpose of choice' might be taken to mean the actual purpose someone has in preferring one item of a kind to another on a particular occasion, and this may or may not be the purpose or interest which people normally have in making such choices. I trust that the need for these clarifications and stipulations will eventually become apparent, and the reader may find it useful to refer back to them.

I was saying that it is at least logically possible that there should be a definitive purpose in choosing among moral reasoning performances. But would such an unchallengeable purpose be compatible with the fundamental 'right' or claim to personal autonomy in moral judgement? I took the position in Section 1 that an unchallengeable purpose for all *moral* choice would be inconsistent with the principle of autonomy, and this point seemed to underlie several other reasons why morality does not constitute an objective standard. But do we not 'reserve the right' to form our own moral opinions about anything whatsoever that logically admits of being morally evaluated? We cannot morally evaluate an earthquake or the behaviour of rats, but can we not morally evaluate human institutions and their purposes? It would be an infringement of our autonomy, then, to be told that the purpose which people commonly have in preferring some pieces of moral reasoning to others (supposing they had such a purpose) cannot be morally evaluated but must simply be accepted.

Such an argument would surely be unsound. Reserving the right to reject the purpose which practically everyone has in choosing among moral reasoning performances (supposing they have one) would go much farther than we have to go to preserve the claim to autonomy. Consider the following points. Intuitively, we do not have the right to ignore facts which seem to us to be morally relevant. Intuitively, we do not have the right to make up our minds about moral questions in any way we like, as in a snap judgement when there is time to inform ourselves, or in a mood of complete selfishness. And these two restrictions seem to be just as important and inescapable as the assumption of personal autonomy. But notice that they still leave each person free to form his own substantive moral judgements. They do not logically demand a certain substantive evaluation while excluding contrary evaluations. This is very unlike the situation which would obtain under an objective standard of substantive moral evaluation where, as we saw in Section 1, it might often be possible to prove to a person that his own well-informed, disinterested, and most deeply felt moral judgement is false, and that (for example) some action which he thinks abominable is really his moral duty. The only substantive restriction would seem to be that we could not take moral exception to that purpose in choosing among moral reasoning performances, nor of course to the standard of reasonableness which it demands. But I shall discuss this point more closely later on.

Granting for the moment that logically there could be an unchallengeable purpose in choosing among specimens of moral reasoning, is there such a purpose in fact? One would be inclined to say that there is not if it seemed intuitively obvious that one *is* permitted to challenge *any* candidate purpose which might be advanced, even in a context in which we are evaluating a moral reasoning performance. But surely this is not obvious. It is a debatable answer to a rather abstruse question which no one could formulate without a good deal of prior philosophical reflection. And some philosophers might wish to answer that question by saying that there *must* be *some* point to this activity of giving, accepting, and rejecting reasons for moral judgements, even if it cannot be to certify the truth or probable truth of such judgements because (as we shall continue to assume in this Part) they do not admit of truth or falsity. On the other hand, one might plausibly argue that if there were such a purpose we would surely all know about it. Or at least those of us who are not complete novices at moral reflection and reason-giving might be expected to know about it, just as we know the purpose (the objectives to be attained) in choosing among family cars when we go to buy one, even though we may not stop to think of it but only of the familiar criteria which it generates. Therefore, inasmuch as it seems doubtful *what* that purpose might be as we begin this discussion, it is at least doubtful that there *is* any such purpose.

For a start, let us ask whether it would be possible to set up or legislate such a purpose. It seems that this would be possible if it were done by universal agreement. If everyone were to decide and agree that the purpose of accepting some specimens of moral reasoning while rejecting others is *P*, so that good moral reasoning is precisely reasoning for our moral judgements in such a way as to further *P*, then *P* would literally and obviously be the purpose in choice for this activity. Of course, coming to such an agreement would *change* the evaluation of moral reasoning performances into a rather different sort of activity from what it has been heretofore if the purpose thus agreed upon required a standard quite different from the one which is now commonly recognized, viz. the standard described in Section 2. So it would *not* be possible to legislate the purpose of moral reasoning *as we know it* unless we were careful to adopt a purpose which in fact demands the existing standard, or at least something quite close to it. But if the purpose adopted did require that our moral reasoning performances be reasonable in the ways described in Section 2, then (supposing the description is roughly accurate) we could go on reasoning in morals just as we have in the past, and we would have an answer to the question which we are mainly concerned with in the present section. That is, we could explain why our standard of good moral reasoning is a valid standard, i.e. an objective standard not open to challenge when we are evaluating pieces of moral reasoning.

This takes us rather far into Wonderland, no doubt. There is no such universal agreement and there isn't likely to be. Moreover, a determined sceptic about moral reasoning who wished to set up an absolute bar to this answer could do so merely by refusing to participate in such an agreement himself. So the point I have just made would not trouble him.

Let us therefore retreat into one of the nearer provinces of Wonderland and suppose that *practically* everyone were to agree upon a certain purpose for moral reasoning, a certain objective or coherent set of objectives to be served in giving and accepting some reasoning performances as good and sufficient while eschewing and rejecting others as bad and insufficient. And let us suppose that the purpose thus agreed upon did demand the existing standard as I have described it. Nearly all people would have agreed upon purpose *P* because they desired the state of affairs which *P* contemplates, and because they wished to clarify moral discourse. Furthermore, the existing standard is needed to accomplish that purpose, as people would have discovered, because its observance (the giving and accepting of reasoning performances which it indicates are good, and the eschewing and rejection of those which it indicates are bad) is far more likely to bring about that state of affairs than any other means they might adopt, including the observance of any other standard of good moral reasoning. Finally, let us suppose that *P* is in turn 'needed' by the existing standard if it is to be a valid standard, which we commonly suppose it to be. Like any objective standard, it needs a vindicating purpose, and *P* is the only one in sight which fills the bill. In summary, let us suppose that the vast majority of people were to discover that the existing standard of good moral reasoning presupposes *P* in just that way, and were therefore to adopt *P* explicitly as their purpose in choosing among moral reasoning performances.

What would be the logical situation of someone who eccentrically refused to join in this agreement, declaring that it is morally wrong to try to bring about the state of affairs which is contemplated by P? First of all, I do not see how we others could force him to play our 'game', and we could not say that it is morally wrong of him to refuse to play. Judgements of moral right and wrong could only be made within the game, about the 'players' and their actions. Or more precisely, such judgements would *call* for playing the game when it is time to give reasons for them, and the eccentric would be free to ignore any claim on our part to have given good reasons for such a judgement about him inasmuch as the standard of good reasoning would be part of a game which he refuses to play. But secondly, and by the same token, this eccentric would not be saying anything intelligible in our game if he said '*P* is morally wrong.' At best he would be calling on us to play a different game if we wished to understand and evaluate what he was saying. It is doubtful whether his statement would be intelligible even then, since it is at least very difficult to devise a coherent game of this kind all on one's own. But however that might be, we would not know the rules of his game, we would not be playing it with him, and we would have no intention of learning it or playing it. Having found a clear sense for 'valid standard of moral reasoning', and being in actual possession of such a standard, we the vast majority would stick close to our own sense and standard. If this be tyranny of the majority, then so is every language, and so is practically any game (in the literal sense of 'game') which is played by many players. In order to speak or play, you must accept the basic rules followed by others. But notice once again that in accepting and following the standard of moral reasoning described in Section 2, one would not be committed to any substantive moral evaluations, but would remain free to make up one's mind in whatever way seemed best.

Since it is still highly unlikely that *practically* everyone should reach an agreement of the sort just described, it may seem pointless to ask what the logical situation would be if they did. But let us pursue the matter a bit farther and ask whether there *is* some possible objective or point to the evaluation of moral reasoning performances which *would* do the trick if practically everyone *did* agree to adopt it. Can we think of a purpose which would demand the existing standard as I have described it, and which is 'needed' by that standard if it is to be a valid standard?

I think we can. It seems to me that the existing standard would be required if, in adopting, offering, accepting, and rejecting moral reasons and arguments, we had the following objectives: to reach agreement in our autonomous moral views and judgements, and to foster mutual respect even when we fail to reach agreement. To show this, I shall attempt in the next few paragraphs to explain two things: first, why observance of the standard which I have described in Section 2 would definitely further these objectives; second, why it would probably do so more effectively than would the observance of any other standard of good moral reasoning. After that, I shall also point out why it would seem to be the case that just this purpose is required if the standard described in Section 2 is to be an objective standard and hence valid. That is, I shall attempt to explain that no other purpose which might plausibly be assigned as our purpose in choosing among moral reasoning performances does require this standard.

(1) The first point involves us in psychological questions, rather than logical or conceptual ones. But I think they are

easy questions to answer without special knowledge or expertise. Is it not obvious that the chances of two or more people agreeing on some moral question will normally be much improved if their views are well informed, disinterested, and communicated to one another with reasons which have been tested in the way that standard requires? When people take a disinterested stance and base their judgements on roughly the same ample body of relevant facts, then two great obstacles to moral agreement are overcome, as I said before: selfishness and ignorance. The *communication* of their judgements and reasons will also provide other favourable conditions for agreement. It will then be more likely that they will structure moral problems in similar ways; and no doubt there is an important element of non-logical persuasion in many of such communications. Finally, if the discussants nevertheless fail to reach the same moral opinion or at least mutually consistent opinions, it seems obvious that they will be more likely to respect one another as moral persons despite their conflicting views than under any other conditions of substantive disagreement. True, there can be no guarantee of this, especially if the issue under discussion is one of great practical importance on which feelings run high. But even then there will be one *reason* to respect one's opponent despite his hateful opinion, namely, that he has formed it unselfishly and rationally.

(2) Our next question is whether there is any other standard of moral reasoning the observance of which would promote the mentioned objectives as well as, or better than, observance of the standard described in Section 2. And first, what other standard is there to consider? I take it that anyone who knows how to engage in moral discourse would normally admit that we *ought* to be well-informed and disinterested in our moral judgements, that we *ought* to be sincere in the reasons we give for them, etc. But some people (a certain minority of moral philosophers) think the results thus obtained may be overridden by the application of some further test. These philosophers hold that while the results of

such reflection are quite likely to be sound, and while we may often have to be content with them in practice, they are nevertheless subject to correction in the light of some supremely general principle which the philosopher in question happens to regard as the fundamental principle of morality. This would be a principle which has no 'other things being equal' qualification, and from which all other moral principles can be derived in the light of non-moral facts. Further, it would be a principle by recourse to which all apparent conflicts between the derived principles could be resolved. In other words, it would be the principle by which all moral evaluations are ultimately determined. The most popular principle of this sort among philosophers is of course the principle of 'utility' in its various formulations.

I think it must be admitted that the application of such a test would help to promote a certain kind of moral agreement very efficiently. After all, if there is indeed a supremely general principle which validly determines the answers to all moral questions, then the *truth* of a moral statement will consist in its deducibility from that principle in conjunction with relevant non-moral facts. Application of the principle will not merely increase our chances of agreement but will guarantee agreement in the absence of empirical or deductive error. The second objective, mutual respect in disagreement, will be otiose in the ideal case where there is no such error. But in many real cases where it will be possible for two utilitarians (for example) to disagree, their common use of a utilitarian method will undoubtedly promote such respect.

It is essential to notice, however, that the use of such a standard or method would not promote agreement in fully autonomous judgements, or indeed mutual respect between fully autonomous persons, and these are the objectives we are considering. Under a supremely general and hence unchallengeable principle of morality, one could not judge autonomously in a strong sense. That is, one's judgement could not extend even to basic principles. At best one would be autonomous in the weak sense that one had the right to do one's own casuistry and make one's own mistakes in applying unchallengeable principles. In using a method of reasoning which directs us to apply a supremely general principle of moral choice, we would always face the possibility of having to accept a moral evaluation which strikes us as wrong. We could not use the 'intuition' to correct the principle; we would be forced to accept every deductive consequence which the principle had in conjunction with non-moral statements known to be true.

This possibility of having to accept intuitively unacceptible judgements is not remote, or of concern only to people of eccentric moral views. We might all be forced to swallow implausible moral evaluations, as W. D. Ross has famously pointed out.[2] If we can really purchase a penny's worth of net favourable utility for the human race by breaking a sacred trust, then we ought to break it. Nor is this trouble overcome by the device of rule utilitarianism.[3] Rules derivable from the principle of utility will give conflicting directions in many cases, just as 'ordinary moral rules' (many of which are supposed to be roughly so derivable)[4] conflict with one another. Hence they will need to have *ceteris paribus* clauses, and we will be thrown back to the principle of utility if we are to resolve such conflicts and answer the moral questions which generate them. Then, if the facts of the case are such that action *A* will have the greatest utility among actions open to us, we must favour *A* and the rule which endorses it, no matter how deep our conviction may be that some other rule takes precedence in the circumstances, and that *A* is terribly wrong.

Apparently we must conclude that no standard of demonstrative moral reasoning would further the mentioned objectives. And it is only a demonstrative method, I submit, which would even seem at first glance to rival the standard of

[2] For references, see Appendix II.

[3] Cf. David Lyon's criticism in *Forms and Limits of Utilitarianism* (Oxford: Clarendon Pr., 1965).

[4] Notice that, of the philosophers who believe in some demonstrative method of ethics based on a supremely general principle, we are really concerned only with that sub-minority who definitely intend their theories as explications, not as substantial reforms of 'ordinary' morality.

Section 2 in this regard. For what non-demonstrative method other than the method prescribed by the latter standard would do so even nearly as well? To reflect, decide, and argue in the way that standard prescribes is *ideally* suited to produce agreement or mutual respect between morally autonomous persons.

To complete the argument that the existing standard described in Section 2 would be required by the mentioned objectives, one other thing should be made explicit, although it is fairly obvious. It seems highly probable that these two objectives would seldom if ever conflict, i.e. require conflicting ways of reflecting and arguing. Surely the kind of moral reasoning which is most conducive to agreement between autonomous persons is just the kind that would most efficiently promote respect between them if they should still disagree—at least if they were not highly eccentric persons. Hence these objectives require the same criteria, and the purpose of promoting both of them is a coherent purpose.

Finally, we must cover the third major point which I mentioned above for this phase of the argument, namely, that the existing standard of good moral reasoning would not only be required by the mentioned objectives for the reasons just given, but also needs to have these objectives if it is to be an objective standard and thus demonstrably valid. The point would be that there is no *other* plausibly assignable purpose in choosing among moral reasoning performances which would demand these same criteria, this same standard.

What other purpose needs to be considered? If we ask someone, or stop to consider ourselves, what purpose is served in choosing among specimens of moral reasoning, of offering or accepting some and rejecting others, one answer that might plausibly be given is that we hope to show the truth of certain moral statements and the falsity of certain others. But this purpose does not demand our described standard, for satisfying that standard never enables us to show the truth or falsity of moral statements. And if it *were* possible to show their truth or falsity, reasoning in accordance with our standard would be (for that purpose) superfluous. The criteria of good moral reasoning would be something quite different, perhaps that one has invoked the objective standard(s) of substantive morality with factual accuracy, or that one has so invoked the divinely created standards of substantive morality. Now, besides the purpose of *certifying the truth or falsity* of moral statements, and the purpose of *justifying* one's moral statements (the notion I am attempting to explicate), what other plausibly assignable purpose is there to consider? There is none that I can think of.

It should be added as part of the explication that the purpose of promoting agreement and mutual respect is itself, surely, a plausible purpose of moral reasoning, i.e. of choosing among moral reasons and reasonings. I think it can safely be said that people who engage in moral reflection and reason-giving do often wish to achieve agreement and foster mutual respect. Moreover, it seems very likely that these objectives *would* quite *typically* be desired by people who engage in this sort of discourse and recognize the criteria we have described, if they were to stop and think of it. And I am myself unable to think of any other goal that (*a*) is widely desired by such people, or would be if they considered the point, and (*b*) also demands these same criteria. Indeed, it seems very unlikely that there is any other objective which meets these specifications.

If what I have been saying is correct—if, to summarize, (i) the standard described in Section 2 *is* the existing (commonly recognized) standard of good moral reasoning performances, and (ii) it *would* best permit the attainment of those mentioned objectives, and (iii) the purpose of attaining those objectives is itself 'needed' by the standard if it is to be a valid standard, then we seem to have identified *the* purpose which moral reasoning as we know it presupposes, in the sense of 'presupposes' used earlier. Of course, it is not *literally* a purpose which people always have in mind when offering, accepting, and rejecting moral reasons; although, as I have said, some people probably do have this purpose, literally. But one might nevertheless claim that it is the *point* of moral reasoning, meaning by this that it is the purpose which we might well have, and indeed ought to have if we claim that such choices can be correct or incorrect; that is, if we claim, in effect, that such choices are determined by a valid standard. Here I take it for granted that the 'point' of an institution or activity need not be the explicit purpose or intention of the people taking part. The tradition in ethics which looks for the point of substantive moral evaluation has not looked for the purpose which people explicitly or consciously have in all of their moral choices, and would put itself out of court if it did. Nor have I relied on the literal sense of 'purpose' when arguing in Section 1 that substantive moral choice lacks a coherent, all-governing purpose.

There is a weaker and a stronger sounding claim which we might now wish to make. The weaker sounding claim is that we have at least shown how people *could* establish the recognized standard of good moral reasoning as an objective standard. They could do so by voting, in an overwhelming majority vote, to adopt the purpose in choice which I have identified. This would not bring about any important change in the existing evaluative activity and recognized criteria of evaluation, in contrast to the deep changes which would accrue from the adoption of a fundamental and henceforth unchallengeable purpose in substantive moral choice. But if we are allowed to speak of an 'immanent' purpose or 'point' of moral reasoning, why should we not make the stronger sounding claim that we have identified *the* purpose which the recognized criteria of good moral reasoning *do* subserve? How better could one identify the immanent purpose or point of a set of value criteria than by identifying the purpose which they presuppose, in the sense of 'presuppose' which I have been using, viz. that it in fact requires them and that they in fact need that very purpose if they are to be valid criteria? And indeed, the two theses would seem to amount to the same thing for all practical purposes. To say that people could validate the commonly recognized standard by agreeing to adopt such a purpose is very much like saying that it *is* the immanent purpose, given that they do wish to hold that the standard is valid, and given that no other purpose but this one would do the trick, and given that they find it perfectly agreeable.

Can we really say that the purpose which has now been identified is *unchallengeable*? Suppose we point out to someone that his moral reasoning on a certain occasion does not satisfy the standard described in Section 2. His reasons strike us as biased, insincere, or based on faulty information, and he has to admit they do not satisfy that standard. (For present purposes we may assume that he will be honest about it.) Can he nevertheless deny that his reasoning has to pass the test, that the standard which I have described *is* the standard of good moral reasoning? Can he take the position that, although the purpose we have identified may require such a standard, he is free to reject that purpose?

Not if he also takes the position that in moral reasoning as we know it, and as he claims to practise it (not in some other imaginable form of discourse), one *can* reason well in support of one's moral judgements. For, in order for that to be possible, there must *be* a valid standard of good moral reasoning. Otherwise, 'good moral reasoning' and 'arguing well in morals' will lack any appropriate sense.[5] But in order for there to be a valid standard, it seems that there must be a purpose requiring the criteria which people who know how to engage in this activity commonly do acknowledge—unless (to mention the only other possibility we have managed to uncover) valid standards of reasoning can exist by legislative fiat, which is absurd. And the purpose which we have identified seems to be the only one in sight which could serve as that definitive purpose. So I would seriously suggest that anyone who thinks it is possible to reason well in morals—and who but a hard-headed sceptic does not?—is logically barred from challenging or rejecting that purpose when the occasion is one of evaluating moral reasoning performances.

What about other occasions? If someone abstains from

[5] No doubt they would still have hortatory uses, and perhaps such paradoxical senses, respectively, as 'reasoning which I urge you to accept' and 'being persuasive in morals'.

even claiming that we can reason well or poorly in morals, will he be able to take moral exception to that purpose? Not if he is to be wholly consistent, it would seem. A moral objection is one for which he can be asked to give reasons. In making a moral statement, he at least undertakes that good reasons could be given for it, even if he is not able to give them himself. So in saying that such a purpose is *morally* objectionable, he at the same time seems to presuppose that it is acceptable, for there is no good moral reasoning without it.

Now, to be sure, no one is barred from entering a *non-moral* objection to this purpose. Let us suppose that it interferes with some other purpose or interest of mine. I may happen to think that moral agreement is a bore, and not care two straws whether people who disagree respect each other. If so, I may have a reason to ignore this purpose or even to attempt to frustrate it. But then if I am to act consistently, it seems that I should give up making moral judgements. If I try to have it both ways, saying that such and such another standard of moral reasoning is the one I recognize because it is demanded by such and such another purpose which I prefer, then I shall only be talking to myself, like the man in Near Wonderland who stood out of the practically unanimous agreement on the purpose of moral reasoning.

All of this may seem to add up to a tall and startling claim. But I think it follows safely enough from what I said earlier in describing the existing standard of moral reasoning, and in presenting an analysis of objective standards and evaluative truth. Everything depends, of course, on how accurate and convincing those discussions were. But is it really so startling, after all, to be told that one cannot, logically, take moral exception to the purpose of reaching moral agreement and promoting mutual respect?

Many readers will now press the objection, mentioned at the beginning of this section, that I may have identified a valid standard for evaluating certain items which I have called moral reasoning performances, but that this is a misleading name for them. It will be said that the standard which I have identified is not really a standard of reasoning but of persuasion. Hume remarked that moral approbation and disapprobation can be confused with judgements of reason because of their calmness; a latter-day Humean might say that our standard of moral 'reasoning' only analyses and, as it were, codifies the moral sentiment of reasonableness. It cannot be a standard of rational justification because, in Hume's words, reason is the faculty which judges of truth and falsehood. Hence, we cannot explain the rational justification of moral judgements in terms of such a standard.

I think this is incorrect, a too miserly restriction of the notion of rational justification, even if not so miserly as in Hume's critique of induction, where justification is limited not only to the sphere of truth and falsehood but to the performance of deductions. Yet, it is obviously an important objection which we must seriously consider. It will require some preparatory illustration in the next section before I can hope to answer it in Section 5. Here I shall only add a brief remark to fix our present bearings.

We have gone on conceptual safari to find the elusive purpose of moral reasoning when everyone knows that the purpose is to justify moral statements. Or at least that is the purpose of 'justificative reasoning', our topic throughout Part I. Readers unfamiliar with this sort of affair might therefore want to know why we have not addressed ourselves more explicitly to that purpose, and why we have not asked whether *it* demands and is required by the standard described in Section 2. Is it because that purpose really demands more than such a standard can give, as the Humean critic would complain? Well, it is a fair question whether this standard of reasoning does enable us to justify moral statements, but there are good ways and bad ways to raise the question. Surely 'justification' is not some state of affairs or condition of statements which we can identify independently of reasoning, and then go on to inquire whether the observance of this or that standard of reasoning would be well calculated to produce it.

A more useful approach would be to inquire into the meaning of 'rational justification' or the notion of justificative reasoning, and then consider whether, in conforming to the standard which has now been explicated, one exemplifies that notion or not. I think one does, and I shall attempt to explain this in the remainder of Part I. I shall attempt to show that what the use of this standard enables us to accomplish, as disclosed in the foregoing discussion, is itself the rational justification of moral statements.

Finally, a word on the opening complaint that, in prescribing the standard described in Section 2, one only endorses 'Western liberal morality'. This complaint is importantly mistaken in two ways, but there is also a bit of truth in it. First of all, if the foregoing discussion is correct, we have not *morally* prescribed anything. Indeed, we have not *prescribed* anything, but have only drawn attention to reasons why a commonly accepted standard of good moral reasoning or persuasion, call it what one must, is in fact a valid standard. Secondly, I would deny that Western liberals, whoever they are exactly, have any patent on this standard, and the label is therefore misleading. But thirdly, there may very well be groups of people in the world who do not recognize this standard in their moral reflection and reason-giving. Indeed, there most certainly are. For after all, 'moral' and 'morality' are words of many meanings. In some of them, merely feeling bound by rules of social behaviour would be enough to qualify as having a morality. No doubt there are many people in 'Western' culture whose notion of morality is largely heteronomous: they feel bound by some substantive standards merely because these standards have been issued to them by their 'moral superiors'. To such people, moral reasoning is casuistic analysis in the application of legislatively valid standards. But I see nothing very troublesome for our project in this. If we finally manage to throw some light on *one* type of morality and moral reasoning, surely a most important type, then this is perhaps all that can be reasonably asked of us.

4. An Analogy: Judicial Reasoning

We have now answered the objection, stated in an emotivist idiom at the beginning of the last section, that in recommending the standard of reasoning which was described in Section 2 one only makes a new moral judgement which needs to be defended like any other. To preface our work in this section and the next, it may be useful to mention a different kind of objection in which our account is likened to the emotive theory itself. The objection points out that the emotivists hold a 'relevant' moral reason to be one which may be expected to 'influence' the preferences or attitudes of one's audience,[1] because it is impossible to show the *truth* of one's own preference or attitude. The only serious difference between their theory and ours, it may be thought, is that they candidly admit this is reasoning only in a manner of speaking, and by no means valid reasoning.[2]

There really are other important differences, however, between our account of good moral persuasion and that found in the most detailed and representative emotive theory. Stevenson's test of relevance in the article just cited does not incorporate the commonly recognized criteria of reasonableness, but on the contrary, violates them. It does not require that we advance only reasons or arguments which have passed

[1] Cf. C. L. Stevenson's 'The Nature of Ethical Disagreement' in H. Feigl and W. Sellars, *Readings in Philosophical Analysis* (New York: Appleton–Century–Crofts, 1949 , and in his own *Facts and Values* (New Haven: Yale Univ. Pr., 1963), esp. at pp. 589 and 4, respectively.

[2] See esp. Chap. VII in Stevenson's *Ethics and Language* (New Haven: Yale Univ. Pr., 1944).

the test of reasonableness in our own reflection. Whether we mention all of the salient facts or only those which may be thought to support our moral statement, and whether we appeal to our interlocutor's disinterested judgement or attempt to play upon his fears and prejudices, will depend on the exigencies of the rhetorical situation and other variable factors. Does he have the sort of intelligence and temperament that are more likely to be influenced by reasonable appeals, or not? And do we simply prefer to be reasonable ourselves, or not? And do we wish to inculcate *this* attitude in others, or not?[3] In contrast, the account given in Sections 2 and 3 not only accepts the ordinary criteria of reasonableness as binding in every case, but attempts to explicate them as a demonstrably valid standard.

It would be desirable, however, to show that our account is not only a plausible explication of the ordinary standard of good moral persuasion, which the emotivist account cannot be, but that it also does specify a standard of rational justification.[4] Accordingly, I shall attempt to defend the following thesis in this section and the next. An objective standard directing us to use reasons and arguments of a kind which are in fact well calculated to secure the reasonable agreement of others to our own reasonable moral judgement, or at least to secure their respect for us in reasonably making that judgement, is a standard of rational justification. To give reasons and arguments of that kind for that purpose *is* to justify one's moral judgement, as I shall endeavour to explain, even

[3] Ibid., at pp. 156–7. See the discussion of these points by Carl Wellman in 'Emotivism and Ethical Objectivity', *Amer. Phil. Quart.*, vol. 5 (1968), reprinted in W. Sellars and J. Hospers, *Readings in Ethical Theory*, 2nd edn. (New York: Appleton-Century-Crofts, 1970).

[4] The phrase 'rational justification' is redundant if we understand 'justification' in the strong sense which has been of primary interest to philosophers and is our own main concern. But there seem to be closely related but weaker senses (e.g. offering reasons or alleged reasons, or *attempting* to justify in the strong sense). I often use the phrase 'rational justification' in order to avoid these latter senses, and to acknowledge that we are not to take the short way with our problem and hold that moral argument surely is a form of justification because people are *said* commonly to justify their moral assertions by giving reasons for them. It could be that this common observation is true only when 'justify' is being used in one of the weaker senses.

though the truth or probable truth of moral statements cannot be established in this way, or perhaps in any way.

I intend to argue for this thesis with the aid of a fairly extensive legal analogy. This will be a comparison of moral reasoning with judicial reasoning in difficult cases where there is no uniquely correct or true decision to be rendered, but in which the judges are nevertheless said to justify their judgements in oral and written opinions. My argument will be in two parts. First there will be a description of judicial reasoning in difficult cases, showing that we lack a method of identifying true legal conclusions in such cases for reasons which are closely analogous to those which seem to rule out truth in morals. It will also be pointed out that the major criteria of good reflection and argumentation are practically identical in moral and judicial reasoning, although the law also has more specialized, professional criteria. We shall also suggest that the standard of good judicial reasoning in such cases can be vindicated—can be shown to be an objective standard—in a way that is closely similar to what we have seen on the moral side of the analogy. This will take us to the end of the present section. In the second half of the argument, consisting of Section 5, we shall consider whether this common form of good persuasive reasoning actually does fall under the notion of rational justification or not. It will prove convenient to concentrate mainly on the judicial analogue in that discussion, but I shall try to show how the main results apply equally to moral reasoning.

Some writers on jurisprudence have suggested that *no* case has a uniquely correct decision under the law, but this is a minority view and probably incorrect for reasons noted in Appendix III. It is enough for present purposes to point out that *many* difficult cases, quite possibly a majority of appealed cases, are not legally determined in the sense that there is only one legal argument and judgement supported by the facts of the case and the authoritative standards, i.e. relevant statutes, precedents, and recognized principles. In saying this, I do not mean to rely on the fact that different judges with much the same view of the law affecting a given case may easily differ on points of detail concerning its proper disposition. I mean that substantially contrary views about how the principal issues of the case should be decided may be equally sustainable. Yet it is commonly said that the judges write opinions 'justifying' their judgements in such cases, as they do in other cases. And many an opinion coming from our more distinguished judges has been offered as a model of reasoning at a high level of competence, even though it has been given to justify a judgement (or a dissenting view) in just such a case.

Why do cases often lack legally true decisions? One reason is that legal standards (like moral principles) may 'intersect' and conflict in given cases, and there may be no second-order legal standard telling us how we must resolve the conflict. Just as in morals, we may have to rely on our own best 'judgement' in such cases because there is no general criterion or test to which we can appeal. To be sure, some statutes and even some well developed rules of case-law come equipped with general 'exceptions' which will enable us to dispose of some apparent conflicts. But often the conflict is real, and the judge must rely on his own judgement in deciding what sort of exception would be the more reasonable to allow in the circumstances of the particular case, and of course in similar cases which may arise in the future.

A second source of legal indeterminacy is found in the 'case of first impression' for which no controlling statute or binding precedent or recognized principle can be found, but which is nevertheless thought to present a 'justiciable' question, one that an appropriate court can be called upon to answer. Here the court will have to invent a rule for the case. It will do so if only by giving its reasons for deciding the case as it does decide it. And the substance or content of the rule which ought to be invented and applied to the case may well be something on which two good judges could differ. Neither may be able to point to important legal objectives which argue convincingly in his favour, or to markedly stronger analogies in the past resolution of other legal problems. Similarly, we may very well have to make up our mind on what is morally required of us in a given situation even though no previously embraced moral principle seems applicable to it. This can happen through 'moral growth': coming to appreciate some moral problem to which one has previously been insensitive. According to the description of moral reasoning given in Section 2, there will be no one principle which we *must* then embrace and apply, even if there should be a consensus among others who have already considered the problem.

A third reason why a legal case may have no single correct decision is that the highest appellate courts in most jurisdictions occasionally *reject* rules of law represented by their own earlier decisions, and have the acknowledged right to do so. In thus overturning a precedent, they may give the same sort of reason that an autonomous moral agent or 'judge' may sincerely and properly give in rejecting a moral principle which he once accepted, namely, that it no longer seems valid or sound.[5] And judges may of course disagree on whether to overturn a precedent, and on what to put in its place if they do.

Finally, there are striking similarities in the way antecedently accepted rules or principles are *modified* in judicial and moral reasoning. As I pointed out in Section 2, we do not apply moral principles mechanically to new questions falling under them, at least not to moral *problems*, although we may apply them fairly automatically to routine questions. Rather, after reflecting on a problem we decide what principle we will *accept* as morally proper for resolving it or forming a judgement about it. This may force us to refine or qualify our principles, if only to the extent of deciding how their *ceteris paribus* clauses will operate in a type of situation to which we have not applied them before. In law, similarly, it

[5] Of course it is not enough that the old rule or principle conflicts with what the court or the moral agent would now *like* to do, although this may often enough be the real reason. But for purposes of the present discussion, we assume that the courts attempt to follow the standard of good judicial work, just as we assume that the 'moral judge' adheres to the form of decision making and reason giving which is under discussion as a type of reasoning.

is the problematic case which determines the rule, more than it is the antecedently formulated rule which determines how the case must be decided. The point is by now a commonplace of jurisprudence, but let us pause to illustrate the important and legitimate type of judicial lawmaking to which it refers.

A famous illustration of the modification and 'growth' of case law rules or principles is found in the developing law of negligence, beginning perhaps with the Squib case (*Scott* v. *Shepherd*, 1773, 2 Wm. Blackstone 892) and continuing through many leading cases until we reach some grand culmination like Judge Cardozo's opinion in *Palsgraf* v. *Long Island R. Co.*, 1928, 248 N.Y. 339, 162 N.E. 9. Without attempting to give anything like an adequate summary of that development, let us use the illustration merely to suggest how considerations of fairness and reasonableness, rather than any definite second-order legal rules or criteria, must figure in the revision of case law rules.

In the Squib case, the defendant had thrown a lighted squib or explosive into a crowded market house, and the plaintiff was severely injured when two men successively threw the squib away from their stands until it struck him and exploded. In deciding in favour of the plaintiff, the court gave as its reason that the defendant acted unlawfully and the plaintiff was injured as a result. 'A person is liable for the harmful consequences of his unlawful act' seemed to be the rule on which the court relied. But in a later case to which this rule is literally applicable, we may have to consider various facts which seem to point to a different conclusion, or at least to some needed modification in the rule. For example, a defendant's act, while unlawful in the sense of being careless of the safety of others, may not be intentionally mischievous. The rule may accordingly be broadened to cover negligence as well as intentional wrongdoing. In a still later case we may have the further variation that, although the injury was the result of the defendant's negligent act and would not have occurred without it, this effect depended on a long chain of causes and circumstances of a sort which could not have been anticipated by anyone. (In the Squib case it was obvious that *someone* would probably be hurt as a result of the defendant's act.) Hence the court will find it sensible and fair to narrow the rule in this respect by requiring that the cause be 'proximate' rather than 'remote'. In a still later case, we may find that the causal chain is short but includes a second person's independent act of negligence without which the injury would not have occurred. Then the court may consider it desirable to add a further qualification that the injury must be a 'direct and natural' consequence of the defendant's negligence if he is to be made to pay for it. There may then ensue a whole line of cases serving to give these phrases more specific meaning through their peculiar factual complexities and rationales.

Finally, we may have a case where the defendant did act carelessly in a way likely to hurt someone, and where the 'causal chain' was very short, but where the injury to the *plaintiff* was nevertheless extremely improbable. That is, no one could have anticipated that anything of the sort might happen as a result of the defendant's act, not merely that the plaintiff in particular would be the person hurt. This was Mrs. Palsgraf's case. Two railroad guards, helping a passenger board a train which had already begun to move out of the station, caused him to drop a small parcel wrapped in newspapers. It fell on to the track or between the car and the platform; it contained fireworks; and as the train crushed it they exploded, causing a heavy scale standing on the platform many feet away to tip over on to the plaintiff, injuring her.

In refusing to hold the railroad responsible despite the carelessness of its employees, the court emphasized the unforeseeability of the injury to the plaintiff or to anyone situated as she was, and essayed still a further formulation of the applicable rule or principle. In the court's opinion, a defendant's liability must result from a breach of his duty to the plaintiff, a duty not to expose the plaintiff to risks of injury. But this legal duty must be limited to risks of a sort which a person using reasonable care might be expected to appreciate. Notice that such a rule preserves (would have yielded) the result reached originally in the Squib case, even as it denies victory to Mrs. Palsgraf. And the court, through Judge Cardozo, recognized that this rule may also have its exceptions. In a case where the defendant was actually attempting to injure someone, it might not seem unjust or unreasonable to make him compensate someone else whom he actually did injure by his malicious act, even though it was entirely unforeseeable that the latter person would even be endangered by it. Whether it *would* seem just and reasonable might depend on further circumstances, and could be a matter on which good judges might disagree, as they did disagree in the Palsgraf case. And there might be no authoritative legal standard to which one could appeal in order to decide which opinion was correct.

The point, then, is that while the courts need to have, and do have, the power to revise rules or principles of law in certain circumstances, there sometimes is no single correct way for them to do so—no correct content which the revised rule ought to have, and no certain result which the judgement ought to enforce.

To summarize what has been said thus far, it can be seen that the occasions of judicial lawmaking are rather similar to those circumstances in which our autonomy of moral judgement is exercised in the most obvious ways: as when we feel constrained to *adopt* a principle which is new to us; or when we reject principles we no longer consider morally sound; or when we adapt our principles to fit new situations and to conform to new moral 'intuitions',

It is obvious, however, that judges do not have anything like the *degree* of autonomy or discretion which we claim as moral agents and moral judges. Many verbally unchangeable standards are handed to them by the legislature, and there are important professional and political restrictions on what they can do when interpreting statutes and precedents or 'developing' traditional legal doctrines. The thought will therefore occur that there may be uniquely correct results which a court is bound to reach even when performing in its acknowledged legislative role. That is, there may be substantive judgements which a court ought to render, and substantive legal rules or rule modifications which it ought to make in doing so, even when deciding very difficult cases which lack correct decisions under existing law—which lack them, that is to say, except through a new and legally correct exercise of the judicial lawmaking power.

Despite the paradox which may seem to be involved in speaking of the *legally* correct *content* of rules created by judicial *lawmaking*, the idea is plausible enough if we take it to mean that in some cases there are broader legal norms which require a certain kind of specilized lawmaking in the context of a given problem, yielding certain substantive results and excluding others.[6] And someone may wish to suggest that this is always the situation whenever judicial lawmaking is justified, so that in a deeper way all cases do have legally true decisions. But this is almost certainly false, and for a reason which will now be familiar. In order for it to be true, it seems that law, or at least judge-made law, would have to consist of an objective standard or a unified set of objective standards. For in what other way would there *always* be a substantively correct rule which the judges ought to produce unless they *do* normally pursue one all-dominant purpose in lawmaking, and may properly be said to decide wrongly when they fail to pursue it? Yet it seems highly probable that substantive law, like substantive morality, does not constitute an objective standard.

This point has been made rather convincingly by Ronald M. Dworkin in an essay which is all the more valuable for present purposes because it is not concerned with moral reasoning or its similarities with judicial reasoning, and of course does not discuss objective standards or use the term.[7] As he points out, we are all free to *recommend* some fundamental purpose for judicial lawmaking, just (I would add) as we are all free to propose a 'point' for substantive moral

[6] Cf. cases of type three, described below.

[7] See his review article, 'Wasserstrom: The Judicial Decision', *Ethics*, vol. 75 (1964–5), reprinted with minor changes as 'Does Law Have a Function? A Comment on the Two-Level Theory of Decision', *Yale Law Journal*, vol. 76 (1965).

preference, a point which other people may or may not agree to adopt. But anyone much acquainted with law who stops to consider the question will realize how unsafe it would be to assume that judicial lawmaking as we know it—as it figures in our existing legal institutions—does have such an immanent purpose. Dworkin's illustrations remind us that when judges do modify existing rules of law, as they are sometimes entitled to do under the traditional practice, they very often, and even typically, rely on considerations which are not utilitarian in nature or otherwise concerned with bringing about some desired state of affairs. For example, they may give greatest weight to popular standards of fair business practice, or they may follow some recent statutory treatment of an issue which is in part analogous to the one they have to decide. And if we glance back at the kinds of considerations to which the courts have been attentive in revising the principles of negligence, I think we can also see how far-fetched it would be to suppose that these considerations are really teleological, or (more implausible still) that they are directed to the furtherance of a *single* overriding purpose. It could also be pointed out, and Dworkin does point out, that even if there were some fundamental objective or consistent set of objectives which is to be pursued in all lawmaking by the legislature, it would not follow that court's ought always to give it overriding weight in their own specialized and restricted lawmaking.

This completes the first main point I wished to make in this section: that there is no legally true decision in many cases, and for reasons which are very (though not perfectly) similar to those we find on the moral side of the analogy. But perhaps a word of caution should be added to avoid a distorted picture of the judicial process. The main thing we want courts to do is give *the* legally correct decision, and I think it is very often possible for them to do this (see Appendix III). It must also be noted that courts are subject to appellate and scholarly criticism for the ways in which they deal with statutes, binding precedents, and accepted legal principles. And sometimes they are rightly criticized for definite legal error; e.g. for plainly misinterpreting a precedent, for neglecting some relevant statute, for failing to see some obvious and crucial analogy, or for missing the relevance of some well-established legal policy. But often enough the criticism can be based only on disagreement as to what *is* fair or reasonable or practicable, not on any authoritative legal standard or on any well-established criterion of judicial craftsmanship. It may be useful criticism for all that, just as criticism of the work of legislatures may be useful. In like manner, we may be appropriately criticized by others for the ways in which we adapt or modify our own moral principles, notwithstanding our right to make up our own minds in such matters. To criticize moral and legislative decisions is to disagree with them, giving reasons and appealing to other people for careful consideration of those reasons. It is not to attempt to prove their incorrectness by appealing to facts and an objective standard, for it seems rather obvious that there are no objective standards in such matters.

The second point that I wish to make in drawing this analogy, and a point which can be made briefly, is that many familiar requirements of the good judge and good judicial work are closely similar if not identical to the requirements of moral reasonableness described in Section 2. First of all, a judge must carefully study the case before him, taking note of the precedents and statutes and legal principles which have been cited to him, and any other relevant standards which his study may disclose; and of course he must be attentive to all the facts of the case which may have legal significance. This is obviously similar to the requirement that we be reasonably well informed of relevant facts and plausible moral principles when making moral judgements. Second, a judge must be impartial; his decision must be one that he would be willing to render no matter who the parties to the case were, as long as the legally relevant facts remained the same. Third, a judge is supposed to disqualify himself from sitting in a case where his personal interests are involved. And in deciding other cases, he must not give special weight to the interests of his own socio-economic or professional class, or to his own racial or religious group, and so on. Now it is true that in morals we cannot avoid judging matters in which our own interests are involved, but if our judgement is to be universalizable we must give no greater weight or importance to them than if they were someone else's interests. A fourth requirement of the legal judge is that he be sincerely rational. That is, he is not free to reach any result he pleases as long as he can give plausible reasons; he must give the judgement which he honestly thinks is best, and the reasons which he honestly thinks are strongest.[8] This is obviously similar to the requirement that we defend only those moral judgements which we have reached in reasonable reflection, and that we use only those arguments from facts and relevant moral principles which we have ourselves found convincing.

My third and last major point is that the criteria of judicial reasonableness which have just been mentioned can be plausibly vindicated as an objective standard of good judicial reasoning performances in a way that is closely analogous to what we have seen in Section 3. More specifically, I want to suggest that these criteria constitute an objective standard of good reasoning in difficult, lawmaking cases which have no true decisions under existing law. For it is reasoning in *such* cases that I mean to compare with moral reasoning in this section and the next.

Let us begin by noticing that while the foregoing requirements of 'the judicial point of view' are supposed to be satisfied in every case, their importance increases as we move from relatively easy legal questions towards more difficult problems. Here it will be convenient to distinguish four ideal types. The easiest and rarest type of case is one in which the

[8] As one well-known author expresses the point, 'the integrity of the process in which the judge is engaged depends not only on distinctions he may make reasonably, but also on his own belief in the legitimacy and decisiveness of these distinctions.' Edward H. Levi, 'The Nature of Judicial Reasoning', in *Law and Philosophy*, S. Hook, ed. (New York: NYU Pr., 1964), p. 266. For another statement of this point, cf. Louis L. Jaffe, *English and American Judges as Lawmakers* (Oxford: The Clarendon Pr., 1969), p. 38.

facts are not in dispute and any competent lawyer would surely hold that there is but one controlling standard which may simply be applied as it stands to decide the sole issue. Such a 'case' is not likely to find its way into court at all, but it might for tactical or other reasons, and there are minor points in almost any litigated case which are that easy. If it does get into court, we need not be too concerned about whether the judge has a properly judicial temperament, or is even very honest. For it will be obvious to him and to everyone else that there is really no way in which he can avoid the correct result without raising suspicions of dishonesty.

Next, imagine a slightly less easy case, one in which some dialectic of relevant rules or other standards must be reasoned through to arrive at the correct judgement. Let us also suppose that the facts have been stipulated by the parties or are obvious from overwhelming evidence, and that seeing the correct relation between the several standards in the light of these facts is no more than an easy exercise in clear thinking. Now, even in this kind of case there will be some leeway for a biased or corrupt judge to make his judgement and supporting argument (if any) seem legally unskilled at worst. So we are dependent in some measure on his satisfying the foregoing criteria if the correct judgement is to be had from him.

Often, however, the precise interplay of legal standards will not be quite clear. Conflicts may occur; decisions as to their relative 'weight' may have to be made; good sense may seem to demand an expansion or contraction of case-law rules, or the creation of a new exception to avoid an unconscionable result. Yet even in these more difficult cases it may sometimes happen that a wide majority of competent and disinterested lawyers would be in agreement as to the correct rationale and outcome, perhaps because they would think the *preponderance* of broader legal principles and policies requires a particular solution to the problem.[9] Let this be our

[9] This possibility is explained and emphasized in R. M. Dworkin's criticism of H. L. A. Hart's general theory of law. See 'The Model of Rules', *U. of Chicago L. Rev.*, vol. 35 (1967–8); reprinted in *Essays in Legal Philosophy*, R. S. Summers, ed. (Berkeley & Los Angeles: U. of Calif. Pr., 1968).

third type. In it we are still more dependent on the judge's loyalty to the judicial point of view than we were in type two. For an honest and professionally competent judge could still go wrong in such a case if he failed to study it carefully enough, or in a sufficiently disinterested spirit.

It happens not infrequently, however, that there is no such professional consensus about a problematic case, so that almost certainly it has no 'true' decision, no uniquely correct rationale and outcome under existing law.[10] And it seems safe to say that there will be no one decision which ought then to be reached by a more radical kind of lawmaking, if this judicial function is not controlled by an objective standard in the way we mentioned and rejected a moment ago.[11] In this fourth type of case, then, the very notion of the right substantive decision drops out of sight. It will not make sense to speak of the legally right decision as far as the content of the court's reasoning and judgement is concerned, although there are always definitely *wrong* ways to decide a case. But we can still demand that the judge decide such a case only after as thorough a study and as disinterested an analysis as his abilities and the time available permit. If he does so, and does not fall into legal or logical or factual error, then he will have decided the case rightly, in the only sense 'rightly' can have here. Hence, it can be seen that the criteria of judicial reasonableness provide our only legal test that this most difficult type of case has been decided as it should be.

Next, let us observe that the kind of explicit justification which is appropriate in a given case will vary with the difficulty of the case. In cases of type one, a brief memorandum stating the relevant facts and controlling legal standard may suffice. Any lawyer acquainted with the case will recognize that the salient facts and the appropriate standard have been singled out. And laymen who are parties to the case will easily understand how the court's judgement follows from them. But in cases of type two, the judge will need to set out the reasoning which dictates his judgement. Most lawyers

[10] On this point and the preceding one, cf. L. L. Jaffe, op. cit., pp. 36–45.

[11] For further discussion of this point, see Appendix III.

might be able to construct it for themselves if given the facts of the case and the pertinent statutes and precedents, but probably few laymen could do so with any good assurance that they were right. In the third type of case, a more subtle rationale will be appropriate in which the court spells out those legal considerations which seem to dictate certain relative weights for conflicting rules, or a certain revision of existing standards, and so on. This will also be appropriate in the fourth type of case where competent and disinterested lawyers would not be in general agreement as to the effect of the considerations thus appealed to. Since the court, for that very reason, can be said to make law in settling the legal question raised by a case of this type, it seems that judges should be as conscious and candid as possible about the extralegal grounds on which their decision must now rest. Certainly a judge should be candid about the policy grounds of his lawmaking when he is himself of the opinion that the existing law does not dictate any one result.

My reason for mentioning this shift in the kind of explicit justification appropriate to cases of lesser or greater difficulty is that it calls attention to certain background objectives of the judicial process, objectives which I think it clearly does have in addition to the immediate one of adjudicating civil disputes and criminal accusations. It is just because the importance or urgency of these further objectives can change with the difficulty of the case that different sorts of explicit reasons may be in order. Thus, in very easy cases exemplifying type one, there is the purpose of applying the clear and controlling law to the case at hand. We wish not merely to settle the case but to do so according to law. In cases of type two, an obvious further purpose is to make it clear to the parties, especially to the losing party, how the law actually does dictate the result which the court has reached. In the third type of case, an important purpose will be to clarify, reshape, or perhaps create legal standards in a way that certain more general principles or policies of the existing law may be said to require, and to explain how they do require it. Finally, an outstanding purpose in the fourth type of case will be to settle, change, or supplement the existing law and give some carefully considered reasons for doing so. In this way, assurances can be given to the losing party, the legal profession, and the interested public that full and fair attention has been paid to the interests of all concerned and to the considerations which can be advanced for shaping the law in this way or that. Hence they may be persuaded that the judgement in the case and the attendant lawmaking are desirable, or at least reasonable.

Here we find our vindication of the criteria of reasonableness as *the* standard of good judicial reasoning in this fourth type of case. For in *such* cases it would seem that providing such assurances and attempting such persuasion is the *only* purpose of reason giving, and it will be best secured by judicial reasoning performances which satisfy these criteria. This conclusion will ring falsely to many readers of judicial opinions, but for reasons which I think are not really damaging to my contention, and which may even lend it support on second thought. For one thing, cases are seldom definitely earmarked or conceded to be of type four. Courts in their written opinions rarely admit that they are changing the law in any respect, and when they do so they will nearly always be found to claim that the case belongs to our third type, i.e. that fundamental principles of existing *law* definitely require and validate the changes which they are making in specialized standards. More importantly, a case may be of type four because of *certain* legally open or 'lawmaking' issues, while other issues of the case can be disposed of in ways which I have referred to under the other ideal types. But if I have argued correctly in the first part of this section, there surely *are* cases of type four; and *on the lawmaking issues* what other proper purpose of judicial reasoning *could* there be but the one which I have just mentioned?

I shall probably be accused of straining too hard for this last point of my analogy, so let me go a bit deeper and try to say why it is that our judicial institutions, and especially the practice of judicial reason giving, do have such a purpose in the most difficult sort of case. First, I think we should notice that it would be logically possible to devise a legal system and 'decision procedure' which would yield one and only one judgement in any case that might be imagined or presented. Legal scholars sometimes say that it would be humanly impossible to devise a code of laws to cover all cases that could arise, or indeed will arise, in the endlessly varied contingencies of life. But this is not literally true; after all, the code could always direct the judges to toss a coin as a last resort. What is commonly meant by such a remark, or should be meant, is that it is a practical impossibility to invent a complete code which will regulate our affairs more or less as we would *wish* to regulate them. Even a vast body of law consisting of thousands of rules, each equipped with dozens of explicit exceptions and 'weight' indicators, would either fail by a wide margin to provide a clear outcome for every case that could possibly arise, or it would have to employ some kind of toggle-switch device (even if not coin tossing) which would undoubtedly require many a decision we would reject if we could foresee it.

Draftsmen of legal codes have other problems that are relevant here besides the problem of foreseeing cases which they would not want to see governed by the rules they are presently formulating. The legislative policy values or objectives reflected in those rules may themselves change; that is, we may change our opinion about the kind of social order we want, and we surely will change it on points of detail. Even where we do not, the rules we formulate today may become generally unsuited to the realization of their original purposes or values under future economic and social conditions. These are some of the reasons why it is necessary to leave judges some room to legislate, especially if our political legislatures do not engage in fairly continuous surveillance and revision of 'private' law, which they do not. Indeed, for practical reasons they cannot, certainly not with sufficient flexibility to secure adequate justice to litigants.[12] It is often unavoidable that judges should remould or refine rules of law if they are to apply them intelligently, as even our

[12] Cf. L. L. Jaffe, op. cit., esp. Chap. I.

glance at the law of negligence was perhaps enough to illustrate.

Because of this legislative function of courts, and the resulting possibility of arbitrary or unintelligent lawmaking, we need some kind of 'procedural' control in the broadest sense, some operational standard by means of which we may be persuaded that their creations are sound, or at least created in a reasonable way. This need is seen most dramatically in the fact that the losing party in a case of type four can rightly say that law was made and applied retroactively to his disadvantage. If this is sometimes unavoidable in any practicable system of law and adjudication, then we need assurances that it will be done as fairly as may be expected of fallible men. The well-known requirements of the honest and good judge which I have brought together as 'the judicial point of view', or the criteria of judicial reasonableness, will provide that assurance if the public can believe that most judges do try to live up to them.[13]

[13] The foregoing analogy is extended and given further detail in Appendix III, where it is argued that the main structure of moral reasoning illustrated in Section 6, below, is also the main structure of good judicial reasoning, whether in difficult cases or easy cases.

5. The Concept of Justification

PERHAPS we have now seen enough of the similarities between judicial and moral reasoning to begin to concede that *if* the accepted standard of good judicial persuasion in type four cases is also a standard of rational justification, then so is the standard of good moral persuasion discussed in Sections 2 and 3. But our Humean critic will continue to deny the first part of that conditional, and he will also have picked up some new ammunition from Section 4. Indeed, many readers will now surely object that a method of reasoning and a rational method are not the same thing, as I may appear to be assuming. A method of choosing means to attain certain ends may be eminently rational if it helps us choose the most appropriate means to those ends. But the fact that the means to be chosen consist of arguing or 'reason' giving in a certain manner and spirit, and that the end is acceptance by others of certain statements one wants them to accept, is not enough to convert that rational method into a method of rational justification. The pattern of good reflection and reason-giving common to moral argument and legal argument in difficult cases may well be rational in the former sense, but it cannot be in the latter sense, the critic will insist. Why not? Because the statements we seek to 'establish' via this method are never true, and the method employed does not use any kind of inference. There is no claim that one is rationally obliged to accept a certain conclusion *if* one begins with certain premisses. From the facts of the case and the existing body of law, two or more contrary decisions can be 'justified' legally, just as, from a detailed description of someone's action and an array of moral principles one happens to regard as valid, contrary moral conclusions can be 'justified' according to our method. How can this be *rational* justification? Is it not misleading to speak of 'reasons' when one only refers to those considerations which have influenced one to *make* the legal or moral case come out in a certain way?

The question we have to answer, then, is whether judicial reasoning in type four cases, and moral reasoning in support of autonomous judgements, can be accounted reasoning in the sense of rational justification and not merely in the sense of the rational pursuit of certain objectives through 'reason' giving. In order to answer this question, we must try to clarify the notion of rational justification and then see whether or not it applies to the common form of persuasion which has been discussed in the last three sections.

How should we proceed with such a task? I suggest that we take valid deduction and scientific induction as two major paradigms of rational justification, and trace out their major common features, asking at the same time whether our legal–moral form shares those features. No doubt the rational status of induction can still be contested in some philosophical contexts, but I am going to assume that it is not controversial in the present context. I only wish to know whether judges and moral reasoners can justify their judgements in the same broad sense of 'justify' we seem to use when we speak of justifying mathematical statements or scientific statements. To keep the discussion from becoming needlessly abstract or excessively repetitious, let us compare deduction and induction primarily with judicial reasoning, speaking always of the latter as it is used in type four cases (those lacking true decisions under the existing law), and of course restricting the treatment of judicial reasoning to those features which it has in common with moral reasoning. As a precaution, let us also consider from time to time whether the point being made would apply equally to moral reasoning.

1. We may begin by noting certain important characteristics which all three types of reasoning have in common. First, in all of them one gives reasons to support conclusions.

Second, in all of them this must be done in accordance with restrictive rules which discriminate between good and bad reasons. Third, these rules are vindicated by the purpose of reason-giving which operates in the particular field. That is. they are well calculated to enable us to achieve such purpose. Let us first comment briefly on deduction and induction in this connection. The main purpose of deductive reasoning is to spell out the meaning and implications of given statements or sets of statements, be they statements of what we know, believe, guess, suspect, assume, or what not. A rule of deductive inference will be acceptable only if it assures accuracy in such explications. We have such assurance about such a rule as *modus ponens*, for example, since its validity is directly apparent from the meaning of 'if ... then ...' Similarly, the purpose of inductive reasoning is to settle on true beliefs about objective matters of fact, or at least to maximize our chances of doing so. And there is no doubt that the inductive rules of common sense and science do enable us to do these things. While the rules discriminating between sound and unsound inductions have not been clarified to anything near the extent that the rules of deduction have been clarified, and while the debate continues among philosophers as to *how* we know that the rules of either sort enable us to achieve our purposes, no one can doubt that they really do.[1]

In judicial reasoning, the judge gives reasons for his conclusion which consist of facts of the case and legal standards which together entail that conclusion when they are deployed in a certain order with certain relative weights and refinements tailored to the case. And, more importantly, the judge gives reasons for *choosing or settling upon* that particular arrangement of salient facts and weighted legal standards (including, perhaps, new standards), saying why he finds it best

[1] The problem, of course, is that it would be circular reasoning to claim that we know from experience which rules of induction are reliable, at least if we have to rely on those very rules in making such judgements on the basis of our experience, as would seem to be the case. And it would also be circular reasoning to claim to know via deductive tests that our rules of deduction guarantee accurate explications of the implicit meaning of statements.

for the case at hand.[2] Now the restrictive rule for judicial reasoning is that in offering reasons of the *latter* sort the judge must only offer those reasons which he has found convincing, or at least more convincing than any others, in a process of reflection which satisfies the criteria of judicial reasonableness. In Section 4, we have just pointed out the objectives which vindicate this rule. If it seems a strange rule of reasoning which introduces biographical requirements concerning the reasoner, we must be careful not to slide into an exclusively deductive model. There is also a biographical requirement in the basic rule of induction. Even if probability is a 'logical relation' between our data and our hypothesis, we are justified in taking the probability coefficient as the measure of the credibility of the hypothesis only if we have included in the data all the relevant evidence which has come into our possession to date.

2. Despite these very broad similarities, there will still appear to be a chasm separating good judicial persuasion from our two paradigms of reasoning. If one asks why this is so, perhaps the most natural answer will be to repeat the main objection as stated at the beginning of this section: the judicial method is not a form of inference and it is not designed to help us reach, or approximate to, the truth. Offhand, both of these features seem essential to a method of justification, even if not to a rational method of settling disputes and clarifying or revising the law. But I do not think this answer will stand scrutiny, and in criticizing it we should be able to put our finger on a more plausible reason why judicial persuasion is generically different from deduction and induction rather than being a third species of rational justification.

Consider first the matter of inference. Deduction and induction are actually very different kinds of inference—so different, in fact, that it can be misleading to speak of inductive inference at all without calling attention to the diff-

[2] For illustration of what it is to make such a selection and give such reasons, see the discussion of cases in Appendix III.

erence. This is because the word 'inference', like 'logic' and 'valid', is heavy with allusions to deduction, at least in the philosopher's lexicon. It would be better to speak of induction rules and deduction rules as two different types of *rules of support*, and some writers have done so. Now, good judicial persuasion involves a third kind of rule of support which we have just stated, and even if that rule differs widely from the others in some ways, it is like them in being an efficient rule given the very different purposes of the reason-giving or conclusion-supporting activity in which it figures.

Secondly, there is considerable ambiguity in the objection that deduction and induction are tied to the notion of truth while the judicial method is not. In one way, all three of them are tied to *logical* truth. Many philosophers would agree that induction and deduction are both connected to logical truth in that not only statements about the deductive validity of an inference, but also statements that a certain hypothesis has a certain probability on certain evidence, are logically true or logically false. But, of course, the same can be said of statements to the effect that a certain judicial decision is justified in view of the way the judge has in fact reached and defended his judgement. Granting that the correct method of justifying legal conclusions is such and such, the statement will be logically true or logically false.

A more interesting point is that while both deduction and induction *are* related to truth in ways that the judicial method is not, in some of these ways deduction and induction also differ from each other, so that the relations in question cannot be regarded as essential features of reasoning. Consider material truth or agreement with natural fact. Induction is pragmatically bound to this notion while deduction is not. Ideally, we can calculate the probability of an hypothesis from statements of the evidence with the aid of the induction rules, so that to this extent such rules can be used independently of the truth of such statements. But since the main purpose of induction is to increase our chances of settling on objectively true beliefs, the truth of such statements has to be ascertained. This is not the case with deduction;

that is, its main purpose does not require that we establish the truth of the premisses. To be sure, deduction has an essential role to play in empirical inquiries, and it may be that the deductive sciences would never have developed very far without the spur of such inquiries. But it is possible to carry on some of these sciences with complete indifference to any question of material truth. Hence, if we are to take deduction as one of the paradigms of justificative reasoning, it cannot be an essential aspect of such reasoning that it be carried on for the sake of gaining or certifying materially true beliefs.

What about truth in the more general sense of correctness against contraries? How do our three types of methods compare on that? If it is a question of certifying the *conclusion* of an argument as uniquely correct, then deductive and inductive reasoning are in hardly any better position to do this than judicial reasoning is, and in one respect worth mentioning they are in a worse position. The conclusion of a sound inductive argument can be false, and an indefinitely large number of different conclusions can be validly deduced from the premisses (in various systems of deduction), including mutually contrary conclusions if the premisses should happen to be inconsistent. But in many legal cases of type four we can at least say retrospectively what *the* correct decision was, namely, the decision which the court actually did reach while satisfying the criteria of reasonableness.

However, deductive reasoning can certify the unique correctness of an *argument* against all of its contraries, given consistent premisses. I use the term 'argument' here in the sense of one or more premisses, *P*, and a conclusion, *c*, which is asserted to follow from it or them. The point is that deductive reasoning can certify an argument of the form '$P \rightarrow c$' against any of the form '$P \rightarrow$some contrary of *c*', given that *P* is self-consistent.[3] Similarly, inductive reasoning

[3] Of course, valid arguments in another sense of the term 'argument', viz. the deductive reasoning itself which purports to take us from *P* to *c*, will not usually be *uniquely* correct. The importance of this distinction and the fact that it has been frequently overlooked are developed in John Corcoran's 'Con-

can (ideally) certify that a data-and-probability argument of the form '*D*⟶the probability of *c* is *phi*' is correct against any of the form '*D*⟶the probability of *c* is other than *phi.*' But there is no third analogue to be found here for judicial reasoning. In judicial reason-giving, the rule of support referred to above is not the sort of rule which we can apply to see whether it *does* allow '*P*⟶*c*' *rather than* '*P*⟶some contrary of *c*'. Obviously, it allows both. Following that rule, one judge can 'reason' his way from *P* (which we must conceive as a statement of the existing corpus of law plus all the facts of the case) to *c* (a statement of legal conclusions about the case, on which the court's legal judgement or order will rest), while another judge can reason equally well from *P* to some contrary of *c* which would be the basis of a radically different or substantially contrary judgement or order.[4]

This seems to be the really crucial difference between deductive and inductive reasoning on one side of the alleged abyss and judicial persuasion on the other. One might plausibly maintain that it is essential to any method of justificative reasoning that it be able to certify the unique correctness of *arguments* in this sense. For one reasons that *c* is justified on the basis of *P*, inasmuch as it follows from *P* and *P* is true. But how can *c* be justified in this way if *not-c* or some contrary of *c* follows just as well from *P*?

Another initially plausible argument against our thesis is the following. If we were to allow as a form of justificative reasoning any method of giving statements for the 'support' of other statements as long as this is done in accordance with rules that are suitable for achieving whatever purpose the method might have, this would open the door to all sorts of irrational methods. Doesn't astrology, for example, have its

---

ceptual Structure of Classical Logic', *Phil. and Phenom. Research*, vol. 33 (1971–2).

[4] It should be noted that the fact that both *c* and *not-c* can be properly arrived at on the basis of *P* does not here depend on the fact (though doubtless it is a fact) that *P* is inconsistent. Even if the corpus of law were entirely consistent, different judges could justifiably reach opposite conclusions about a given case while satisfying the standard of good judicial reasoning described in Section 4.

own rules that are recognized and applied by those who devote themselves to this 'field of reasoning'? Or, to take a more widely respected 'discipline', is it not often said that theology has purposes which are quite different from those of science? Perhaps its special modes of argument are appropriate to those purposes. Would not such a concept of reasoning force us to admit that good theological arguments can justify statements about the gods?

3. Addressing ourselves to the latter argument first, we must ask what *are* the purposes of those reason-giving activities? If the purpose of astrology or palmistry is to foretell the future, then their methods or standards are not suitable, for they do not actually enable us to accomplish that purpose. They would have to be ruled out in favour of the methods of common sense and science, with a corresponding restriction on the kinds of future events we can rationally claim to foretell. But if their present purpose is to furnish amusement, then their methods might be very well suited, or they could be changed a little to make them suitable to this purpose. Who could then complain of them? Something rather similar can be said of theology, although our modernizing theologians will understandably shy away from the point. If the purpose of theological argument is to certify beliefs about questions of fact, then its traditional methods are not suitable and must be replaced by the methods which we know are suitable to that purpose. This would no doubt end in severe restriction or abolishment of the traditional subject matter of theology. But if religious people were now to agree or understand that religious discourse has purposes which are fundamentally expressive and poetic, not cognitive, they might be able to develop suitable rules or methods in aid of such purposes, and so go on talking about 'God' in ways that no one could criticize as irrational.[5] However that may be, one can

[5] The rub in this, no doubt, is that many cherished qualities of religious expression that have been associated with *believed* myths would then be lost. Perhaps this is why religious modernists are reluctant to say quite clearly what the point of theological discourse now is in their opinion. Traditionalists would

choose whatever example of pseudo-science one likes and it will not exemplify the concept of reasoning mentioned in the last paragraph. If it did—if its methods actually were suitable for pursuing its goal of knowledge—it would not be a pseudo-science but a real science.

Now let us ask why it is that the possibility of unique correctness in arguments seems essential to the notion of justificative reasoning. Is it not because (i) the clearest mark of an irrational method in co-operative knowledge-seeking activities or would-be *sciences* is the absence of interpersonal checks, and because (ii) it is impossible either to have such checks or to be rationally confident of one's own cognitive claims unless we can have uniquely correct arguments, in the above-indicated sense? If we lacked assurance not merely that *c* does follow from *P*, but that *not-c* does not, then although we could show that *P* is true, we could not know or justifiably believe *c* on the basis of *P*. Hence (to make the general point) we could not know that any *c* is (non-logically) true unless we could directly observe that what it says is the case *is* the case. On the other hand, when we do have a method in which uniquely correct arguments are possible and identifiable, we can establish the truth or probable truth of *c* on the basis of *P*: truth when our method is to deduce *c* from a *P* which is known to be true, and probable truth when our method is to argue inductively from a *P* which is known to be true. And, of course, the purely formal sciences also need unique correctness in arguments for some of their own cognitive purposes. Thus, given that *P* is self-consistent and that we want to know whether *c* is implicit in *P*, we can get the answer by deducing *c* (or *not-c*) from *P*, but only on condition that our method will not enable us to do both.

Thus it would appear that the main purpose of the empirical sciences, and certainly a major purpose of purely formal science, would be frustrated if their methods did not normally guarantee that we cannot arrive at mutually inconsistent conclusions from the same self-consistent evidence or

---

have no trouble choosing between supernaturalism and a banalized literary genre, but both alternatives will be distasteful to the modernist.

premisses. And more particularly, it is necessary that different people correctly applying the methods of science to test a conclusion by reasoning from the same available evidence or premisses should normally be guaranteed against certifying opposite results. The word 'normally' is no doubt an essential qualification here. But even when opposite results *are* validly obtained from the available evidence by different investigators or theorists working in some new or unsettled area of knowledge, we ought to say that the evidence is as yet inconclusive, not that the theory they disagree about both has probability *phi* and lacks it, or that empirical arguments really lack unique correctness in our sense. They have it very typically. Otherwise we could not have the stock of inferential knowledge we certainly do have, either in the sciences or in everyday cognitive affairs.

The important point to notice is that the absence of such a guarantee does not interfere with the purpose of judicial reasoning in cases of type four. The purpose there is not to gain or certify knowledge. It is not to show that certain statements are true or probable, or that they are implicit in other statements. On the contrary, it is presupposed in this ideal type that there are no true legal conclusions to identify or certify; and to the extent that any issue in a real case is classifiable to this type, there is no legal truth or knowledge that can be in question concerning it. The purpose is rather to *persuade* one's audience (litigants, legal profession, public) of the *desirability* of one's judgement and legislative product, or at least to reconcile them to one's reasonableness in rendering that judgement and creating that bit of law.

Let us summarize and draw the obvious conclusions. Unique correctness in arguments is a desideratum made necessary by the purposes of deduction and induction as cognitive methods, but it is not required by the purpose of judicial reasoning in difficult cases lacking true decisions under existing law. Its absence does explain why 'serious astrology' is not a method of rational justification, because the purpose of serious astrological argument is the same as the purpose of scientific argument: to certify knowledge of, or probable belief about, material facts. But its absence does not show that the standard of good judicial persuasion in type four cases is not a method of rational justification, since reasoning in such cases has no cognitive purpose and thus no need (in that connection, at least) of uniquely correct arguments in our sense. The same point applies, of course, to the standard of good moral reasoning explicated in Sections 2 and 3. That standard also does not provide a method of giving or identifying uniquely correct arguments for moral statements. For in light of what was said there, we must conceive of *P* as consisting of all the facts about the subject of our moral evaluation which we regard on due reflection as in any way relevant, plus all moral principles which we regard as relevant. And it will then be possible for one person to conclude, in compliance with the standard, that *c* is the correct evaluation to make, while another person (or the same person at another time) may come equally well to a contrary conclusion. But our supposition was that moral statements are neither true nor false, and hence that the purpose of moral reasoning is not to certify moral statements as true or probably true, but to persuade others to agree with them, etc. So there is no need on that account for unique correctness in moral arguments, and our standard of good moral persuasion is not disqualified on that account as a standard of rational justification.

4. Perhaps it will be said that the mere fact that there is this difference in purpose, and hence in the *need* for unique correctness in arguments, is enough in itself to show that judicial reasoning in very difficult cases ought not to be called reasoning in the sense of rational justification. But how does it show this? We *could* perhaps shape the notion of justification so as to apply it only to argumentation in support of knowledge claims or probability claims. But what need is there to do so? We needn't do so in order to exclude irrational methods, as we have seen. Should we do so in order to exclude such things as astrological amusements and theological poetry from the denotation of 'justification'? They

will be excluded anyway by their primary amusement aspect or poetry aspect. It does not seem to me that *any* sacrifice of our other intellectual needs or interests would accrue from applying the term to judicial reasoning, and I think definite advantages might be claimed for it. First, it would clarify and sharpen our ideas. In the concept of justification which we have sketched from deductive and inductive reasoning, the important requirement of interpersonal checks and uniquely correct argument floats freely, as it were, through the general concept, while the usage here recommended would serve to tie this requirement down to those species of justification where it is actually needed. And a cognate advantage of more obvious importance is that this would save the common opinion and usage—common among lawyers, certainly—that judges *can* give very good or very strong reasons for their decisions even in the most difficult cases, not just 'some sort of reasons or alleged reasons', to recur to the weak sense of 'justify' mentioned earlier. For surely, to give very good or very strong reasons for one's evaluative conclusion *is* to justify it rationally.

One might therefore propose to reshape or reform the notion of justification or justificative reasoning so as to include good judicial reasoning in such cases among the things this notion comprehends. But the same considerations argue just as well that it is already included. We conservatively built up the notion of justificative reasoning from deduction and induction, leaving judicial 'reasoning' out of it so as not to assume prematurely that the latter use of the word employs the same concept. And it was in the concept thus built up that we found the generic requirement of unique correctness in arguments and interpersonal checks. But we saw that no mischief is to be expected from extending that somewhat artificially obtained concept to judicial argument in the way proposed, while limiting such requirement to the justification of knowledge and probability claims. And from this fact, I think we can now see that it would have been correct to use judicial reasoning in legally open cases as a third paradigm in building up the concept, just as the usage referred to at the end of the preceding paragraph would suggest that we should. So it seems to me that we are not making any substantial revision in the ordinary notion of justificative reasoning, but only a useful specification of that typically vague, non-technical concept.

Again let us notice in passing how the point applies equally to moral reasoning. People surely believe and say even more commonly that it is possible to give very good or very strong reasons for many of our moral judgements. So the strong notion of justification is being employed, and the usefulness of specifying the general concept in the way that I have just described is again illustrated. One also sees in retrospect, therefore, that it would not have led us into error if we had taken 'moral reasoning', as this has been explicated in parallel with 'judicial reasoning', for still another paradigm of rational justification.

5. Finally, we must consider the important objection that, if what I have said so far is correct, the emotive theory of ethics may also be said to offer a method of rational justification. As conceived by the emotive theory, moral argument is not intended to establish the truth or probable truth of moral statements, so it is not vulnerable in the way serious astrology or serious phrenology are vulnerable. *Its* goal is to produce agreement in attitudes, and the emotivist's criterion of a good reason or a good piece of moral argument is that it is likely to influence attitudes in the way intended by the person using it, i.e. towards agreement with the attitude expressed by the moral statement which he is defending. So it has a 'reasoning rule' which discriminates between good and bad reasons, and the observance of that rule is well calculated to attain the objective which this activity has in view. Thus it is a method of rational justification, according to what I have said up to this point, even though it sometimes licenses special pleading, the exploitation of fear, prejudice, ignorance of fact, etc.[6]

It is not a sufficient reply to this objection to point out, as I

[6] See the second paragraph of Section 4.

did at the beginning of Section 4, that the emotive theory's account of moral argument cannot be an acceptable explication of moral reasoning as we know it. For I think it would still reduce our own account of justification to an absurdity if the criterion of relevance given by Stevenson would, in any case, *be* a standard of rational justification according to that account. And such a result would undermine my whole project in this first Part, which (as I said in the Introduction) is to show how reasoning has a more important role in moral discourse than either Hare or the emotivists have managed to explain.

The objection gives us the clue we need, however, to round out our discussion of the concept of justification by adding a further condition to those which have been specified so far and correctly restated in the objection. What condition shall we add? If we are intuitively convinced that the existing standards of good moral and judicial persuasion do constitute standards of rational justification, we will naturally look for one or more additional features which they share with each other and with the other paradigms, and which seem essential to good reasoning when we attend to them. So let us do this.

It should be pointed out first that moral and judicial reasoning, as I have described them, not only follow rules the observance of which is well calculated to attain the respective purposes of these two reason-giving activities, but that they also have very similar rules because their objectives are very similar. And while in each case the objective is, in part, substantive agreement, it is also significantly unlike the objective which is furthered by Stevenson's rule of relevance. In consequence, their rules of reasoning are quite different from his, and of course the class of reasons which will count as good reasons is also quite different. His rule tells us to use whatever facts and arguments will be psychologically effective to produce the attitude we want to produce in our interlocutor or audience. In contrast, the rule of good moral reasoning and the rule of good judicial reasoning in legally open cases tell us to use all and only those facts and arguments which we have honestly found most appealing when we have been well informed of relevant facts and substantive standards, and have considered the question at hand from a disinterested and psychologically normal point of view. They tell us this because the purpose of choosing and offering reasons is, in each case, to persuade our interlocutor or audience in a *reasonable* way to accept our judgement, or at least to convince them that it is a judgement which we *reasonably* hold.

These additional common features show that our standards of moral and judicial reasoning satisfy a more general requirement which the standards of good inductive and deductive reasoning will also be found to satisfy, but which the emotivist's standard for moral reasoning does not satisfy. It is a requirement which is difficult to state concisely, but perhaps the following characterizations will be sufficient for our purposes. In order to constitute a standard of rational justification, a standard of good reasoning performances must not only be an objective standard in the way I have repeatedly explained; it must also be accompanied by the following assumptions. The statement one seeks to justify must be considered to have its own objective status, to be in some sense sound or valid or true quite independently of one's own feelings, desires, or interests. To be sure, we *may* believe it, or feel that it is sound, or be strongly attracted to it, or desire that it should be true or valid, or have some special interest in defending it. But none of these subjective factors or relations can determine its truth or soundness or validity, marking it off as a statement we *should* defend as against its contraries. Rather, the relevant rule of reasoning tells us how to identify certain objective factors or considerations which give a statement that status, that claim upon our rational acceptance whether or not we care to accept it. It is true that the emotivist's rule also tells us what facts and standards to cite as our reasons, namely those which are likely to induce others to accept a certain moral statement. It also tells us what moral statement to defend, namely, any moral statement we may feel like defending. And this is no doubt the gist of the matter. Under a method of rational justification, the statement to be justified *must not* be any statement one likes.

The kind of external control that is imposed by reasoning rules in a true method of justification can best be appreciated by noticing the sorts of arguments we would otherwise be permitted to make. In 'justifying' a statement of fact as probable in some degree, we could omit that part of the data which tends to drive the probability down to something lower. In defending a claim that conclusion *c* is strictly entailed by premisses *P*, we could proceed by any successive lines of proof our audience might be induced to accept, however low its logical sophistication might be. And in defending a moral judgement, we could offer any facts or arguments that might be expected to move our actual audience to accept the judgement, regardless of whether a well-informed and impartially reflective audience would be so affected by them, or whether we sincerely accept them ourselves when considering the subject of judgement from the moral point of view.

The point probably needs to be emphasized that it is not just Stevenson's account of moral relevance which thus runs afoul of this last requirement of rational justification. I doubt that some other version of the emotive theory that was more intent on preserving moral common sense could add the requirement of reasonableness to that of psychological efficacy in determining the relevance of moral reasons, or that it could substitute the former requirement for the latter. It seems that no version of the emotive theory could do either of these things unless it were prepared to go on and show that reasonableness is not just another moral value or attitude which may be disputed or avoided like any other, but has a privileged status in moral discourse. Stevenson seems to have been clear on this point in *Ethics and Language*, despite isolated passages suggesting the contrary. And as recently as his presidential address of 1962,[7] he did not think it possible to go on to show such a thing.[8] If anyone does succeed in showing it, as I have attempted to do in this first part of my essay, the result may be sufficiently different from other ethical

[7] Cited at p. 4, above.

[8] Both points are well documented by Carl Wellman in the article cited at p. 76, above.

theories as to require a label of its own—different not merely from the classical emotive theories of Ayer[9] and Stevenson, but also from more recent theories which have correctly reported that there seem to be bad though efficacious methods of persuasion. While it is all very well to point out that reasonableness seems to be a privileged value in ordinary moral discourse, it is also highly desirable to *explain* its logical privilege if we possibly can.[10]

It may be useful to summarize the long argument which comes to an end at this point. When our examination of objective standards and evaluative truth seemed to disclose, in Section 1, that moral statements can be neither true nor false, we resolved to inquire whether such statements can nevertheless be rationally justified, as we normally assume in everyday thought and talk. After describing various commonly accepted criteria of good moral reflection and argument in Section 2, and considering what fundamental purpose in choice these criteria might presuppose, I attempted in Section 3 to identify the purpose which they necessarily do presuppose. If I have succeeded, this shows that the criteria in question constitute an objective standard of good reasoning, that is, a standard which will permit us to make true evaluations of moral reasoning performances. But it still remained to show that the 'reasoning' performances thus found to be good are rational justifications of the moral statements which they are given to support, rather than *merely* efficient means to produce certain desired effects, i.e. moral agreement or respect. More precisely, the question was whether supporting a moral statement in the way best calculated to produce such effects is rationally justifying it. Our discussions in Sections 4 and 5 seem to have shown that it is. The concept of justification which I have attempted to specify or unfold in Section 5 does apply to moral reasoning in compliance with that standard, just as it applies to judicial reasoning in compliance with *its* own standard in legally open cases. It is hardly

[9] Chap. VI of *Language, Truth and Logic* (2nd edn.; London: Gollancz, 1948); also pp. 20–2.

[10] For further illustration, see Appendix IV.

surprising, of course, that our standards of moral and judicial reasoning should satisfy that concept when, in the last analysis, the concept has been abstracted from them. But it has not been abstracted *only* from them.

The reader may now be left to judge whether I have managed to explain how moral statements can be justified.

PART II
Moral Truth

6. Paradigms of Moral Truth

IN trying to understand the logic of morals, we should do what we can to accommodate the widespread conviction and usage that many moral judgements or statements are not merely reasonable but indisputably true, and that certain others, if anyone cares to entertain them, are just as clearly false. Ethical theories of the naturalist type can claim some credit on this score even if they give insufficient weight to personal autonomy in the *way* they conceive of moral truth. On the other hand, those theories which have paid more attention to the autonomy of the moral agent or judge, and have accordingly rejected naturalism, have hardly begun to do justice to the notion of truth in morals. While the intuitionists of thirty to sixty years ago accepted it verbally, they notoriously did not explain it, and various emotivists and prescriptivists have pretty well given up on it. Some recent anti-naturalists have thought that truth is an indispensable notion in morals because it seems too paradoxical to deny that various moral statements *are* true; but what it *means* to say of a moral statement that it is true remains highly obscure. My ambition in this Part is to consider what sort of basis (what type of standard) *this* form of evaluative truth might have, so that we might at least find a clear sense for 'moral truth' and cognate expressions. I shall not here be interested in deciding which moral statements *are* true, except incidentally to that purpose.

It will not be necessary to take back anything asserted in Part I, although in this section and the first part of Section 7 it will temporarily seem that I must. I do of course withdraw the provisional assumption, retained throughout the last four sections, that evaluative truth, whether in morals or in any other subject matter, must always consist in the entailment of an evaluative statement by one or more statements of fact together with a standard which is either objective or legislatively valid. That assumption was not necessary to what we did in those sections; it merely accompanied the argument that even *if* there is no such thing as moral truth one might still manage to explain how moral statements can be rationally justified.

Let us begin by examining one or two moral statements which I think practically everyone would say are obviously true—everyone, that is, but certain moral philosophers while they are philosophizing. Let us grant that they are true, and attempt to explain how one would show that they are true if called upon to do so. After that, let us briefly discuss more doubtful moral questions on which it would be difficult and perhaps impossible to establish the truth. In light of these discussions, and in light of our previous elimination of objective and legislative standards, let us then conclude the present section by suggesting a third type of basis or standard for moral evaluation. The conception of moral truth thus proposed will be developed at length in Section 7, and one more consideration in its favour will be pointed out in Appendix III after we have completed our legal analogy.

To common sense it seems perfectly obvious that some actions are morally right and others wrong, so obvious that one could explain conclusively why they are right or wrong. It may be hard to give conclusive arguments in moral *problems,* where sincere differences of opinion can easily occur; but surely one *could* prove a great many moral judgements on easy questions where there is no such disagreement. Here is the way Mr. G. J. Warnock expressed this idea in a book published several years ago:

One could argue conclusively that some course of action would be, say morally wrong if one could show that that course of action would lead *quite certainly* to certain consequences, which would constitute *indisputably* some serious harm to some innocent person or persons and that there would accrue *quite certainly* no good to anyone which could possibly be held to outweigh those harmful consequences. It is not that there are no cases which satisfy these conditions; it could be shown, for instance, with this sort of conclusiveness that it would be morally wrong for me to induce in my children addiction to heroin. But, of course, when *all* the relevant considerations point *indisputably* one way, it is unlikely to occur to anyone that the argument is worth stating; the question, in fact, is scarcely likely ever to be raised. Nevertheless, that such an argument, if stated, could be really demonstrative, seems to me clear; and anyone who, if such an argument is put to him, denies that the conclusion follows—who holds, while conceding the facts, that, for instance, it would *not* be morally wrong for me to induce in my children addiction to heroin—shows either that he has not really followed the argument, or that he does not know what 'morally wrong' means.[1]

Let us take the moral judgement referred to in this passage and attempt to prove it in the way the author apparently thinks it can be proved. If I understand him correctly, the argument would run as follows.

1. Other things being equal, it is morally wrong to cause serious harm to innocent persons.
2. Inducing in my children addiction to heroin would lead to consequences that constitute serious harm to innocent persons.
3. There would accrue no good to anyone which could outweigh those harmful consequences.

Therefore, it would be morally wrong for me to induce in my children addiction to heroin.

Does the conclusion follow from the premisses? Some doubt might be entertained on this point since the accrual of countervailing good to someone might not be the only way in which things can fail to be 'equal'. So let us rewrite premiss 3 as follows:

3. There is nothing about the present case which could justify

[1] G. J. Warnock, *Contemporary Moral Philosophy* (London: Macmillan, 1967), p. 70.

causing those harmful consequences; that is to say, other things *are* equal.

Now since premisses 2 and 3′ are undoubtedly true, and since it would seem absurd for anyone to question the moral principle expressed in premiss 1, the argument seems to be demonstrative, a valid deduction from premisses known to be true. Notice that the truth of the conclusion does not consist in its entailment by facts and a valid universal standard. Instead of such a standard, we have in premiss 1 a moral criterion or principle with 'other things being equal' in it.

Let us ask how we do know that these premisses are true. Not that there would be any practical need to explain this; probably no one *would* ask us how we know these things. But for present purposes it is necessary to consider how such a question should be answered.

As for the first premiss, I would say about *it* what Warnock says about his whole argument: anyone seriously questioning it could hardly be said to know what 'morally wrong' means. I shall not here attempt to explain just *how* the meaning of that phrase is connected to 'causes serious harm to innocent persons', but if the reader has any doubt that premiss 1 *is* self-evident, let him read it again.[2] Notice that without its *ceteris paribus* clause, premiss 1 would not be self-evident but obviously too general and false. To use an unpleasant example which precisely fits the point, it might be necessary and right to shoot an insane person to keep him from blowing up a whole trainload of innocent people in the next moment. Avoiding harm to people apparently *cannot be left out of account* in moral evaluation. That an action avoids such harm does not suffice to make it right although it counts in its favour; and that an action harms someone, even someone innocent, does not suffice to make it wrong in all circumstances, although it counts against it and always *tends* to make it wrong. To put this another way, the prevention and

[2] A promising explanation is offered in the book by R. W. Beardsmore mentioned in the Introduction and discussed in Appendix II. I shall return to this question in Section 7.

avoidance of harm to people is apparently *an* object of morality as we know it, even if not *the* object. While there are other objects, and accordingly other moral principles which sometimes come into conflict with the principle announced in premiss 1, there will be individual cases in which there is no doubt at all that the latter principle controls; and this is such a case. It seems that 'there is no doubt at all' should be taken rather literally here. It is not as though there were one supreme object which indicates that there *should* be no doubt, like the basic purpose in choice which tells us how to adjudicate conflicts between the several value criteria appearing in an objective standard. It is just that no one *would* have any doubt in such an extremely easy case, certainly no one who considered the matter from the moral point of view as characterized in Part I.

Premiss 2 certainly looks like a statement which could easily be checked and confirmed. For the sake of the illustration, we may suppose that the children are very young and thus innocent by definition. And we may safely assume that heroin addiction would be seriously harmful to them through disruption of their normal socialization in the type of society in which they will probably have to live, whether or not it would cause serious physical harm. But more on premiss 2 in a moment.

As for premiss 3′, Warnock would no doubt be entirely justified in asserting that other things *are* equal. I am quite sure that I would be so justified if the example pertained to me and my children. There is just nothing about my children or their relations with other people or things which even remotely suggests to me that there could be any good consequence of causing them to become addicted, or that I should cause them to become addicted for some other reason. They have no disease which can only be treated with addictive doses of heroin; there is no religious doctrine or bit of revelation that I know of, according to which it is my duty, like Abraham, to cause them this harm; and so on.

It is true that universal negative statements like premiss 3′ are always evaluative. Even if we know of no reason why the moral consequence generally attaching to the principal description (that common to premisses 1 and 2) should not attach in the present case, so that there is nothing to 'weigh' or evaluate for that possible effect, we still must have judged that the moral significance of all other true non-moral descriptions of the subject being evaluated is nil. And the *ceteris paribus* clause in a moral principle cannot be construed as equivalent to a closed list of exceptions with fixed weights so that it could be a purely non-evaluative question whether there are any countervailing considerations in the case sufficient to override the effect of the principal description. But even though premiss 3′ is evaluative, one may very well be entitled to believe and assert it.

If one had to explain in some detail why Warnock would be entitled to assert premiss 3′ it seems that the explanation would be approximately the following. He is in position to know all about the case, to have a sufficiently thorough knowledge of any facts that might be relevant to the rightness or wrongness of the course of action described. Hence, he *would* no doubt be aware of any fact that *could* possibly constitute a countervailing reason, a reason cancelling or at least weighing against its wrongness. But being imaginatively attentive to the facts of the case, and considering the matter impartially and calmly, he is aware of *no* such reason. And since the argument in which premiss 3′ figures is intended to justify a moral judgement and not merely a claim that he has consistently adhered to his own preferences, he must feel that none of the facts *should* strike *anyone* as such a reason, or at least not as a sufficient reason. In short, one is not entitled to say that other things are equal merely because one is not prepared to give any countervailing reasons. Rather, one must know of no such reasons, being well informed of the facts and considering them in the way required by the standard of moral reasonableness described in Section 2.

Notice that contrary evaluations are not *logically* excluded. Highly eccentric evaluations like that of some madman who thinks it a father's duty to cause his children to become addicted will only be psychologically excluded. They will seem obviously unacceptable to anyone, or practically anyone, who views the matter in the way just described. Not only is it a safe bet that Warnock would be justified in asserting premiss 3′, but it would also seem to be correct (linguistically normal) to say that he knows that premiss 3′ is true. Once again, *I* certainly know that there isn't any reason why it would be morally permissible for me to cause *my* children to become addicted to heroin. I am not restricted to saying 'probably there isn't' merely because there is no finite list of absolute exceptions, or some other moral algorithm which I could use to demonstrate that there is no such reason.

There are, of course, highly eccentric opinions not only about the sorts of considerations that could justify inflicting serious harm upon the innocent, but also about what constitutes harm. Bearing this in mind, it can be seen that premiss 2 of the argument also has its evaluative element.[3] For all I know, there are people (perhaps some addicts with an easy and secure source of supply) who think daily euphoria from heroin is a great enhancement of life, even in spite of the disadvantages of addiction. Far from agreeing that there are no countervailing considerations in our hypothetical case, such people would not even regard addiction as harmful. Or one could imagine a society in which the highest honours and privileges are reserved for a priestly caste of life-long heroin addicts. In such a society, the great honour of addiction might count as a *prima facie* reason why it is right to cause one's children to become addicted. But Warnock, being the sort of person he is, living in the kind of society he does live in, and having the sort of feelings he has about the harmful effects of heroin addiction, would dismiss such considerations as ridiculous if they occurred to him, and would see nothing but harmful consequences. This would be a very reasonable judgement on his part, and it could be justified in the same way that premiss 3′ can be justified. Indeed, the two judgements overlap. Finding no beneficial effects for the children is part of finding no factual considerations indicating values

[3] The point is also discussed in Appendix II.

to offset the harm. And again, it would be quite correct to say that Warnock *knows* it would be harmful to the children to cause them to become addicted.

These, then, are the ways in which we know that the premisses of the argument set out above are true. In concluding this part of the discussion, it may be noted that the second premiss of a moral inference—that which describes the subject of our moral judgement—can sometimes be purely descriptive. For example, such an inference may begin with the premiss that it is wrong, other things being equal, to cause severe physical pain to someone, and this may then be followed with the purely descriptive premiss that such and such an action does so. It should also be noted that the third premiss is probably always needed in justifying a moral conclusion by appeal to facts and principles. This is because no moral principle (no candidate for premiss 1) will be quite safely true without a *ceteris paribus* clause; or so it would seem. It is wrong to tell a lie, or to steal, cheat, rape, or kill; but perhaps not absolutely so, not in every conceivable circumstance.

In the foregoing illustration, all of the relevant considerations point indisputably in the same direction. Let us now consider one or two moral questions which are not so completely one-sided but nevertheless do have obviously true answers. Suppose I have promised you that I would do something, and you have relied on my promise and will suffer a moderate loss if I fail to do it, but that unforeseeable circumstances now make it disastrous or even fatal for me to do it. Practically anyone would agree that I am not morally obliged to keep my promise, even if I am unable to make good your loss. Or, seeing that the insane person will certainly blow up the train unless we shoot him, practically anyone would agree that it is morally right to shoot him even though doing so will cause serious harm to an innocent person. In these cases there *are* substantial countervailing considerations, and they clearly are sufficient. We must therefore reject the 'other things are equal' premiss, and with it the conclusion that it would be wrong to break the promise or shoot the man. So we replace the rejected inference with one we can accept. For example:

(1) Other things being equal, one ought morally to do what one easily can do to prevent mass destruction of human life.

(2) Shooting this one lunatic now is required to prevent such mass destruction, and I easily can shoot him.

(3) Other things are equal; that is, the fact that it will harm him seriously is not a sufficient excuse for failing to do it, and there is no such excuse.

Therefore, I ought to shoot him.

The reasoning that would be required to justify my accepting the premisses of this argument is the same as that described a moment ago. Thus, premiss 1 could hardly be questioned by anyone who knows what 'ought morally' means. Premiss 2 is an empirical statement that could be highly probable (the trestle appears to be mined; he has repeatedly threatened to blow up the train; he is reaching for the detonator, etc.). And premiss 3 represents my honest judgement of the relative weight of the two evils involved, the same judgement anyone would make. Depending on the circumstances, and above all on how confident one could be of premiss 2, this argument could also be demonstrative—a valid deduction from premisses known to be true—even though there are facts weighing tragically against one's judgement.[4]

Before passing on to doubtful moral questions, let us pause to relate this more detailed account of moral reasoning to what was said in Part I. Otherwise there may be some unclarity as to the sense in which 'reasons' is being used. In the foregoing account, it appears that moral principles (like 'it is wrong to harm the innocent, other things being equal') and facts (like 'this harms the innocent') are reasons for particular

[4] Notice that even Warnock's example is not absolutely one-sided. After all, the children will presumably have euphoric periods as they are becoming addicted. But this is a negligible value which we (informed and reasonably reflecting people) will recognize but not regret sacrificing.

evaluative statements (like 'this is wrong'), and that statements of the reasons deductively entail the conclusion when joined to the premiss that other things are equal. But wasn't it suggested in Part I that the fact that a person has accepted a moral statement in accordance with the requirements of Section 2 is a reason for that statement? The answer is that in both Parts of this essay it is intended that principles and facts are reasons for a moral statement, whereas the fact that a person has made or accepted the statement in accordance with the requirements of Section 2 is a reason, or rather *the* reason, why *he* is justified in making or accepting it. The statement is then also said to be justified *as his* statement.[5] How these reasons for different kinds of things relate to one another can be summarized as follows.

As part of one's moral judgement-making and decision-making, one considers and adopts certain reasons, i.e. facts and principles which one finds salient and controlling when considering the subject of evaluation in the manner required by Section 2. Then, in justifying one's judgement or decision to someone else, one gives these reasons, as well as any other reasons one may have for regarding *those* reasons as true and controlling. (We have just been explaining what these other reasons are like.) Thus, a person and his judgement (*qua* his) are justified if and only if he has followed the procedure of Section 2. And he justifies his judgement (*qua* content) to others by giving those reasons and further supporting reasons. He asks his interlocutor to see whether those reasons are not convincing to him also, viewing the subject of evaluation in accordance with Section 2. This request is normally tacit when it is understood that the parties are engaged in a *moral* debate or discussion. Finally, if one's interlocutor does appreciate the fact that one has satisfied the requirements of Section 2, this may help to assure his respect, even if not his acceptance of those reasons and the moral statement which they entail.

Let us now briefly turn to cases where the relevant considerations not only point in opposite directions but, in doing

[5] See page 49, lines 11 to 16.

so, leave us with a moral question that is difficult to answer. Sometimes moral dilemmas are not only occasions for deep regret because some important value must be sacrificed, as in the train case, but are also difficult intellectual problems. Careful reflection may be necessary before we can be sure *which* value should be sacrificed, if we ever can be sure. The considerations on either side may be much more nearly equal than in the last example, so that people could easily disagree about their relative importance. For example, I might have to choose between (i) helping a person who is in serious distress and (ii) keeping my promise to someone else who will be harmed if I do not keep it. My doubt may be relieved by learning more of the facts; but perhaps not. Or someone else might judge differently than I would, though we were both fully informed. Recall the illustration in Section 2 of the man who had very strong reasons for going to the science convention, and also very strong reasons for not going. He and his wife had opposite but equally reasonable opinions about whether he ought to go.

We may also be in serious doubt as to whether a certain principle is morally valid, either to serve as our first premiss or to indicate countervailing facts. Many moral principles that people sincerely accept are, of course, not self-evident like the principles which I have mentioned so far in this section. Consider the principles that contraception is wrong, or the principle that non-therapeutic abortion after the first several weeks of pregnancy is wrong, or the principle that civil disobedience in a democracy is wrong. We are not apparently forced by the very meaning of 'morally wrong' to accept them or to reject them, and of course people often disagree about these and many other principles.

The fact that people are often in moral doubt or disagreement does not prove, of course, that they would remain in doubt or continue to disagree after mature reflection. And surely there would be *less* disagreement if people did reflect more than they do. But since there is no official canon of valid moral principles, and no official table of moral weights and measures, it is always *logically* possible that people should disagree even when they are well informed and otherwise judging reasonably. No doubt this will also at times be a *psychological* possibility or probability, if only because of differences in temperament and moral training.

Now, in these difficult cases, *must* some one judgement nevertheless be true? *Are* there answers to the moral questions posed by such cases which are correct to the exclusion of all contrary answers? Must either the sick scientist or his wife be mistaken in their equally informed and reflective judgements? It strikes me as very implausible to say so. Is it not far more plausible to think that there simply is no *true* moral judgement to make in response to many a difficult question—no one judgement which 'agrees with the moral facts', whatever that might mean? To be sure, it is not only *very easy* moral questions which seem to admit of true answers. I think it would also be commonly thought that many a moral question which demands serious reflection does have a true answer. It is important to reflect on moral problems confronting us because we want to avoid acting or judging *wrongly*, and it seems that we sometimes do succeed in such reflection. But this might be accounted for by pointing out that the correct answer to a moral question may not *become* obvious until the facts of the case have been investigated and considered by a reasoning mind. Sometimes we will remain in doubt or disagreement even though we have all the pertinent non-moral facts and deductive relations well in hand. And I doubt that people commonly think that *every* moral question, no matter how difficult, no matter how evenly balanced the arguments pro and con may seem to be, has a correct answer which excludes all contrary answers, even though we may never be able to tell what that answer is. I daresay that anyone who has ever been torn by a really difficult moral dilemma would think such a view naive. And other people would probably have no opinion on the point unless they were philosophers puzzling over the epistemology of morals.

If there are no true answers to many difficult moral questions, what is it that differentiates these questions from those which obviously do admit of true answers? In both types of questions, it is entirely possible to construct valid deductions in our three-premiss form; in both, such arguments can use verifiable non-evaluative premisses; and in both, the evaluative premisses will often be justifiably accepted and asserted by the person who is judging the case. The only notable difference, it would seem, is that in the easy cases *practically everyone* would agree, while in the difficult cases there would probably be considerable disagreement or doubt. More precisely, there would be agreement and disagreement in these respective cases *among people who are qualified to judge and have properly judged.*

If we were looking for a *sign* of moral truth which we could rely on, we might therefore naturally look for a consensus among people who have actually considered the subject of our evaluation in the way described in Section 2. Yet, what is it that possession of those qualifications equips one to judge, lending authority to one's judgement and especially to the consensus of people so equipped? Can we establish that authority by independently checking the truth and falsity of various moral judgements and showing that such a consensus of reasonable people is normally a reliable guide? This is just what we apparently cannot do, of course. The whole discussion up to this point leaves us entirely in the dark about how such an independent determination should be made. We have only found that we had better stop chasing the will-o'-the-wisp of an objective moral standard, which utilitarians and other naturalists still find attractive.[6]

In this situation, if we are going to take common moral thought and discourse seriously and continue to say that moral statements are very often true or false, I suggest that we try out the following idea even though it is sure to jar very badly at first on many philosophical ears. The truth of a moral statement may simply consist in the fact, or result directly from the fact, that such statement would represent the consensus of those people who might consider the moral

[6] The model of moral legislation is no longer very attractive even to philosophers of theological orientation, for reasons briefly mentioned in Section 1.

question to which it is addressed and form a justified moral opinion about that question. In our main paradigm of true moral judgement, we found that one is *justified* in thinking it wrong to cause one's children to become addicted to heroin if (*a*) one has reflected properly, and (*b*) the relevant facts and principles make one feel that it *is* wrong or properly to be condemned. And what else is there in the example to make this a *true* judgement—to make it a fact that such behaviour *is* wrong—except the fact that *anyone* who might consider the matter properly would be practically certain to concur? I find it hard to imagine what else moral truth *could* be based on but such a consensus if we must reject (i) the notion that morality is the product of some absolute legislator, and (ii) the idea that it is all designed to further some one indisputable purpose.

Notice that we have already found it natural and correct to use 'know' in a way that is compatible with this use of 'true'. If we know something it must be true; and we observed that, in the illustration, Warnock is not merely justified in thinking there is no reason why it would be morally permissible for him to turn his children into heroin addicts, but surely knows this to be the case, knows that other things *are* equal. How is it that we can say this? I suggest that it is because anyone who similarly knew all about the case and considered the facts in a morally reasonable way would be practically certain to agree that there is no such reason, and that *this* is also an obvious fact.

My suggestion is not that the moral truth about something is whatever the overwhelming majority of people think about it, or would think about it if we asked them. It is rather that a moral statement is true if and only if practically everyone who might consider it *in the proper manner* would concur in it. Accordingly, it could easily happen that a certain moral statement were true even though the majority of people rejected it, not having informed themselves on the question, or not having considered it attentively and impartially, etc. And it is even logically possible that everyone should reject a certain true moral statement, no one having properly considered it. Notice also that according to this suggestion many moral statements are neither true nor false, since on many moral questions there would be no consensus among well informed people judging reasonably. But whenever there would be such a consensus, any moral statement to the contrary would be false.

One must consider the following points, however. The fact that everyone agrees, or would agree that a certain proposition *p* is true cannot make it true—cannot make it the case that-*p*. Nor is it true, in general, that something can be made to be the case by the fact that everyone *holding a justified opinion* on the matter would agree or think that it is the case. These are important aspects of the ordinary notion of truth, and they hold good for evaluative truth under objective and legislative standards. What does make it the case that-*p* in those kinds of evaluative truth is that *p* follows from non-evaluative facts and a valid standard. How then might the idea of a consensus be eked out with some further objective element which would account for the feeling and common usage that moral statements like those in our paradigms are certainly true, not just thought to be true? I think this further element could take the form of semantic rules. It could be that certain moral criteria or principles are part of the very meaning of 'wrong', 'ought morally', etc., and that in rejecting or questioning them we would not only misuse these words but also deviate from the communal patterns of approval and disapproval which have validated these principles.

This suggestion jibes with what we found it correct to say about the principles figuring in our paradigm arguments. It is also worth mentioning that many philosophers have thought it plausible that there are necessary connections between predicates of moral value and non-evaluative descriptive predicates. If these connections cannot be fixed by some all-controlling purpose in moral choice, as I have argued they cannot, perhaps they are fixed piecemeal as we learn to live the form of moral life into which we are born. To learn to live a certain way of life is to learn to have the same sorts of moral experiences under given conditions that other people living that life normally have—to approve and disapprove similar things morally, i.e. from the moral point of view. People living that life will agree that—or, rather, will have learned from an early age that—certain features in an action make it a wrong action, 'wrong' being the word one uses to express moral disapproval and to indicate that something is *properly* disapproved and discouraged. The lesson that lying is wrong, for example, will have been learned just as soon, and as just as important a lesson, as the lesson that 'lying' means telling an untruth in order to deceive.[7]

Criteria of excuse and mitigation will also have been learned, as will criteria of moral rightness in several senses—what we may do, ought to do, or deserve praise for doing. And therefore criteria for the justification of actions that would otherwise be wrong will also have been learned. Now, in a large number of instances, only a single criterion will apply. Or if two or more apply they will often do so in concert: with no conflict of 'right-making' and 'wrong-making' features, and no significant excusing or mitigating features if the action be wrong. These are the very easy moral cases we all know how to judge correctly, and do judge correctly nearly every day, at least to ourselves (and whether or not we act accordingly). This was illustrated in our first paradigm. Furthermore, in many cases which are not *entirely* one-sided, we who have learned to live a certain form of moral life would still apply our moral criteria with virtual unanimity, as was illustrated in some of the other examples. But as I said before, there seems to be no statable rule or second-order criterion which we follow in doing so, and we soon run into cases where there would be persistent doubt or substantial disagreement among us even though we were completely informed of the relevant non-moral facts and were otherwise in compliance with the standard of reasonableness.

Why restrict the test of moral truth to those sharing one form of moral life? The reasons for this restriction cannot be

[7] Cf. the discussion of Beardsmore, Phillips, and Mounce in Appendix II and the books cited here.

made fully explicit until the second half of Section 7. But it should be pointed out here that the paradigms by which the consensus notion of truth was introduced already illustrate the need for such a restriction. This was explicit in the heroin case, where we had to admit that in a society very different from ours it could be right, *prima facie*, to cause one's child to become addicted. It was not obvious in the case of the threatened destruction of a train, but I suppose this is because we so naturally assume that failing to save many lives when one can easily do so would be regarded as wrong in just about any society.

Stated so briefly, this doctrine of moral truth is of course rather vague, but many apparent disadvantages of it will easily come to mind. Let us end this section by listing the more important of them. For convenience of reference I shall call them numbered objections, although they are not so much arguments against a definite conception of moral truth as considerations we shall have to bear in mind as we attempt to present a clear and plausible conception.

First, I expect anti-naturalists to throw up their hands and exclaim for the thousandth time that moral truth—the question, for example, whether a certain course of conduct is morally right or wrong—obviously cannot be determined by the mere meanings of words, by the fact that people use moral and non-moral terms in certain ways and in certain inferential sequences. Even non-evaluative truths are never determined by the mere meanings of words unless they are tautologies or analytic statements conveying no information.

Second, many people will find it implausible that some moral evaluations are neither true nor false.

Third, many people will also find it implausible that a moral statement can be true at one time and false at another, as our proposal obviously allows, and not merely that popular moral *opinion* can change.

Fourth, despite the addition of semantic rules to the consensus notion of moral truth, I think it will still be objected that our proposal subverts the ordinary concept of truth by making truth parasitic to justification, rather than conversely.

Here a consensus produced by applying a certain method of justification is to be our criterion of truth, but the acceptability of a method should really depend on whether it is a reliable guide to the truth. Our suggestion seems to allow that something can be made to be the case—e.g. that a certain action can be made to be wrong—merely by someone's justifiably thinking it so. The suggestion seems to confuse the truth of a statement with the conditions under which someone would be justified in saying that it is true.

Fifth and finally, this conception of moral truth, and perhaps any recognition that there is such a thing as moral truth, will be said to conflict with the strong claim to personal moral autonomy which we have emphasized throughout this essay as an essential ingredient in moral judgement, or at least in the type of moral judgement which we have been attempting to elucidate. For it would seem that, under our proposal, one could prove to a person that his own best judgement about some moral question is wrong, i.e. that his own justified judgement is contrary to the consensus.

In developing the idea that a certain form of consensus is the basis of moral truth, I shall attempt to answer the first four of these objections in the following section, saving the last for our concluding section.

7. Two Aspects of 'Truth' in Morals

THE first objection—that the truth of moral statements cannot be determined by the mere meanings of words—is no doubt correct in one important respect to which I hope to do justice in the second half of this section. But first I beg attention to another respect in which it is not correct.

Let us first point out some types of statements which are not as dependent for their truth on the normal use of words as I think moral statements are, although they are of course partly dependent on it. All of these are statements which can very well be false even though they use words just as words normally are used. In science and everyday empirical belief, we are usually interested in explaining and predicting events, and possibly controlling them, not in describing particular entities, although we of course have to be able to make such descriptions and make them accurately if we are to give our explanations and make our predictions. We may be interested in the material question whether all *F*'s are *G*'s, and the truth of the statement 'All *F*'s are *G*'s' cannot consist in or follow from the fact that the consensus of scientists or other people would be that all *F*'s are, indeed, *G*'s. If we determine that individual *a* has property *F*, then whether or not it will prove to have *G* is also independent of any such consensus. The consensus cannot make it have *G*, except perhaps in resolving borderline doubts. (*a* falls in fact within the 'penumbra' of '*G*''s previously determined meaning, and now we extend the 'umbra' to include it.) In many a case, something *F* will definitely be *G*, or will definitely not be *G*, and while the consensus of competent people judging carefully would be reliable authority to the effect that it is (or is not) such a consensus could not make it so.

Now, the truth or falsity of any moral evaluation will of course depend on non-moral facts which obtain or fail to obtain quite independently of any consensus; but in taking *moral* reasoning and truth for our special study, we are primarily concerned with the relation between those non-moral facts and the moral statements whose truth or falsity is in question. We are interested in what the truth of a moral statement consists *given* all the possibly relevant facts of a non-moral sort concerning the individual action or other subject of evaluation. I mean to explicate *that* notion of moral truth. Therefore, the appropriate analogy is not with contingent generalizations, explanations, or predictions, but with empirical classifications in which we assign some empirical property *F* to some empirical referrent *x* in light of all the (possibly relevant) properties which *x* in fact has other than *F*, the correctness or incorrectness of such predication then being entirely dependent on the meaning of '*F*'. More concretely, statements like 'That action of Jones (of which we are otherwise fully informed) is wrong' should be compared with statements like 'That object before us is a table' or 'That other object before us is a person', and not with statements like 'That table will still be in this room tomorrow' or 'That person will never marry', not to mention statements about casual connections, laws, or empirical probabilities.

It is not hard to see that the truth of 'This object before us is a table' (if it is a true statement) is intimately connected to the fact that all or practically all properly qualified people *would* say that this object is a table: that is, people who, being in position to observe this object, knowing how to use English and using it normally, might seriously consider and say whether or not this object is a table. To be a bit more specific, the truth of the quoted statement does not *consist in* the fact that such people so described and situated would make such a statement, but in the fact that this object *is* a table. But the latter fact is mentioned by using the word 'table' in its ordinary meaning, and this meaning depends upon what people so described and situated would say about this object and many other objects.

Let us consider this point in a little more detail. 'This is a table' is true if and only if this *is* a table. But can we say that this object (pointing to some paradigmatic table) *is* a table if and only if practically everyone, being in position to observe and using English normally (etc., as above) would say that it is a table? Suppose they *wouldn't* say it. Wouldn't it still *be* a table? That is, wouldn't it still be what we now call a table, even though it wouldn't, under that supposition, be properly referred to with the English word 'table'? There is one condition under which it would, and another condition under which it would not then be a table. If this sort of thing (pointing) still had the same *uses*, which of course it would if it really remained the same sort of thing (i.e. what we now call a table), then only the word 'table' would have been discontinued, and some other word meaning the same thing would have to be used to refer to it. But if people did not refer to this sort of thing (pointing) with the word 'table' or any word or phrase having the same meaning, but used some other word of an entirely different meaning, then of course this sort of thing (pointing) would not have the same uses as it now has, for it is *the uses of a thing* (in a broad sense of 'uses') which determine *the meaning of the words* we use to refer to it.[1] And if it did not have the same uses, it seems clear that this sort of thing (pointing) would not then be a table but a useless object, or perhaps a device for warding off evil spirits, or just some curiously arranged wood we can build a fire with.

Similarly, wouldn't this action (referring to a particular sadistic killing of a human) still *be* what we now *call* wrong even if practically everyone who might consider it from the moral point of view would say it is 'not wrong', although we may grant that the word 'wrong', under that supposition,

[1] The view of naming, using, and communicating about objects which I take for granted in this paragraph is well developed by R. Doorbar in 'Meaning, Rules, and Behaviour', *Mind*, vol. 80 (1971).

would not be the correct word to use in morally characterizing the action? Yes, it would still be what we now call wrong if the people who take the moral point of view towards things continued to have the same 'uses' for it: that is, if they continued to have the same evaluative response to the sadistic killing of humans. And if they did so, they would need to refer to it in evaluative terms which mean that it is properly to be condemned, and which express condemnation.[2] But if they would not so characterize it with a synonym of 'wrong', but would use some value term of an entirely different meaning—one expressing mild approval, for example—then under this more radical supposition it *wouldn't* still be wrong, just as this table I am now writing on wouldn't still be a table under the corresponding radical supposition. True, the act referred to would still be a sadistic killing of a human, at least if we continued to have use for the kinds 'human', 'killing', etc. But it wouldn't be wrong and it wouldn't be murder ('murder' being a condemnatory word).

This will seem very hard to accept, even absurd. But I think its absurdity is an illusion traceable in part to one's failure to realize *how* radical the supposition is from which it follows. It is extremely difficult to shake oneself loose from the *actual* meaning of 'wrong' even when engaging in philosophical fantasy. Also, it is part of our normal scheme of ideas that a thing can very well be wrong even if someone (or, just conceivably, everyone) denies that it is wrong. But this has only specious relevance to the fantasy, in which it is supposed that *everyone judging disinterestedly and with full information* would deny that the sadistic killing in question is properly to be condemned. And indeed, this last remark does make it obvious that moraliy as we know it could scarcely exist under this supposition. So it is doubtful whether it makes sense to say that certain actions would nevertheless *be* wrong—or indeed that they would *not* be wrong, meaning

[2] For a view of 'table' and 'murder' quite similar to this, see Julius Kovesi, *Moral Notions* (New York: Humanities Pr., 1967), Chap. 1, esp. pp. 2–3, 6, 14–15, 20–1.

by this that they would be morally permissible rather than that 'wrong' lacks sense here.

This conclusion will still seem hard to accept, however, because one wants to say that some things *really ought* to be morally condemned *whether or not* the people following this or that form of moral life do condemn them or would condemn them from the moral point of view. Perhaps sadistic killing of humans would be condemned in every way of life that humans live, but that isn't what *makes* it wrong; or so one wants to say. Furthermore, it seems that some things which *are* wrong would not be so condemned in some ways of life, while some other things that are not wrong at all would be. But I must postpone discussing this until the second half of the present section.

Let us turn to the second objection that moral statements must be either true or false. Here the analogy with empirical descriptions is again helpful. Consider cases where it would not be clear to everyone who is in a position to observe and knows how to use English (etc., as above) whether the word 'table' applies or fails to apply. The statement 'This object is a table', made in such a case, would be neither true nor false, unless we were to stipulate that anything which is not clearly and safely a table is a non-table. But in a very large number of cases, there would be no doubt or disagreement. The many cases in which there has been no doubt, and the indefinitely many cases where there would be no doubt, serve to fix the meaning of the word. If there were any practical need to provide ourselves with a working definition (probably there never would be with the word 'table' except for limited technical purposes, as in the furniture industry) we might do so by extracting general criteria from various paradigm cases and checking them against other paradigmatic tables. The resulting list would then classify some of our previously doubtful cases as tables and some as non-tables, while many others would remain doubtful, assuming we had devised a list of characteristics which together make something a table *ceteris paribus*, rather than a list of necessary and sufficient conditions. And even a list of the latter sort would of course leave some cases in which 'This is a table' would be neither true nor false inasmuch as the words used to make the list would have their own vague edges of meaning, and so on.

All of these elementary points can of course be made about practically any non-technical word or combination of words used to refer to empirical entities and properties. So, for each of a large number of common words and combinations of words, there can be a large number of true statements, a large number of false statements, and a large number of statements which are neither true nor false. This may not be true of the precisely defined predicates and well-formed formulae of logic and pure mathematics, but it is true of the kinds of words and statements we are concerned with most of the time.

I think this leads to part of an answer to the plausible objection that moral evaluations must be either true or false. After all, the non-evaluative descriptive words figuring in our moral criteria will also be vague or ambiguous. It may be neither true nor false that a certain piece of behaviour was a 'promise'; it may be a borderline case whether or not someone said something 'intending to deceive'; and so on. Furthermore, we have already seen that when moral criteria conflict there is no well-established higher-order criterion directing how the conflict must be resolved, and there may also be no likely consensus of properly reflective people.

I observed earlier that along with the intuition that a moral statement (like any statement) must be true or false, there is an opposite intuition which may have its appeal if we have ever experienced a severe moral dilemma. And now I think we can see why it is the latter hunch which is probably correct. Notice, first of all, how we commonly ignore the fact that many empirical descriptive statements which might be made with our existing language apparatus are neither true nor false. This is only natural and is usually harmless since there is never any need to make the vast majority of such statements. When occasionally they are made, there is usually no practical issue attaching to them, no need to say whether they are true or false. And if there is, we normally adjust our language to permit it. This may tend to foster the illusion that all statements are either true or false, as from the viewpoint of formal logic they ought to be. Even in legal and moral evaluation, where we are more frequently involved with practically important though logically indeterminate questions, there may be some pressure of habit to ignore or deny it, a pressure which is abetted in the legal analogue by a judicial institution which can give us, in any case, an *official* answer to such questions, usually accompanied by the more or less sincere claim that it *is* a law-determined answer. And there is an analogous effect in morals. When we finally take our stand on some difficult moral question, we may prefer to think that we have solved our dilemma and decided rightly, rather than merely cutting the Gordian knot, as we may actually have done.

This is not a complete answer to the 'excluded middle' objection, however. Many people will say that there are right and wrong ways, after all, to sharpen our moral criteria or principles, just as they will say that although many conventionally recognized principles are undoubtedly valid, some others may very well not be. But this broaches the topic which I have postponed to the second part of the section.

The third objection—that moral truth cannot change—will also be taken up as part of that postponed topic. What about the fourth objection—that I have confused the truth of a moral statement with the conditions under which we would be justified in saying that it is true? To answer this, I shall proceed by showing how that distinction is marked in the case of evaluative statements which are true by virtue of objective standards, and then point out the partly similar and partly different way in which it is marked in the case of moral statements.

As an example of the first kind, let us take the statement 'This is a good car', said of one of the more expensive models received new from the manufacturer. The statement means (something like) 'This is a car you ought to choose over many others, if you are choosing among cars as such.' The condition under which we would be justified in believing or saying that the statement is true is that we know or have good reason to believe that this car satisfies the criteria of a good car. But what we mean in saying that the statement 'This is a good car' is true is that in fact this is a good car. Now that last fact, if it is a fact, depends on two other facts which we may distinguish, viz. (1) the fact that such and such criteria *are* the criteria of a good car, and (2) the fact that this car satisfies them. It may be noted in passing that fact (1) depends in turn on the purpose we have in choosing among cars. Thus it is easy to see that the fact we mean to assert when we say that the statement first quoted above is true is not at all the same condition or fact under which we would be justified in saying that it is true. They are, respectively, the fact that this is a good car, and the fact that we know or have good reason to believe that this car satisfies the criteria of a good car. In this case, then, our analysis does not confuse the truth of a value statement with the condition under which we would be justified in believing it or saying that it is true.[3]

Now let us consider the statement 'That act was (morally) wrong', said of a certain act performed by a certain person on a certain occasion. This statement means (something like)

[3] The same point can be made, *mutatis mutandis*, about value statements which are true by virtue of legislatively valid standards, e.g. the statement 'This is a poor Airedale' from the illustration in Section 1. I leave this as an exercise.

It may be useful to spell the point out for empirical descriptions or classifications of the sort referred to a few pages back. If we were to say that the statement 'This animal before us is a mammal' is true, we would mean that the animal is in fact a mammal. The condition under which we would be justified in believing or saying that such quoted statement is true is that we know or have good reason to believe that this animal does have the characteristics of a mammal. The fact which constitutes the truth of the quoted statement is thus very different from the fact which constitutes the condition under which we would be justified in believing or saying that it is true. These are, respectively, the fact that this is a mammal, and the fact that we know or have good reason to believe that it has the characteristics of a mammal. Arguably, the latter fact is identical to the fact that we are justified in believing that this animal is a mammal, although I am more inclined to say they are different facts. But anyway, we have not confused this fact (that we are justified, etc.) with the very different fact that this is a mammal.

'The agent ought not, morally, to have performed that act' or 'That act is properly to be condemned, viewed morally.' Now, the condition under which we would be justified in believing (holding, saying) that such statement is true is that we know or have good reason to believe that the act in question satisfies the criteria of wrongness in an act. And if we were to say that such statement is true, we would mean that in fact the act was wrong. The truth of the statement (if it is true) consists in the fact that the act *was* wrong. Now *that* fact (that the act was wrong) depends on (1) the fact that such and such criteria are the criteria of wrongness in an act, and (2) the fact that the act in question satisfies them. But now, what does fact (1) depend upon? Not, in this type of evaluation, upon the fact that people have some coherent and controlling purpose in choosing morally among acts, a purpose which requires certain criteria and regulates their application in concrete cases. Rather, according to our account, fact (1) depends on the fact that people living a certain form of moral life commonly feel that acts of certain kinds are properly to be condemned, and commonly do condemn them, from the moral point of view. And fact (2) depends on the fact that practically anyone living that life who was well informed about the act in question and judged it reasonably would hold that it is wrong or properly to be condemned. More specifically, fact (2) depends on the fact that there would be such a consensus that the act was wrong for certain controlling reasons, i.e. because it had certain characteristics which were held to be of controlling moral significance in the particular act. For example, it was a slanderous lie, and no good excuse or justification could be found in the other facts concerning it, even in the fact (let us say) that the liar had been slighted by his victim, or had promised someone that he would tell this lie. To know how to apply conflicting criteria in easy cases is to know their nuances. It is to be able to resolve the conflict in the way practically anyone living this moral life would be sure to resolve it in this case if he were thoroughly informed and disinterested.

Thus it should be easy to see that the fact we mean to assert when we say that that moral statement is true is not at all the same as the condition or fact under which we would be justified in saying that it is true. These are, respectively, that the act in question does satisfy the criteria of a morally wrong act, and that we know or have good reason to believe it does.

Here a word of summary may be useful. We began with a thesis having the following form, in part. 'If and only if practically everyone qualified to judge would hold that-*p*, then *p* is true. We do not mean that it *would* be a good *sign* that *p* is true if there were such agreement. Rather, we mean that the *fact that there would be* such agreement (wherever it is a fact) *does make p* true—does make it a fact that-*p*.' Taken quite generally, this is of course ridiculous. The fact that qualified people would hold that something is the case cannot, in general, make it the case. But our thesis includes a further point about the type of statement, namely, that it classifies something according to its moral value, based on all the relevant non-moral facts. Now where everyone, or practically everyone who properly considered such facts *would* hold that the subject of the statement has moral value *F*, anyone who actually *does* say that such subject has *F* will be using '*F*' correctly to make a true statement. This follows from the nature of the statement and from the qualifications required for considering the matter 'properly'. Further details must be added, but the main point should now be reasonably clear from the analogy of empirical descriptions. If practically everyone who knew English and took into account all the relevant considerations as to whether this thing I am writing on is a table *would* say that it is a table, then, necessarily, anyone who actually *does* say that this thing is a table will be using the word 'table' to make a true statement.

It is no doubt a somewhat elusive idea that in order for some concrete action to 'satisfy the criteria of wrongness', it must not only be the case that it has one or more 'wrong-making' characteristics, but that its having them should 'control' or be the dominant consideration in its moral evaluation. What *is* controlling in the particular case depends on what the consensus (of properly qualified judges) would be about that very question in that very case. And this may give someone the impression that, according to our account, whether an act *does* satisfy the criteria of wrongness *will* depend, after all, on whether someone thinks it does. But that would be a false impression because we are not concerned with what anyone actually thinks about the particular act, as far as our account of truth is concerned, but with the meaning and effect of the criteria.

Whether a certain feature of an act is wrong-making at all will depend on what sorts of acts people leading a certain form of moral life will typically condemn. And the meaning and effect of the criteria of wrongness thus constituted and used will also depend on what sorts of mitigating, excusing, and justifying conditions they typically recognize and how much weight they typically give them in various circumstances. This latter judgement, though an essential ingredient of moral evaluation, cannot be reduced to any formula, as I have repeatedly insisted. But that does not alter the fact that there *would* be a consensus about *many* such cases among people who do live a common form of moral life.

Though it will involve some repetition, let us illustrate these statements with others a little less abstract. We may observe that a person who has learned to live the morality of his own group will almost infallibly make true moral judgements about the *easiest* moral questions. Even if he quite fails to satisfy the standard of reasonableness, he is likely to *judge* such cases correctly (however he may then act) if he is informed of the non-moral facts. After all, he knows very well that lying, cheating, stealing, raping, maiming, killing, and so on, are wrong. But in cases where there are countervailing facts to attend to, and in which there is nevertheless a true judgement to be made, he is not quite so likely to make it unless he judges disinterestedly. When our own interests and partialities are allowed to affect our decision more than they should, we begin to exaggerate or minimize the weight of various relevant facts, as illustrated by the college admissions case in Section 2. But when *has* someone given too much or too little weight to a relevant fact, and how is this known? In many cases it simply is obvious; we just *do* know if we stop to think and have been brought up right. In other cases it is not obvious and we do not know. In a particular case it will be obviously all right to break our date for golf to help someone in distress; in another case it will be obviously all wrong to break a certain promise to one person in order to help another (and perhaps ourselves) in a certain way. And in many another case, informed and reasonable people would disagree about whether it is right or wrong. In so far as the existence and meaning of moral criteria, and hence the proper application of the words 'right' and 'wrong', etc. depend upon what the consensus among such people would be about all sorts of cases, breaking one's promise in the last cases mentioned would be neither definitely right nor definitely wrong.

II

But *do* moral criteria or principles depend solely on such a consensus? We are still left with the thought that the criteria thus constituted might be morally invalid. To express this in terms of the fourth objection, which we were just discussing, the conception of truth here expounded holds that a moral proposition *p* is true if and only if people of a certain description would think or say that-*p*; but while this may be correct for empirical descriptions or classifications of the type referred to above, it will not do at all for moral classifications. A moral statement of the form 'X is wrong' might very well be false even though the description of the consensus (notably the 'qualifications' of the people among whom the consensus would obtain) is such as to assure that 'wrong' is being used just as the people living a certain form of moral life normally do use it. Given that 'wrong' is the word to express condemnation *and* to say that something is *properly* to be condemned, it is logically possible that the people living that life should all sometimes misapply the word. It is possible that they should use it to condemn some things which ought not to be condemned, and to refuse to condemn some other things which are morally inexcusable, saying they are *not* wrong. Indeed, this has probably happened many times, as where some group of people have recognized certain morally invalid criteria (e.g. that taking humans for sacrificial victims is necessary and right) along with certain valid criteria which practically all human groups will be found to recognize (e.g. that killing a member of the group is wrong in the absence of an appropriate excuse or justification).

This point has great appeal and must be taken very seriously. Surely it would be wrong to rule it out entirely, committing ourselves to moral conventionalism. Yet other considerations argue strongly against it. For one thing, the objection uses a notion of evaluative truth which remains utterly mysterious. I take it that we have eliminated objective standards and legislative fiats as possible bases of the validity of moral criteria, and now any consentient basis would also be ruled out. Moreover, our examination of paradigmatically true moral evaluations did seem to yield a consentient basis. The judgements we considered surely are true if moral judgements ever are true, and their truth seemed to rest on the *common* use and *typical* application of certain criteria of moral approval and disapproval, and on nothing else that was apparent. If it be replied that those examples involved conventional criteria which happen to be morally valid, the rejoinder must be that it does not seem possible to give any clear sense to this last use of the value predicate 'morally valid'. How are we to determine the correctness or incorrectness of saying, for example, that communal disapproval of murder is morally valid, and communal approval of human sacrifice is morally invalid? It remains *totally* obscure how we are to determine this, even though we have managed to become tolerably clear about various ways in which value statements can be true or false.

How are we to give proper recognition to all the conceptual elements involved in this puzzle? Can we allow, at one and the same time, that (1) moral statements are true if they apply the communally recognized or 'established' criteria correctly; but nevertheless (2) that the correct application of moral criteria will not yield true moral evaluations unless those criteria are themselves morally valid; and yet (3) that it does not make any clear sense to speak of the moral validity or invalidity of the criteria recognized in a given form of moral life, at least not the most basic or general of such criteria?

It seems to me that if we are to accommodate all three of these notions, we can do so only by recognizing distinct levels or major aspects of moral thought and talk in which they can be legitimately said, or about which they can be separately true. I suggest that it will be correct to say that moral statements made at one level (called the first level hereafter) can be true in the way described in the first part of this section. Most moral discourse seems to be carried on at this level, to which I think ethical naturalists have given most of their attention. But at a second level, to which I think ethical non-cognitivists have given most of theirs, it will also be correct to speak of the moral validity or invalidity of any basic moral criterion of the first level, whether it be merely proposed for discussion or already established in communal life. (I shall indicate shortly what I mean by 'basic' here.) Since there are no fixed substantive criteria to be applied in moral discourse at the second level, the statements made there will not be true or false, although they can be defended and justified in the way described in Part I of this essay. Before developing these suggestions, I shall briefly mention a number of other reasons why there apparently are two distinct levels of moral thought which we have found this philosophical motive to distinguish.

The examples in Section 6 plainly illustrate moral thought at the first level; and they also seem to show that we commonly do think and say that everyday moral judgements are *true*. They also illustrate the kind of semantic links which were described by Beardsmore *et al.* and discussed above. But the second level of moral discourse is also no mere product of dubious philosophical dialectic, as I think ethical naturalists have sometimes wished to maintain, because there surely is logical room for radical criticism or 'prophet talk' within moral discourse, and indeed for conservative talk supporting recognized criteria. It seems to be linguistically normal to use predicates of moral evaluation to evaluate recognized moral criteria.

This is obvious enough when one moral criterion is criticized as incompatible with some other criterion which the critic regards as more fundamental, and which is itself commonly established. Here we are still at the first level of discourse if it is well accepted that the criterion under attack is supposed to be derivative from, or is required to be compatible with, the second criterion invoked. (See the case of cigarette-smoking, discussed below.) But it is also linguistically possible to evaluate in moral terms those moral criteria which are not commonly thought to have such a derivative or dependent status by the people whose lives they regulate. To vary an earlier example, if you, a Roman Catholic layman, tell Pope Paul that his principles concerning artificial birth control are wrong because they conflict with utilitarian criteria which he and you both recognize, you are arguing at the second level because neither the Pope nor the moral community to which you both belong have thought that utilitarian criteria are always controlling, or controlling in such a matter as this. In asserting that they *ought* to be controlling in this matter, you are making a statement which many Catholic people have recently wished to make, and surely can make without violating any rules of moral discourse. But it is a statement which has no standing at the first level of discourse since it rejects a moral criterion (that artificial birth control is wrong) which until now (the present generation) has had basic or absolute status in the moral life of Catholics.[4]

Lest my suggestion seem a weak compromise that leaves the important issues untouched, I must add some essential details. I think they will show why ethical naturalists are definitely right on some points but definitely wrong on others which I take to be more fundamental.

[4] By a basic moral criterion, then, I mean one that is accepted and used whether or not it is thought to be compatible with other moral criteria. This does not mean that a basic criterion cannot be 'outweighed' by other criteria in particular cases, but only that it cannot be invalidated *as* a criterion no matter what facts are adduced (in discourse at level one).

1. Many ethical non-cognitivists would no doubt say that the 'moral' statements whose truth I recognize at the first level are really 'hypothetical' statements. By this they would mean that *if* we accept certain criteria or principles which we need not accept in view of level two, then certain subjects are to be morally evaluated in certain ways. This is true enough, although I doubt that anyone satisfying our procedural criteria *will* fail to grant the substantive criteria invoked in our paradigms. It is hard to imagine anyone bothering to universalize his judgement if he does not think it wrong to cause serious harm to innocent persons, or to fail to save many people from death when he easily can. But the statement is misleading in so far as it suggests that moral statements at the first level are either not evaluative if true, or not true if evaluative. That they are evaluative, and that they can be true in as strong a sense as any non-moral evaluative statements can be true, will appear, I think, from the following considerations. A moral statement made at the first level can be true not merely in

Sense I: that *if* you accept principle P, and *if* you agree that it is the controlling principle in the present case, i.e. that other things are equal, then, the non-moral facts being so and so, you must accept the moral statement,

but also in

Sense II: that *since we all do* accept principle P; or rather, since P is an essential feature of the meaning of 'morally wrong' (or 'right', 'obligatory', etc., as the case may be); and since the present case is indeed a paradigm application of P—just the sort of thing we mean by an indisputably wrong action—we must accept the moral statement.

Without stopping to sort out the various meanings of 'hypothetical', I am inclined to think that moral statements which are true in Sense II are less hypothetical than those which are true merely in Sense I and not Sense II. But the important point is that moral truth in Sense II is no *more* hypothetical than is evaluative truth deriving from an objective standard, although this may seem doubtful at first glance. When a value statement is true pursuant to an objective standard, there can be no question that principle P is to be accepted, or that it is to control the present evaluation. Both of these points will be determined by the fundamental purpose in choice and other matters of fact. It is not necessary that they be commonly or typically recognized, although in many cases they will be. But the whole affair rests, after all, on a certain consensus, namely, the consensus that a certain fundamental purpose is to be served in choosing among items of the kind which is in question. Moral evaluation at the first level differs from this in that the consensus operates piecemeal. That is, we know what criteria of value are controlling in many cases even though we cannot calculate or deduce this from some over-arching purpose. We know it merely because we know the practical meaning of the moral criteria in the way of life we have learned to live. We know how they unquestionably would apply in a great many easy cases, including cases we have never yet encountered or imagined. That is, we know how anyone living that life would be practically certain to apply them in those cases if he were informed of the facts and made a sincere moral judgement.

It can be seen in this way that value statements which are true pursuant to objective standards, and moral statements which are true at the first level of discourse, are both hypothetical in the rather tenuous sense that they presuppose a consensus, either a consentient purpose in choice or a consensus as to the kinds of things which are to be morally approved and disapproved. But I think it would be a mistake to conclude from this that *no* value statement is categorically true after all. I suppose it does show that, as an earlier generation of philosophers might have put it, there are no values in the world without valuers, and no inter-personally true values without *common* purposes, interests, preferences. But we needn't deny this in order to hold that some motor cars and some quarterbacks really and truly are better than some other motor cars and some other quarterbacks, or that some actions truly are wrong, e.g. the cold-blooded murder for gain mentioned at the beginning of Appendix III, or causing your children to become heroin addicts for the pure hell of it.

2. The fact that the great bulk of moral thought and talk goes on at the first level is important enough to list as another major point in the naturalist's favour. That it is a fact seems obvious enough when one considers the myriad of easy and usually unspoken moral judgements we all make, beginning in childhood and continuing throughout our lives. It should also be emphasized that even most criticism of existing moral standards seems to be conducted at this level. Important changes in recognized criteria can be brought about without any reflection or discourse at the second level, as the following will illustrate.

Because of the statistics on lung cancer and heart disease that have been published during the past decade or two, many people would now judge that it is in some degree morally wrong to influence children to become habitual smokers of cigarettes by smoking in their presence. Many of these same people had no such opinion thirty or forty years ago. Let us simplify the illustration by ignoring the point that even then there were some grounds for thinking cigarettes unhealthful. With this simplification, we can say that someone who was reasonably well-informed and judged reasonably of the matter forty years ago might very well have judged that it was not wrong to smoke in the presence of children. But anyone who is well-informed and judges reasonably today is likely to conclude that such behaviour is wrong in some degree, even if by force of habit he continues to engage in it.

It might be thought that this only shows that moral principles apply differently in the light of changing knowledge, not that there has been any change in the principles themselves, e.g. in the principle that it is wrong to influence children to acquire harmful habits, or in the more general principle that it is wrong to harm others or expose them unnecessarily to harm. Yet *one* principle will have been dropped: the principle that it is all right to smoke cigarettes in the presence of children. This is a significant change since it reverses the proper evaluation of a type of behaviour millions of people engage in every day. And it will not have been brought about by any radical criticism at our second level of thought and discourse, but by realizing and pointing out that this principle is not in fact compatible with the other principles just mentioned. These latter are of course firmly established and rarely if ever questioned by anyone. Also, the principle that smoking cigarettes in the presence of children is morally innocent was dependent upon them. That is, in the (artificially simplified) moral life of forty years ago, anyone who was challenged about smoking cigarettes before children would have said that it was all right *because* it is harmless.[5]

This kind of illustration will also provide most of our answer to the third objection listed at the end of Section 6, namely, that if there is such a thing as moral truth it never changes. For, granting our simplification, it was not *wrong* to smoke cigarettes before children forty years ago, not something properly to be condemned. Rather, it was *harmful* in ways which were then unknown and unsuspected. But now it is wrong or properly to be condemned because now we do know what harm it can do. Surely no one but a philosopher committed to an ethical theory far removed from common moral opinion has ever thought that the rightness or wrongness of an action can depend on consequences which are completely unknown and unsuspectable at the time of the action.[6]

[5] The illustration isn't perfectly neat even with the mentioned simplification, though I think it serves our purposes well enough. For one thing, it may be that there would still not be a consensus among properly informed and reflective people about the moral impropriety of smoking cigarettes before children. (After all, they will see it a thousand times anyway in old movies on television etc.) But if the reader is unhappy with the example, he can easily substitute one of his own. Any example will do in which there is no reason at time t to think that behaviour of a certain description is harmful or otherwise objectionable, while at $t+n$ there is overwhelming evidence that it is inevitably and severely harmful, and that the harm it causes probably wouldn't occur without it.

[6] Thus I think we are entitled to make it true by definition that the non-

Conceding this kind of moral change, someone will nevertheless say that the most basic and general principles of morality cannot change; for example, the principle that, other things being equal, it is wrong to harm another person intentionally. But this rejoinder is a statement at the second level of discourse, and if I am correct in asserting that it therefore lacks any possible truth value, it cannot show that morality never changes and that our account of moral truth is therefore incorrect. What such a statement does 'show' (count as evidence for) is that the person making it is firmly committed to the moral criteria which he cites as 'unchangeable' or 'really valid'. I share such commitment to the criterion just mentioned, as do all the people who live any of the forms of moral life with which I am acquainted. But this does not show that one or more of those forms of life *could* not change, or *ought* not to change, even as to such a basic criterion as this one.

3. There is one more point that can be given to the naturalist, although he may prefer to avoid any more victories like the last one. Scoring this time against ethical intuitionists rather than non-cognitivists, the naturalist is entitled to point out that the first level of discourse is the *only* place where moral truth is to be found. Putting it another way, the sort of consensus-presupposing truth that we find at this level of discourse is the only sort of moral truth which there is any good reason to think exists. To say, in the deeper sort of criticism which places one's utterance at the second level, that such and such a basic moral criterion is valid or invalid, is to use a very natural kind of moral rhetoric, but it is not to make a statement that can be true or false. At least there is no reason to think such a statement could be true or false in view of everything that has been said in the course of this essay. But I do not wish to deny that it can be an extremely important statement, marking some major departure from an exist-

---

moral facts which are 'possibly relevant' for morally evaluating something (see the third paragraph of this section) do not include facts which are unknown and unknowable at the time the evaluation is made.

ing way of life, or affirming one's allegiance to a way of life.

This point also carries a serious disadvantage for the naturalist, however. If he wishes to say that *the* basic criterion which he explicates at level one is morally valid, no doubt he is entitled to do so. But he will be philosophically confused if he thinks he is thereby making a true statement, or even a possibly false one. It may be that more astute naturalists, profiting from the discussions of the past seventy years, would no longer make this mistake. Even J. S. Mill may not have made it,[7] although for reasons urged repeatedly in earlier sections (not specifically against him) he surely was mistaken in his claim to identify *the* basic moral criterion. But then the naturalist must pay an increasingly heavy price for this clear-headedness, as will be shown in point 4 (no doubt the final price is already obvious).

Why is it so natural, if inevitably 'bewitching to our intelligence', to use predicates of moral value at the second level of discourse, rather than simply declaring our moral allegiance or disaffection in words more appropriate to this purpose? One reason, I think, is that it is perfectly possible to be morally justified in one's opinions and assertions at this level. In making a moral evaluation (say, of someone's action) we may reconsider the accepted force or typical application of some acknowledged principle; or we may reconsider the principle itself, even a basic one. And in reaching a reasonable (or unreasonable) judgement of the action, we may reaffirm, revise, or reject that principle. But since we are primarily

[7] The sentence in which he says that the fact that happiness is universally desired is 'not only all the proof which the case admits of, but all which it is possible to require' in order to show that happiness is desirable, can be read as a conscious attempt to avoid just this kind of mistake. That is, he may have meant that it is not logically possible to require that a basic, accepted moral criterion should be shown to be 'really acceptable' or 'morally valid' since it lacks sense to say of such a criterion either that it is valid or that it is not.

But if Mill did mean something like that, he immediately blurred the point merely by leaving it stand that he was out to show that happiness was 'desirable'—even apart from his notorious comparison of desirability with visibility and audibility in the same paragraph. *Utilitarianism*, Ch. 4.

judging an action, the vocabulary of moral evaluation will seem more appropriate than that of allegiance to, or disaffection from, this or that principle or criterion. And this may continue to be so even when we come to evaluate basic criteria as such. For we *can* evaluate them morally in the sense that we can make factually informed and otherwise morally reasonable decisions to accept or reject them. The procedural criteria of morality—the criteria of reasonable reflection, judgement, and argument—seem to be unchallengeably valid at both levels of moral thought. Indeed, they seem to be even more important at the second level than the first, for reasons which I have attempted to explain in Section 3.[8] Now, when one notices how infrequently we consider whether to accept or reject basic moral criteria, and how frequently we make other evaluations, whether in morals or elsewhere, for which fixed substantive criteria really are available, it is not surprising that value words suitable in the latter type of evaluation should be used in the former also, turning up in phrases like 'really right' or 'not really valid' applied to the basic criteria themselves. Another point to remember is that it will often not be clear on which level a critical moral discussion is moving, even to someone forearmed with our distinction.

4. For the above reasons, it must be conceded to the ethical naturalist (1) that moral statements can be true or false at the first level of discourse, and (2) that by far the majority of moral statements and unspoken moral judgements are made at that level of thought and talk. But we can concede these things only if we also insist (3) that there is an important class of moral statements made at another level which are not true or false because they are not bound by communally established ties between value predicates and non-value predicates. In the moral philosopher's jargon, these latter state-

[8] That is, the need to promote agreement and mutual respect in disagreement is even greater at the second level because our 'right' there to deviate from established basic criteria opens up new possibilities of disagreement.

ments are not bound by naturalistic definitions, even though whole communities are found living by those definitions. We have already given several reasons to acknowledge the 'reality' or legitimacy of this latter class of moral statements, but one further point may be made in this connection.

The question whether our second level is 'real' is the question whether there is a philosophical need for it—whether the idea of such a level can help us recognize and understand important features of ordinary moral thought and talk better than we could without it. Here I think a certain *disanalogy* with law is illuminating. In legal theory there is no need to distinguish such a second level of discourse in which predicates of legal evaluation are applied to established rules of law. With an obvious exception to be mentioned in a moment, no one can really doubt that a legal judgement will be correct *as* a legal judgement if it correctly applies the 'conventional' rules or criteria, i.e. those forming part of the existing system of positive law under which the matter being judged happens to fall. To be sure, we can and do make 'meta-legal' statements about the legal validity (existence in the system) of this or that rule. But there is no good reason to think that the legal validity of the rule also depends on its satisfying the rules or criteria of some higher law which exists independently of human convention or enactment. Whether a rule is legally valid will depend entirely on that institution or 'living convention' which we call the positive law or legal system, and we verify such metalegal statements by reference to other criteria within the system, criteria which Professor Hart refers to compendiously as the rule of recognition.[9] To attempt to show the *legal* validity or invalidity of some rule of positive law by reference to a supposed body of absolute law would be to argue at a level strictly analogous to our second level of moral discourse. And no legal theorist needs to do that unless (like some Natural Law people, notably Thomists) he quaintly refuses to admit

[9] H. L. A. Hart, *The Concept of Law* (Oxford: The Clarendon Pr., 1961), *passim.*

that anything properly called a law can be morally objectionable.[10] Neither does the plain citizen or plain lawyer need to conjure with the notion of absolute law when he wants to know what the law of the state requires or permits or is silent about, or when, having found these things out, he wants to evaluate the law morally or politically.

In sharp contrast to all this, it seems to be perfectly appropriate to ask whether this or that principle of conventional morality is morally valid, and to ask this even about basic principles, as in the birth control example. Indeed, it is sometimes a matter of great seriousness and urgency to ask and (in a way) answer such questions, although they are seldom if ever asked about some quite general basic principles, such as the principle that it is wrong to hurt others without a good reason. The birth control example also calls attention to the fact that we may find ourselves living or trying to live more than one form of moral life at the same time. We will then be under pressure to choose between their basic criteria when these criteria conflict, i.e. to *drop* certain basic principles, not merely subordinate them to others on particular occasions. This is no doubt a very large reason why moral discourse at the second level is more common in modern 'pluralistic' society than in traditional and homogeneous cultures. So we must reserve an important place for it on our map of moral discourse, even if we cannot find a clear sense for the evaluative statements which are made at this level.[11]

[10] Such a refusal is inevitably confusing because of the dominant modern use of the word 'law' to refer to social norms which differ from the principles of morality, though overlapping them in content. But Aquinas's usage is not as mischievous as that of some modern Natural Law theorists who use the term 'Natural Law' to refer to any basis for moral or political criticism of positive law, and who also slide in and out of Aquinas's use of 'law'.

If we do follow Aquinas, the point being made in the text remains valid but becomes more difficult to express and thus, perhaps, more difficult to see. For if we refuse to say that a rule conflicting with (absolute) morality can be a law, then we will need our second level to discuss the 'moral–legal validity' of alleged laws. But we will not need it when considering whether a certain alleged rule of public order (to make a weak stab at finding a synonym for 'a law' in its dominant modern sense) is or is not part of a system of such rules which is in effect among a certain group of people.

[11] Just as the foregoing disanalogy helps to show why we need to recognize a

Let us now attempt to say plainly why it is that the ethical naturalist, after some victorious campaigns, loses the war to his non-cognitivist opponent. The naturalist's main ambition, I take it, is to identify fixed descriptive (non-moral) criteria for morally evaluative terms, thus enabling us to identify true answers to moral questions. He does find relatively fixed criteria in moral discourse at level one, and he may succeed in convincing himself that they are finally or absolutely fixed if he is able to ignore discourse at the second level. But if we point out to him the existence and importance of the latter type of discourse, then in order to keep up his principal ambition he needs to think that moral statements at that level can be true or false. He needs to take seriously a notion of moral truth which philosophers and the philosophically minded have long been attracted to, and have long found deeply puzzling, namely, the idea that there are *moral criteria or principles which ought, morally, to be accepted and used by all human beings and groups.*

For reasons which have developed during the course of this essay, and which I have lately recapitulated,[12] it does not seem possible to give any clear sense to such an expression. Obviously it has important hortatory and 'performative' uses like urging others to accept a principle, or joining in their commitment to a way of life. And some may hope to give it a literal meaning by saying that certain basic criteria are so universally accepted by human groups that any way of life which lacked them could not properly be said to constitute or include a morality. But this seems quite futile. How, in the first place, are we to identify the favoured few among moral criteria? To say that moral criteria X, Y, and Z are essential to any morality sounds like rhetoric raised to the second power. The term 'morality' itself probably lacks sufficiently definite reference to permit us to collect our samples and extract their 'essence'. But even if we could get our samples through some

---

second level of moral evaluation, another important disanalogy between law and morals concerning the *basis* of evaluative truth argues for our consensus interpretation of truth in morals. See the last topic in Appendix III.

[12] Cf. p. 143.

taxonomic convention, and then read off the basic moral criteria which they have in common, this would not satisfy a philosopher who wanted to use the above italicized expression as though it did make sense. Or at least it should not satisfy him. Suppose we found a group of people who could then properly be said to lack a morality because they did not recognize certain criteria for the evaluation of actions, etc. We would still be unable to show that they were morally wrong in not recognizing those criteria. Indeed, we would still be at a loss to explain acceptably what it could even mean to say 'they are morally wrong in that regard'.

Is it a matter for regret that there is no good reason to believe in moral truth of the mysterious sort that philosophers and others have long been puzzled about? On the other hand, is it really of any use to speak of moral truth based on 'relatively' fixed criteria, as I have just been doing? We shall return to these questions at the end of our next and final section. To end this section, let us again summarize.

We needed to restrict the test of truth to those living a common form of moral life because it is only by virtue of the semantic ties holding between moral and non-moral predicates among the people of such a group that we could find any sense for 'true' as applied to moral statements. It was only in this way that we could conceive the condition under which a moral statement would apply *valid* moral criteria, and the condition under which it would fail to do so. That is, such validity cannot be legislative or objective, as we have argued, but perhaps it can be communal or consentient. Yet we have also admitted that it is possible for a person (even a member of the group living that life) to reject such semantic ties. We have even admitted that it is linguistically normal for a person who does reject one or more of them to apply the words 'valid' or 'true' to other criteria which he prefers, and to moral statements which apply the latter criteria accurately. Although we have denied that 'valid' and 'true' have any clear sense in these applications, we have recognized their expressive uses there. We have also conceded that a person may be *justified* in rejecting communally existing criteria and adopting new ones for himself. And we have tried to explain in Part I what 'justified' means here.

These concessions to various aspects of ordinary moral thought are jointly possible, we have argued, only through a device of 'levels'. To avoid paradox one must observe the distinction of levels and avoid crossing from one to another without realizing that one is doing so. Someone might wish to object, for example, that under our account a person may be justified in saying

(1) I know that *p* is false, yet I believe in it and I am justified in believing in it;

or in saying

(2) I know that *p* is true but I am justified in rejecting it;

where *p* is some moral statement. But these forms are actually forbidden by our account because they do cross levels without warning. They attempt in an illicit way to say something which is not at all logically odd when expressed without level ambiguity (and which can be said without any technical references to levels). That is, they attempt to say, respectively

(1′) I know that practically all people following our way of life, if they were fully informed and properly reflective, would disbelieve in *p*; yet on full information and proper reflection I believe in it;

and

(2′) I know that practically all people following our way of life, if they were fully informed and properly reflective, would believe in *p*; yet on full information and proper reflection I do not believe in it.

Along with this restriction against level ambiguity in using 'true', 'justified', and related words, we have also ruled against any supposition that 'true', 'false', 'really right', 'absolutely wrong', and so on, have sense at the second level. Perhaps there will be some feeling that these are 'artificial' rules that people are not commonly aware of and do not commonly invoke to correct one another logically. But if our levels are 'real', as I have argued, then the distinction needs to be respected. And it is a familiar point that the rules of logic which are most useful in practice are just those which people often do violate and need to have explained to them. Common references to truth in morals are anything but clear as matters stand, and I suggest that these restrictions will be conservative of ordinary discourse by helping to make such sense of these references as *can* be made. I think it would be more paradoxical and disruptive either to attempt to eliminate all predications of truth in morals, or to attempt to save them by eliminating the assumption of personal autonomy and the deeper sort of critical moral discourse which I have called discourse at the second level. But these seem to be the only alternatives to our restrictions as a way of achieving a coherent view of the expression 'moral truth'.

A great deal more would have to be done to develop an adequate logical and semantic analysis along the lines proposed in this section. But perhaps the foregoing will at least suggest that matters could be worked out coherently and in reasonable agreement with existing patterns of moral discourse.

8. Conclusions

We have examined the notions of moral reasoning and moral truth in order to see whether it is possible to preserve the common-sense assumption that many moral opinions are true, and that one can often give good and sufficient reasons for them. As announced in the Introduction, I especially hoped to improve on those ethical theories which preserve the assumption of personal autonomy in moral judgement, and especially R. M. Hare's theory which assigns a greater role to reasoning in morals than does either of its major predecessors in this tradition, the emotive theory and intuitionism. I have tried to provide a still larger basis for moral objectivity, partly by exploiting Hare's analysis of standards to identify a valid standard of good moral reasoning, and partly by recognizing certain points about moral truth which ethical naturalists have recognized but have given too great a significance. Let us now briefly consider whether this purpose has been accomplished, assuming that what has been said up to this point is roughly correct. That is, my own arguments and constructions about reasoning and truth in morals are now substantially complete; without repeating them or developing them much further, I now wish to consider what larger consequences they may have for ethical theory if they should happen to be sound. My answer to the last objection in Section 6 is necessarily part of this.

The great problem, of course, is to reconcile personal autonomy and rational objectivity in morals.[1] So it will be a useful preliminary to ask whether we have ourselves managed

[1] Cf. Sections 1.1 and 1.2 of *Freedom and Reason*. Classically, Kant joined this problem to that of freedom and determinism in his network of problems, and its political analogue is found in Rousseau.

to respect the autonomy of the individual, or have finally had to sacrifice it in attempting to preserve the notions of truth and sound reasoning. In this we may take naturalism as our point of reference since it negates personal autonomy in matters of basic principle, leaving the individual with only empirical and deductive questions to answer. How well we may have preserved the claim to personal autonomy will depend on how well we have managed to avoid that position ourselves.

If what I have said in Section 1 is correct, naturalism conceives of morality either as a single objective standard or as several objective standards suitable for several kinds of subjects of moral evaluation, all determined by a single purpose in moral choice, a single objective or closely coherent set of objectives which we seek to further or attain in all of our moral preferences. Accordingly, it would be possible in principle to demonstrate the correct answer to practically any moral question, and to do so in a way that is much more conclusive than are the moral demonstrations in Section 6. That is, one would not merely cite a principle which *no one would doubt* is controlling for the question at hand. One would actually have derived all valid principles from the ultimate purpose of moral choice, and one would appeal to that purpose in order to resolve any conflicts or any vagueness in such principles as they apply to the question at hand. Thus, as we noticed earlier, if someone were to embrace any other moral opinion besides the correct one, it would be possible to demonstrate to him that his opinion is wrong. That is, we could construct a moral argument consisting of true facts, a valid principle and priority, and a valid deductive inference, proving to such a person that his own best judgement is wrong. It would make no difference whether he were imaginatively attentive to all the facts himself, and judged, in the most disinterested and psychologically normal way, that such a principle and priority were morally improper for the case. He would still be flatly wrong.

It is this possibility, jarring so badly as I think it does with common intuitions about the nature of moral judgement, that has been my chief reason for rejecting ethical naturalism as an account of such judgement. And I think it can easily be seen that there is no such possibility under our own account, even though we recognize that moral judgements can be true, i.e. that moral predicates can have fixed non-moral criteria 'locally', or within given ways of life. By our account, a person is always entitled to judge reasonably for himself whether a certain moral principle or criterion is valid, and whether it should be allowed to determine a particular moral question in a particular way. Even if there would be a consensus of fully informed and reasonable moral judges about the question before him—in other words, even if that question does have a certain answer which is true by virtue of the very meaning (locally) of 'right', 'wrong', etc., taken in conjunction with the facts of the case—he is not bound by that consensus and meaning. A moral critic is still entitled by the 'rules' of moral thought and discourse to reject that principle in that application if he finds it objectionable when considering the subject of evaluation in the morally reasonable way.

Such a person would be thinking or speaking at the second of the two levels that we have distinguished, at least if the principle in question were basic in the sense explained in Section 7. But it should also be pointed out that even at the level of moral evaluation in which the basic principles of one's group are never questioned, the autonomy of the moral agent or judge is still preserved for most practical purposes. This is because we will never be able to construct a *moral* argument refuting someone's justified moral judgement, and we will seldom be able to produce *other* evidence that the moral consensus would be contrary to such judgement. In a moral argument we must ask our interlocutor to form his own reasonable judgement, and if he does so it will usually be the best evidence available to him of what the *right* judgement is, i.e. what practically any properly informed and otherwise reasonable person would hold about the matter being judged, assuming there *is* a right judgement to make about it. I admit, however, that it might occasionally be obvious, without collecting any special evidence, that someone's morally reasonable opinion about something is highly eccentric. And this might be shown to him in some rough but substantially adequate way. But if it seems counter-intuitive that we could thereby prove to a person that his own justified opinion is wrong merely because other people who held justified opinions would practically all disagree with him, I can only agree that it *is* counter-intuitive and add that this is why we need to recognize the second level. Presenting such a person with such a proof would only force him into the second level if it did not cause him to change his opinion. If he had the courage of his convictions, he could still disagree with the consensus, although he could not say that it was false and his own opinion true except in a purely rhetorical use of these words.

If it be granted that we have managed to preserve the assumption of autonomy, have we made any advance over other theories in allowing for the objectivity of moral judgements and reasons? I think there can be little question that our discussion, if sound, does represent an advance over both the emotive theory and intuitionism in this regard. For the emotive theory actually repudiates common conceptions of moral reasonableness as a binding standard,[2] while intuitionism is much less venturesome than we have been about *explaining* either reasoning or truth in morals.[3] It holds that when intuitively relevant facts are called to mind, one 'rationally apprehends' the rightness or wrongness of an action; and here our own account is similar. But we have also explained why the intuitively reasonable way of doing this is a valid standard, immune to moral criticism. And we have also tried to take the mystery out of the intuitionist's synthetic necessary connections between descriptive non-moral predicates and predicates of moral value. By our account, the connection is logically necessary at level one because it is

[2] Cf. pp. 75 f., and pp. 105–9, above.

[3] I refer especially to H. A. Prichard's classic statement of intuitionism in 'Does Moral Philosophy Rest on a Mistake', *Mind*, vol. 21 (1912), reprinted in his *Moral Obligation* (Oxford: The Clarendon Pr., 1949).

analytic there; but it is synthetic at level two, and fundamentally synthetic, because we can always proceed to level two and 'break up' the moral definitions which people live by and use in discourse at level one. The intuitionist may wish to reply that even assertions at level two regarding the validity of moral criteria are necessarily true or necessarily false, even though synthetic. But our rejoinder must be that this statement seems to lack sense, and the burden is his to explain it or drop it.[4]

Have we really made progress beyond Hare's theory, however? In his second book he recognizes the standard of reasonableness just as we do, though he does not call it that. Substantially the same requirements are laid down: that we must

[4] Our account of moral truth also has a superficial resemblance to Ideal Observer theories in ethics, so it may be well to point out how different they really are. Such theories are naturalistic, holding typically that moral statements are *about* moral attitudes or responses. ('X is wrong' *means* 'X would be disapproved by an ideal moral observer'. Accordingly, 'X is wrong' is true if and only if X *would* be disapproved by an ideal moral observer.) In contrast, we hold that 'X is wrong' is about X, just as it appears to be, and that it means that X is properly to be condemned. While our theory is partly similar to the IO theories in holding that 'X is wrong' is true if and only if it would be the consensus of properly qualified judges (because the criteria of proper condemnation and the correctness of their application in specific cases depend on such hypothetical consensus) even this is not a close similarity because we restrict this truth condition to level one.

IO theories commonly have no answer to the question, 'How do you *know* that an ideal observer or judge ought to be impartial, dispassionate, disinterested?' But we do attempt to explain this and to avoid the imputation that one only makes a debatable moral judgement in laying down such conditions. Such theories also have the seemingly hopeless defect that we could not know *what* the ideal observer's reaction would be unless we knew his particular background, temperament, physiology—all of which he lacks. But one can often know what the consensus of qualified judges would be. For a good discussion of these and other problems, see Chap. VII, 'Ideal Observer Theories', in Jonathan Harrison's *Our Knowledge of Right and Wrong* (London: Allen & Unwin, 1971).

Like other forms of naturalism, IO theories cannot preserve personal autonomy in a strong sense. If I *could* know what an ideal observer's reaction would be, but had a different one myself when fully informed and properly reflective, I would want to know his reasons and be convinced by them before I could accept his reaction as sound and conform my own to it. In other words, the final appeal would be to my own judgement, contrary to such theories.

be informed of relevant facts, that we must be imaginatively attentive to them, and that we must be able to universalize our judgement and reasons. Also, we have had to admit in the final analysis, just as Hare does, that a person is logically free to adopt and apply any moral principle he pleases, as long as he satisfies those requirements. But if the criticism we have sketched in the Introduction and expanded in Appendix I is sound, and if our own constructive work in Part I is correct (two large ifs, to be sure), then I think we have taken moral reasoning a step farther than Hare did in his outstanding books of one and two decades ago. I shall attempt to explain why this is so in the next few pages, and then conclude with some brief remarks on moral truth.

If the criticism referred to is valid, it will always be possible to trivialize Hare's universalization requirement, that is, to satisfy it while defending any moral statement, however outrageous. We must satisfy his criterion of relevance in describing our act and giving our reasons why it is all right for us to perform such an act; but we can always do this in such a way as to be practically certain that the principle thereby entailed will never have another application, and so can never hurt us. Even without taking advantage of this weakness in Hare's relevance criterion, many people will often be able to universalize judgements entailing principles which could very well prove uncomfortable or harmful to them in other cases. For, as Hare explains with a different point in mind, the question is not what the person who is being asked to universalize his judgement *would* say if the shoe were on the other foot, but what he now *can* say. Can he say sincerely, 'Let me be imprisoned if I have been duly convicted of a felony carrying a mandatory prison sentence'? Of course he can! That is, most people obviously can, even as they vividly imagine what it would be like to be put into prison this very minute. This may be partly due to the fact that they have no expectation of being convicted of any felonies; but they do believe, in any case, that convicted felons should be put into prison when the law requires it. For reasons which I shall not repeat here, many people can similarly universalize various other judgements which you or I or the next person might find objectionable, even if we do not find punishing felons objectionable. To use Hare's own example against him, many people can probably universalize a judgement that it is all right for them to put some debtor of theirs into prison to make him pay or get his friends to pay.

If these things are so, Hare's test will not provide a generally effective screen against objectionably selfish judgements or heartless judgements. Incidentally, he usually avoids such independent moral characterizations of the judgements which his test is supposed to exclude.[5] And he needs to avoid them, I take it, because the test itself is designed to furnish the basis of all effective inter-personal argument for or against moral judgements, at least between people who begin a moral argument with no principles in common. He must avoid any appeal or reference to intuitive moral evaluations in stating the universalization requirement and the relevance requirement which is part of it. So he uses the bare restriction that only 'universal' terms may appear in a description of the act and its circumstances. But we who are not under such a limitation can refer, as above, to morally objectionable judgements. And we can give content to the phrase by saying that it refers to judgements practically anyone would say are objectionable if he considered them in the way one ought to consider something when morally evaluating it. Notice also that in unpacking the phrase 'in the way one ought to consider something when morally evaluating it' we do not let ourselves in for the same trouble that we are now badgering Hare about. For although we also require that moral evaluations be universalizable, we are content to say that the person whose judgement is in question should be sincere about which descriptive characteristics he considers morally relevant.[6] The reason for these house-cleaning remarks will soon be obvious, I trust.

[5] But perhaps not entirely. His various references to 'special pleading' would seem to suggest that it is a *selfish* judgement which will be excluded when reasons which can be so characterized are excluded.

[6] See Section 2, esp. pp. 44 f.

Since Hare does not really give us an effective screen against selfish or heartless judgements, his suggestion that we could derive a moral code, or part of a moral code, by applying his test to situations involving many persons is also illusory, as I have argued in the Introduction and Appendix I.

In this situation, it seems that Hare could do one of three things. He could stick to his formulations of the universalization test and relevance requirement even though they accomplish little or nothing towards assuring the interpersonal effectiveness of moral reasoning. Or he could try some new formulations which also avoid any appeal to intuitive judgements of moral relevance, a project which strikes me as unpromising even though some recent writers have continued to pursue it. Or thirdly, he could simply insist that there is, in any case, an important restriction on moral judgement and reasons which he and many other philosophers have meant to refer to with the term 'universalizability', and that even if their formulations have not caught it exactly, we *are* all bound to observe it. And he might point out that when we do observe it or try to observe it, some judgements which we might otherwise make will have to be withdrawn. But this, of course, would be to invoke *our* requirement in Section 2. Thus: if Jones claims that it is all right for him to perform act *X* in circumstances *C*, he must be prepared to allow that it is all right for anyone to perform *X* in *C*, where *X* and *C* are described in those terms, and only those terms, which Jones sincerely regards as morally relevant in this case. This surely would eliminate *many* objectionable judgements (in the sense noted above), even if many others would not be eliminated for reasons mentioned above and discussed in Appendix I.

Wouldn't Hare have as much right as we have to point to this purely intuitive requirement, and leave it intuitive? Yes, with some modifications of his theory. But then he would have a new problem to face. He would need to consider an objection of the following sort, which we may assign to a consistent emotivist like Stevenson.

'Apart from the fact that people do sincerely disagree about the moral relevance of facts, and about what principles they can sincerely accept, why do you insist on sincerity? Is it that you personally prefer that people should be sincere in their moral reasonings? That is an attitude you are free to take, just as others are free not to take it. Many people will no doubt share your attitude, so your chances of agreeing on morally relevant descriptions, and then perhaps on principles, will be higher when you are discussing moral questions with *them*. But there is no proving that this is the correct attitude to take. The best you can do is argue for it persuasively by appealing to other attitudes which your listener may be expected to have. In falling back on intuitive judgements of moral relevance, and in insisting on sincerity, you only illustrate my contention that there are no valid moral arguments, and that whenever moral disagreements *can* be resolved through the discovery or exchange of factual information this is because the disputants happen to share some ulterior attitude or (if you prefer) some ulterior moral principle.'

We have given our own answer to this kind of objection in Sections 3 through 5. While we have left the universalization requirement and relevance test in an intuitive formulation, we have *not* left it intuitive that they are binding on moral judgement and reasoning, even in something close to our own formulation. We have attempted to show that they are part of a standard which is demonstrably valid for moral discourse. If our argument in this regard has been successful, we have thus taken a significant step beyond Hare's theory and any other anti-naturalist theory which may have recognized the requirements of reasonableness, or the moral point of view, without providing an effective answer to the emotivist objection.

Finally, have we added anything to what Hare and other anti-naturalists might easily have said about moral truth if they had thought it worth saying? Possibly not. But they have not said these things, as far as I am aware, and sometimes half-obvious points may be understood better when someone takes the trouble to say them, or says them in conjunction with related points which were not obvious at all. If anyone cares to insist that I have not really shown how moral statements can be true because the 'truths' of the first level can be rejected at the second level and are never true or false there, I am willing to plead guilty to the charge if I am allowed to add the following remarks before sentencing.

First, 'truth' at the first level of moral evaluation is not to be sneered at. It helps us live by giving order to our common life, so perhaps it deserves better than scare quotes. People do speak of moral truth, and if the expression is to have a coherent meaning, I think it must have the one that I have been trying to present.

Second, I have to point out again that it is a very queer notion of truth that we leave unredeemed here, this notion that some criteria of moral evaluation are 'absolutely' valid and *ought* to be recognized by all people and groups of people. No doubt it is an important notion for philosophers to isolate and do their best to understand. But after finding that 'ought' and other value words can occur as the main predicates or auxiliaries in true-or-false statements of various kinds, while their cognitive significance in this use remains totally obscure, I am myself inclined to avoid it on the ground that it really has no literal meaning.

It will be said that we cannot really dispense with the notion of absolute moral criteria; that we will be convinced that certain moral principles *are* universally valid and binding; that we will sometimes have to declare these deepest moral beliefs and assert their truth against other people who deny or violate them. I agree that we may have to defend our convictions physically, and also that there are situations in which moral rhetoric is a better recipe than logical candour. But when we are being quite candid, why must we say that our basic moral criteria are valid or true? We know how to reason morally, and we have seen how to justify our convictions without making mysterious truth claims. Since we can justify our opinions on less fundamental moral questions which pretty obviously lack true answers even in the sense of 'true' that I have explained, why can we not also show our reasonableness in the way we choose and apply our basic moral criteria, recommending them to others who are also willing to consider them reasonably? What further claim do we really need to make if we are speaking literally and candidly?

Even the purely rhetorical application of value predicates ('true', 'really right', 'really valid,' etc.) to one's basic moral criteria is likely to be seriously confusing even though it is logically innocuous in theory. If one clearly recognises that it is purely rhetorical, there is no harm in it. But those who haven't noticed the kind of distinctions we have been making are unlikely to recognize this, while anyone who has noticed them and taken them to heart may no longer feel the need for *this* kind of rhetoric. According to these distinctions, it is simply out of place to use 'true', 'right', 'valid', etc. at the second level of discourse *except* as an expression of personal conviction or fundamental resolve. To use them there as though they had sense is to fall into the ambiguity of levels. And when we realize this, perhaps the one most maddening puzzle in this area of thought will begin to lose its hold on us. Does it not then seem less urgent to assert that our basic moral beliefs are absolutely valid, or that there at least must *be* absolute moral standards? Extremely important as our own reflectively held principles may be, we see after all that there is no literal point or sense to such an assertion, *and* that its emotional point is made and purchased with too much confusion. The expressive force of the assertion seems to depend on its being taken as though it *did* have literal sense, as though we were not *merely* expressing *our* deepest moral choice or commitments. And there are other ways to express them.

Appendices

I. Prescriptivism

ONE of the three or four most notable features of *The Language of Morals*[1] was Hare's introduction of principles to furnish a syllogistic connection between non-moral factual reasons and particular moral conclusions. This was his answer to the emotivists' doctrine that there is only a 'psychological' connection between moral reasons and conclusions, not a logical one. In giving moral reasons, Hare pointed out, one claims that a certain *kind* of fact is a basis for a certain *kind* of evaluation; one necessarily invokes and commits oneself to a principle. The principles one invokes can of course be challenged by other people, and may need to be justified. But Hare seems to have thought that we can avoid both an open regress in the justification of principles and a merely arbitrary assertion of ultimate principles. The first point I wish to make in this Appendix, no doubt a rather familiar point by now, is that Hare did not manage to show how this is so, at least not where the argument terminating in one's ultimate principles is offered to justify a full-fledged moral judgement, e.g. a judgement that some decision or action is morally right.

In order to 'justify a decision completely', Hare says in a much cited passage, we would have to 'give a complete specification of the way of life of which it is a part'. By this he means a complete account of the effects of the decision 'together with a complete account of the principles which it observed, and the effects of observing those principles' (p. 69). While such complete specifications cannot be given in practice, Hare says that we can at least attempt to inform ourselves as fully as possible about ways of life between which we may have a real choice. And the theoretical possibility of giving a complete specification shows why it is not correct to say that principles must be chosen arbitrarily. The decision to adopt such a completely specified way of life (including the principles which are part of it) 'would be the most well-founded of decisions, because it would be based upon a con-

[1] Oxford: The Clarendon Pr., 1952.

sideration of everything upon which it could possibly be founded (p. 69).

This last statement may be true, but there is still a relevant sense in which the decision adopting a way of life would be arbitrary, namely, that it could not be justified by invoking a principle, at least not in such a way as to show that *those* principles of action are the right ones to have, and decisions conforming to them the right decisions to make. Is there a principle saying that the way of life one ought to choose is the one which seems most attractive after full inquiry? Very well, then there will be a certain way of life with certain principles of action that one ought to choose after such inquiry. But other people will be free to choose others. It seems most unlikely that all or nearly all people would be thus constrained to choose the identical package of principles.

If I think that action *A* is obviously wrong, I also think that people who disagree with me are mistaken. That is, I do not merely mean that *A* is wrong 'as far as I am concerned'. So if I give an argument to justify my judgement and this argument begins by showing that the judgement is in conformity with certain principles, it seems obvious that I have to do something more than show that they are *my* principles, or that I have informed myself before adopting them. Presumably, I must give a reason why they are the right principles for anyone to have, thus necessarily invoking a further principle, and so on. On the other hand, I might try to avoid this puzzle by limiting the sort of claim I intend to make in my 'moral evaluations'. In order not to make judgements that go beyond the reach of any possible justifying argument, I may decide that from now on when I say that *A* is wrong I shall only mean something like '*A* is contrary to principles which I accept'. And when I give some factual reason why A is wrong, I shall only mean something like '*A* is contrary to a certain principle, *P*, to which I hereby subscribe.' But the trouble with this is that I shall then have ceased making moral judgements altogether (or at least 'full-fledged' moral judgements) in order to be able to construct complete justifications for the evaluative statements I do make. In either case, I shall not be able to give a complete argument justifying a moral decision or judgement.

In *The Language of Morals,* Hare seemed to have chosen the latter alternative, although he was perhaps not fully aware how high a price he paid in abandoning all claims to inter-personal validity for his 'moral' evaluations. No doubt he was well aware that people do make such claims, and perhaps he did not feel uncomfortable about giving them up. But to anyone who persists in trying to understand how moral judgements can be adequately supported with reasons, it is the highest possible price because it confesses total defeat and abandons this type of evaluation. Its effect if generally accepted would be to abolish morality as we know it and replace it with something quite different. Notice how it leaves us in a thoroughly sceptical position as to the relevance of moral reasons. It can explain why some facts *seem* relevant to support a given moral conclusion while other facts *seem* utterly irrelevant. (It will say that this is because the first are thereby associated with principles which would be widely accepted, while the latter facts are thereby associated with principles which would be commonly regarded as immoral or absurd.) But any fact at all can really *be* relevant 'for someone' under Hare's account as long as that someone accepts a principle which, together with that fact, entails that conclusion. Each person can decide for himself what shall count as evidence for or against his own 'moral' judgement, at least if he is able to accept and (for the time being) live by the principles to which he thereby commits himself.

It was that consequence of Hare's theory which Philippa Foot attacked in her widely discussed articles later in the fifties (see Appendix II), and which Hare himself sought to avoid or soften in *Freedom and Reason*.[2] In this book he still holds that, from a purely logical point of view, any fact can be a moral reason and any principle can be a moral principle. But he tries to show that this does not have the relativist consequences one might expect, since inter-personal reasoning in morals is not carried on from a purely logical point of view. Psychological factors ('inclinations') inevitably obtrude upon the selection of reasons and principles, and to that extent the emotivists were right. But this does not mean that rational participants in a moral debate will normally be free to adopt whatever principles they like. Quite the contrary, according to Hare. The 'logic' of moral statements collaborates with the inclinations of nearly all people in such a way as to force the same principles upon us. Thus 'there can be useful and compelling moral argument even between people who have, before it begins, no substantive moral principles in common' (p. 187).

The second main point I wish to make in this Appendix is that

[2] Oxford: The Clarendon Pr., 1963.

Hare also does not manage to show how *this* is so. But in order to make the point clearly, it will be necessary for me to summarize the well known argument of his second book.

Suppose someone says that he would be morally justified in taking some action which you or I or the next person would consider objectionable because of its harmful or unpleasant effects on others. In view of the logical features of every moral statement, and in view of the psychological make-up of the vast majority of people, we will nearly always be able to prove to such a person that he ought to retract his judgement, at least if he is willing to engage in moral discourse and thereby submit to those logical features. Every moral statement is *prescriptive* in the sense that it entails a certain imperative. So one does not really make (accept) a moral statement unless one is willing to accept that imperative. And to accept it means to obey it or attempt to obey it whenever one is in the situation to which it refers. For example, 'It is wrong to do *X* in circumstances *C*' entails 'Let anyone in *C* not do *X*.' And every moral statement must also be *universalizable*, a feature which can be exhibited as follows: 'Doing *X* in *C* is right (morally permissible)' entails 'Let anyone in *C* do *X* if he wishes', and the latter obviously entails 'Let anyone in *C* do *X* if he wishes, even if this would be harmful or unpleasant to *me*.' Clearly then, one does not make (accept) the statement 'My doing *X* in *C* is right' unless one is willing to accept and act on this latter imperative also.

In Hare's example, I can only judge that it is morally right for me to have my debtor, Jones, put into prison if I can accept the imperative, 'Let any creditor of mine have me put into prison, if he wishes, when he is situated toward me and my situation just as I am toward Jones.' Hare thinks only a tiny percentage of people will be able to accept such imperatives where being *X*'ed is in fact unpleasant or harmful, all things considered, and they are informed and imaginative enough to appreciate this fact. Useful and compelling argument will then consist in supplying such information and giving aids to the imagination after pointing out such entailments or logical commitments to the person who has said that it is all right for him to *X* someone. Only 'fanatics' will be proof against such an argument, and they are actually very rare, says Hare. Consider Hitler's SS men who said it was right to put Jews to death. If we were to trick one of them into believing that he, after all, is a Jew, how likely is it that he would persist in his judgement and march willingly to the gas chamber? We may be sure that few if any SS men were fanatics in the sense that they were able to say *consistently* 'It is morally right to put Jews to death.'

So in *Freedom and Reason* Hare still thinks moral argument is a matter of showing one's personal consistency or questioning the consistency of someone else. But now he has explained more fully what it means to be consistent with one's own principles, and the explanation does bring his theory into somewhat closer agreement with common moral assumptions. We ordinarily assume that a person's moral judgements can be sound or unsound in some deeper sense than mere agreement or disagreement with the principles to which he announces his adherence, and Hare's logico-psychological account does specify a deeper sense. But he wants to go farther than this. He suggests that a certain type of utilitarian normative ethic would be derivable by applying the universalization argument to situations involving many persons, rather than just two. For anyone who will feel the force of that argument when he carefully attends to it (i.e. practically everyone, according to Hare), the result of applying it to such situations would be a set of rules each of which is designed to secure the interests of everyone concerned. That is, one would have obtained each rule after imaginatively placing oneself in the shoes of everyone (or of everyone in a representative sample) who would be affected by the action or actions one is proposing to take. The rule thus chosen would presumably be the one which each of the people concerned would choose under the supposition that he was going to occupy in turn all of the situations of everyone affected.

Rules so derived could be applied to the solution of other types of moral problems besides those which are resolvable by the universalization argument itself. Hare cites the example of a convicted felon who might try to use the universalization argument on a judge who is about to sentence him. The judge could answer by pointing out that crime involves a multi-person situation, and that the rules derived for it authorize and direct him to impose a prison sentence. Hence he would be justified in sending the felon to prison even though he could not himself assent to the imperative, 'Let me be put into prison.' Hare admits, however, that the principles which might be derived under his theory could not cover all moral questions. Indeed, he does not claim to be able to work such principles out. He says that he has only been concerned to 'establish a point of contact' between utilitarianism and his universalization argument, and cannot 'state clearly and exactly what kind of utilitarianism if any will emerge ...' (pp. 122–3).

What non-evaluative characteristics may be allowed into the descriptions of act *X* and circumstances *C*? If everything true about the act and about the agent and his situation may be put in, then I shall always be able to universalize my judgement that doing *X* in *C* is right, because it will always be possible to guarantee by the use of sufficient detail, proper names, and so on, that no one else will ever be in *C* to *X* me. To say that only 'morally relevant' characteristics may be admitted will not do since it can be debated whether a given characteristic *is* morally relevant. What Hare does is limit the admissible descriptive characteristics to 'universal' ones, i.e. to those which contain no reference to individuals and require none. This can probably be justified on the ground that such a reference is easily used to provide a logical guarantee (not merely a high probability) that 'doing *X* in *C*' will have no other instances, in which case the whole point of the universalization requirement would be frustrated. Hare also says that if anyone should attempt to include a 'universal' feature of his act or situation which does not seem to us to be morally relevant, we can point out to him that it could be a feature of another case in which he played a different role, and we can ask him to ignore the fact that he plays the role he does play in the present case. 'This will force him to count as morally relevant only those properties which he is prepared to allow to be relevant even when other people have them. And this rules out all the attractive kinds of special pleading' (p. 107). As long as it is logically possible that he should some time be in position to be unpleasantly or harmfully *X*'ed himself by someone in *C*, our argument will be effective. He will not be able to accept the imperative, 'Let anyone in *C* who wishes *X* me.'

If the reasoning summarized in the last five paragraphs is correct, Hare has finally managed to show how in many cases moral arguments can be successfully completed to justify one's judgements to others, forcing them (if they would be rational) to retract such contrary judgements as they may have made. True, the principles invoked in such an argument are not given general justifications or absolute warrants, but are supported only to the extent needed for the purposes of immediate debate: that is, to show one's opponent that he really does not accept the principle to which his judgement and reasons initially committed him, but some other principle which can now be accepted by both parties to the debate—although it is proposed that generally justified principles might possibly be worked out empirically from this theoretical beginning. But I shall now attempt to explain why the universalization argument will not work in a great many cases where Hare apparently thinks it will work, and hence why the utilitarian ethic which he thinks might be derived for all but a few people called fanatics cannot possibly be derived in this way. Indeed, for reasons to be noted, I think Hare has not successfully explained how the universalization argument will work in even one case.

To show that many people will often be immune to the universalization argument, let me develop a counter-example cited by one of Hare's critics (R. B. Brandt, in a review in *The Journal of Philosophy*, vol. 61 (1964)). A General who says, 'Let Privates work sixteen-hour days in the mess hall', will not be moved to retract his order if his Adjutant points out to him that *he* could some day be a Private and be put on K. P. Even if the Adjutant spells out Hare's argument in full, the General will no doubt insist that he too, if a Private, should perform this time-honoured fatigue. Someone might wish to reply in Hare's defence that the General would not be *entitled* to leave his order in effect because he *would not* willingly accept it if he *were* a Private (what Private ever has?). But such a reply would misread Hare's test. He says that we should not ask our interlocutor what he *would* say or feel if he were in position to be X'ed, but what he *does* now feel and say about such a hypothetical case. (In this way, Hare intends to preclude the reply that of course one wouldn't like being X'ed and might even take *moral* exception to it, but that this is irrelevant to the validity of the moral judgement one is now making (p. 108)). So it is a strong counter-example to Hare's theory that many a General would 'now' feel that it would be proper for *him* to be put on K. P. if he were a Private, and so could now sincerely assent to the corresponding imperative.

Hare seems to overlook an important result of his own distinctions. He recognizes that it is logically possible for a person to assent to the imperative, 'Let me be (painfully or harmfully) X'ed by someone', but holds that this possibility will be realized only very rarely because we will almost invariably have an aversion to being so treated in the hypothetical case. Hence we will not be able to assent sincerely to the imperative. Thus, he says in effect, every SS man will presumably have an aversion to being killed, but it is logically possible that some SS man will nevertheless not have an aversion to being killed-if-a-Jew (pp. 108–10). And any SS man who does have such a rare 'inclination' as that would be proof against the universalization argument. So Hare observes a distinction between (1) being treated in some painful or harmful way, and (2) being treated in that same way but under some further described circumstance. And he allows the logical possibility that one could have an aversion to (1) in a hypothetical case while not having an aversion to (2) in the same case. Indeed, he must allow this if his theory is not to imply the far-fetched proposition that no one can ever consistently judge that he ought to treat someone else in a way that he himself has an aversion to being treated, e.g. that no one can ever consistently judge that he ought to punish his child for the child's own good. Hare's theory allows that I can make the latter judgement on condition that, although I have an aversion, say, to being turned over someone's knee and spanked, I do not have an aversion to being turned over someone's knee and spanked if I am a child and that someone is my parent who thinks I need a spanking—at least not a strong enough aversion to prevent my now sincerely assenting to the relevant imperative.

With this distinction in hand, we can get such results as the following. The General now has an aversion to doing hard labour and being spattered with grease for sixteen-hour periods, but he does not have a (sufficiently strong) aversion to doing-K.P.-if-a-Private. And many a judge who is about to sentence an offender will be able to pass the test without the aid of any derived rules. For he will have an aversion to being put into jail, but not to being put-into-jail-if-a-convicted-felon. The General's belief in K.P. duty and the judges' belief in punishing the guilty will be enough to preclude a sufficiently strong aversion on their part to being *X*'ed-in-*C* even though they do have a present strong aversion to being *X*'ed. Hence it will be possible for them sincerely to assent to the imperative, 'Let me be *X*'ed-in-*C* if I should ever be in position to be *X*'ed-in-*C*.

These results may seem harmless since they square with common moral opinion. After all, we do not want to use the universalization argument to make someone retract a moral judgement with which we agree. But it is probable that many people will often be able to pass Hare's test when they say that it is all right for them to treat others in a way that you or I or most people would say is morally wrong. All that is required is that they should have some interest or belief which is sufficient to outweigh their aversion to being treated that way, considered by itself. Perhaps relatively few people will be able to pass the test when they say that it is all right for them to kill-someone-in-*C*, although even there the unlikelihood of their ever being in position to be killed-in-*C* may permit that interest or belief to have enough relative weight to enable them to pass the test. I suppose that most executioners could pass the test.

Let us consider less extreme cases. (1) A rich merchant is considering whether to ruin a small storekeeper and gain a monopoly in the town by greatly underselling him until this result is achieved. Can he not consistently say that it is right to do this, or that he ought to do it? To be sure, he would not like to lose his trade and be ruined himself, but if he is devoted to *laissez-faire* economics and the principle that business is business, he may not now have a sufficient aversion to being-ruined-in-free-competition. (2) Consider a father who supports his children just well enough to avoid prosecution for neglect, while spending most of his income on clothes, travel, and entertainment for himself, doing so on the principle that we only live once, and explaining that he wasn't treated any better as a child. He thinks he was rightly treated that way for his parents' convenience, and now it's his turn. (3) A man justifies beating a weaker man senseless by saying the latter struck the first blow. *His* belief is that an aggressor deserves everything he gets. To be sure, he is averse to being severely beaten himself, but not (sufficiently) to being severely beaten if *he* is the aggressor and his intended victim proves more than a match for him. This is his principle as a common brawler. (4) Then there is the grower who pays coolie wages to migratory workers when he could easily pay more. He believes in the traditional rates and would not be disloyal to fellow members of the growers' association. He has a general aversion to being paid coolie wages himself if he should have to work for wages, but not (sufficiently) to being paid coolie wages if he should be a migratory farm worker.

The point is that there is no reason to think people will have interests or beliefs that will outweigh their aversion only in those cases where common moral opinion would endorse or tolerate it. Of course, if we require that only commonly accepted 'moral' opinions or interests may be allowed to cancel our natural aversion to being *X*'ed, then our saying that it is all right for us to *X* someone *will not* pass Hare's test except in those cases. But Hare does not lay down such a requirement, nor can he if his argument is to rely only on '(1) facts; (2) logic; (3) inclinations', as he intends (p. 93).

So it seems fairly clear that Hare's universalization argument, rather than being effective against everyone but the very rare 'fanatic', will often be ineffective against quite ordinary people. He seems to be half aware of this when he takes up the counter-example of the judge meting out punishment. As already mentioned, he tries to handle it by invoking the principles of right conduct which would be theoretically derivable as part of the utilitarian normative ethic flowing from his universalization argument. The judge could justify his judgement by appeal to such principles even if he could not universalize it without them. But no such principles *are* uniformly derivable, for reasons which we have just been considering. If someone can agree that he too should be painfully or harmfully *X*'ed in certain situations (agreement which may be made easier by the fact that he is very unlikely ever to be in those situations, although this isn't necessary) then he can apply Hare's argument to multi-personal cases and come out with rules which do *not* take everyone's interests into account. And others can do the same. So there is no reason to think that they will all come out to the same substantive principle concerning one type of action, much less the same array of principles for many types of actions.

When I said before that Hare hasn't successfully explained how the universalization argument will work in even one case, I meant that anyone we use it against will always be technically able to avoid its effect even while complying with all of Hare's requirements. It is obvious that even while restricting oneself to 'universal' characteristics, one can easily make one's own case practically unique, if not logically unique, by listing all kinds of things that others would doubtless think morally irrelevant. Even if I may only cite universal characteristics which I would allow others to cite as morally relevant, I can still make my case unique by forming a long conjunction of such characteristics and insisting on its moral significance. If it be replied that I will not be prepared to allow that complex characteristic to be relevant when other people's actions-in-circumstances have it, why will I not, seeing that they never will have it? Or if it be replied that I will not be prepared to allow others to make their cases unique by *similarly detailed* descriptions, I can respond by pointing out instances in which we would probably all admit that special features and circumstances *do* combine to make one person's act-in-circumstances morally unique. (The same judgement would be in order in any similar case, but clearly there will be no similar case.) We do not want to eliminate the use of detailed descriptions, for we do not want to rule out the recognition of unique moral cases.

It seems that we will always have to judge intuitively whether a certain description amounts to special pleading or describes a case which 'really is' morally unique. And it seems that the best one could do to close this gap in Hare's test would be to require that the person who is being asked to universalize his judgement should at least be sincere in this regard, citing all and only those characteristics which he really thinks are morally relevant. Hare's test has other technical troubles, especially on the point of imagining oneself 'in someone else's place'.[3] These also seem to be resolvable only by falling back on intuitive judgements. That is, it does *seem* to make sense to say that one can imagine (in many cases, anyway) what it would be like to be in another person's shoes and to be affected as that other person would be affected by the action one is proposing to take; just as it does *seem* to make sense that some non-moral facts are plainly relevant and others plainly irrelevant to the moral evaluation of an action (in many cases, anlyway). But it seems impossible to give a flat rule which will recognize all and only those cases in which one can put oneself into another's place, or which will recognize all and only facts which are morally relevant.

To sum up these criticisms, it seems clear that the suggested utilitarian superstructure cannot be built upon Hare's universalization test because the test itself will not have that nearly uniform effectiveness which Hare claims for it, even if we ignore the technical loopholes mentioned in the last two paragraphs. But if we do fill these loopholes in the way suggested (for more

[3] Cf. C. C. W. Taylor's review of *Freedom and Reason* in *Mind*, vol. 74 (1965), pp. 280–8; and H. S. Silverstein, 'A Note on Imagining Oneself in the Place of Others', *Mind*, vol. 81 (1972), pp. 448–50.

details, see Section 2), it seems obvious that the universalization test will be effective *sometimes*. No doubt there are fair-minded people who, after having said that it is all right for them to *X* someone in certain circumstances, can sometimes be led to admit that it would not be all right because, on second thought, they can see that they would not only *dislike* being *X*'ed themselves but that it would be *wrong* for anyone to X them in similar circumstances. But in saying this, we have already revised and loosened Hare's argument, replacing its test of relevance with an intuitive test, and replacing its 'finding that one could not accept the imperative "Let me be *X*'ed-in-*C*"' with a primitive judgement that, all things considered, a certain action is morally wrong. The requirement that our moral judgements and reasons must be intuitively universalizable in this way is then open to the emotivist's objection which I have restated in Section 8 after giving my own answer to it in Sections 3 through 5.

II. Descriptivism

In her well-known papers of the late 1950s, Philippa Foot examines certain value concepts which are at least near-relatives of moral concepts, and she argues that *they* are tied conceptually to non-moral descriptive notions. From these discussions she tries to make her way towards the conclusion that moral concepts must be similarly tied. For example, she points out that the usual criterion for applying the concept *rude* is, roughly, that offence was given by behaviour showing disrespect for someone; and she argues convincingly, in my opinion, that we cannot use this concept unless we retain this criterion. We would be misusing the word 'rude' if we purported to assign our own criteria, saying for example that noisy (though not disrespectful) behaviour is what we shall condemn as rude.[1] Similarly she shows that *pride* is 'in-

[1] 'Moral Arguments', *Mind*, vol. 67 (1958). In 'On Morality's Having a Point', *Philosophy*, vol. 40 (1965), D. Z. Phillips and H. O. Mounce disagree with Foot, citing for illustration an anecdote from Malcolm's memoir of Wittgenstein in which Moore objects to Wittgenstein's 'rudeness' in losing his temper and interrupting him during a philosophical discussion. 'Wittgenstein, on the other hand, thought Moore's view of the matter absurd: philosophy is serious business, important enough to justify a loss of temper; to think this rudeness is simply to misapply the judgement. Here, one can see how standards of rudeness have been influenced by wider beliefs; in other words, how the judgement, "That is rude", is not entailed by the facts.'

This comment by Phillips and Mounce seems to overlook the point that while the sort of behaviour which gives cause for offense (no one need actually *be* offended for behaviour to be rude) will vary with the group and the occasion, *giving cause for offense by showing disrespect* might nevertheless be the criterion of *rude*. Perhaps Wittgenstein was right, and his behaviour did not violate the standard of mutually respectful behaviour recognized in Cambridge philosophy seminars. Or perhaps Moore was right; it depends on what the standard was. If it is doubtful whether Wittgenstein was rude on that occasion, I imagine he would have been rude beyond question if he had not merely interrupted Moore but had done so by pounding the table and calling Moore a bastard.

This point, by the way, is entirely compatible with what I have said in the

ternally related' to certain sorts of beliefs, namely, that the thing one is proud of is (*a*) in some way one's own, and (*b*) some sort of achievement or advantage. So a person who said he was proud of the sky or of the fact that he could wiggle his fingers would be misusing this notion, unless a special background of fact could be filled in to bring the object of his 'pride' under (*a*) and (*b*), as might conceivably be done for finger-wiggling (the person has been paralysed, etc.).[2] Of course, one could decide to reject the concept of pride or the concept of rudeness and stop using these words. But as Foot points out, once we do accept the question 'Is this behaviour rude?' we cannot validly refuse the conclusion that it is rude, given that it caused offence by showing disrespect for someone.

She then wants to urge that a somewhat similar situation obtains once we agree to use words like 'ought', 'right', 'wrong', and so on. If we agree to discuss points of etiquette or points of morality at all, we cannot avoid the non-value criteria that are standard for their respective value concepts. So we cannot decide for ourselves which principles of morality we will accept, if we are to use the language of morality correctly.

What are these criteria in morality? She does not claim to know precisely, but she does maintain that saying it was someone's duty to do something surely involves the idea that it matters or would be harmful if it were not done. 'How exactly the concepts of harm, advantage, benefit, importance, etc., are related to the different moral concepts, such as rightness, obligation, goodness, duty and virtue, is something that needs the most patient investigation, but that they are so related seems undeniable ...'[3] This remark and a favourable reference to Bentham in the same essay suggests that Foot would take general utility as her guide in such investigations. But in 'Moral Beliefs' an egoist line is suggested when she attempts to tie the cardinal virtues to notions of personal benefit—not only in the cases of prudence, temperance,

main essay. If the facts are thus and so, then infallibly one has been rude. But it is not even part of 'conventional' morality that a rude action is always a morally wrong action.

[2] Or even for taking pride in the sky. If a speaker believes that he created the sky, he is deranged but not misusing words when he says he is proud of the sky. C. D. MacNiven, 'Strong and Weak Descriptivism', *Mind*, vol. 81 (1972). Foot's discussion of pride is in 'Moral Beliefs', *Proceedings of the Aristotelian Society*, vol. 59 (1958–9).

[3] Moral Arguments', pp. 510–11.

and courage, where the connection is fairly easily made, but also in the case of justice.

A point to be noted is that the descriptive reasons *for being* just or courageous, etc., are of course different from the descriptive reasons one might give in claiming that someone *is* just or courageous, and it is these latter reasons which would invoke the criteria of justice and courage. Now some of the virtues, at least, do have fixed descriptive criteria just as surely as rudeness does. A temperate person will have certain characteristics and not others, and so will a chaste person or a physically courageous person. We must observe the standard criteria in saying that someone is chaste or courageous if we want to use these terms literally and correctly. But a complicating point is that we can certainly reject some of these laudatory concepts (indeed, all of those just mentioned except justice, it would seem) without rejecting morality or refusing to speak in moral terms. Thus a pacifist might take the position that the behaviour or characteristics for which soldiers are called courageous do not deserve to be praised or encouraged, that no one should even consent to be a soldier, and that if anyone does find himself a soldier in battle he should throw down his arms and not fight. This would be to reject the virtue of (military) courage. Other people would question the desirability of those attitudes and behaviour patterns which entitle one to be called chaste. The objection could certainly be phrased in moral terms without violating any rules of moral discourse. We could not assign this praising term on the basis of very different criteria without abusing language, but we could reject the value concept *chaste*, the virtue chastity. And in general, we could reject many commonly accepted moral principles or standards by which such and such non-moral descriptive concepts are constituted the criteria of such and such morally evaluative concepts without in the least abandoning morality or correct moral talk.[4] The objection might therefore be made that Mrs. Foot's analysis commits her to moral conventionalism.

She can meet that objection, however, by insisting that the most general moral concepts such as *wrong, right, morally desirable*, etc., are bound to the notions of human good and harm which (she argues) are themselves fundamentally descriptive, non-moral concepts. Presumably, if someone thought it *wrong* to en-

[4] Cf. Hare, *Freedom and Reason*, pp. 187–9

courage the attitudes and habits constituting chastity, this would be because he thought they (and hence their praise) are harmful, or more harmful than beneficial. Whether or not they really are harmful, such a person would be misusing the word 'wrong' unless he thought they were. Or so Mrs Foot might argue. And she does argue that logically you cannot set up just any sort of behaviour as a virtue, e.g. clasping and unclasping one's hands, without filling in a special background connecting such behaviour with human good and harm, as through a belief in its magical efficacy. So her reply to the charge of conventionalism could be that popularly accepted ties between moral statements and non-moral descriptive statements are open to criticism in terms of *the* fundamental tie: that between moral approval and disapproval on the one hand, and the tendency of an action to produce human good or harm on the other.

Another point to consider, however, is that the most general moral concepts might be tied to notions of human good and harm only in the sense that human good and harm cannot be *left out of account* in any general moral argument, i.e. any argument the conclusion of which applies one or more of those most general moral concepts to some subject of evaluation. It might be the case, for example, that any action harming someone, or any practice that is more harmful than beneficial in its effects, is wrong *in so far* as this is so, but that this fact about the action or practice does not guarantee its wrongness. Even *harmfulness all things considered* might not guarantee its wrongness because other notions besides good and harm might also be essentially involved in moral evaluation. Here one thinks of the parallel idea plausibly emphasized by Ross[5] that an action may be wrong even if its harmful effects are less than, or equal to its beneficial effects. If we are to describe and analyse moral thought as we find it and not as some philosophical moralists might wish to see it reformed (and this is what Mrs. Foot does want to do), it seems that we must save a place for the notion that each person has finally to decide for himself which 'duties' cannot be subordinated to considerations of utility. In sum, it does seem that we are not to lay down *moral* rules for ourselves *in disregard* of their harm, benefit, importance, etc. (although *why* this is so has not been explained); but *how much* weight we ought to give to these

[5] Cf. *The Right and the Good*, p. 39; *Foundations of Ethics*, p. 104 (Oxford: The Clarendon Pr., 1930 and 1939 respectively).

considerations also seems to be a legitimate topic for moral reflection.

This last point is similar to Phillips's and Mounce's well-known criticism of Foot concerning *harm*,[6] which I think is sound and severable from their remarks about *rude*. What is good or harmful to someone can depend on what his moral beliefs are; it is not always the other way around. You cannot prove to the orthodox Catholic housewife that she ought not to have a large number of children (citing the harmfulness of such a course of conduct as judged by your physiological and economic criteria of harm) when she believes that having many children is a great honour and good in itself, well worth the risks and disadvantages which you point out. So even if moral evaluative notions are securely and exclusively tied to notions of human good and harm, it seems that the latter notions are not exclusively descriptive (non-evaluative) as Mrs. Foot wishes to maintain. Or to put it my way, even if 'human good and harm' does refer to a notion which is purely descriptive and non-evaluative in the last analysis (which is doubtful), one still must recognize that maximizing human good and minimizing harm does not *seem* to have a monopoly as 'the' point of morality. Someone may wish to set up other objectives which rival or override in his mind 'the' objective which you or I may consider fundamental for determining the truth or validity of moral principles. And he would not seem to be guilty of any logical offence in doing so, however strong our moral disagreement with him might be. Indeed, *common* morality seems to be determined by objectives or values which frequently conflict, as may be seen from the trouble Utilitarians have always had incorporating justice and other special rules of obligation into their systems.

I take it that Mrs. Foot would not claim to have proved her point, and the considerations just referred to seem to show that she definitely has not. Surely she is right in insisting that not just any reason can be a moral reason, and not just any principle can be a moral principle.[7] But she has not shown that the difference

[6] In the article cited above. also in the book by these authors cited below.

[7] It may be helpful to give the obvious answer to an obvious objection here. In the end, I have myself said that any criterion or principle for evaluating something in moral terms will be logically acceptable as far as its substance or content is concerned. But we must satisfy certain procedural criteria in adopting or holding it, and especially in using it. These criteria, moreover, are said to derive from 'the' point, not of substantive moral preference, but

between good reasons and bad reasons (or between moral principles and non-moral principles) depends on 'the' point of morality, or what that point is.

Another prominent strain in Descriptivism has been the so-called practice theory. It tries to find necessary fact-value connections within *various* practices, moral and non-moral, rather than tackling the whole institution or practice of morality. The analyses which have been given of these narrower and more specialized ties have been somewhat clearer than Mrs. Foot's earlier and broader work, but the effect has been to render the whole approach less plausible. For the practice 'theory' is really the suggestion *that*—rather than even a tentative explanation *how*—these definite and plausible piecemeal results might be assembled into a coherent system for all moral practice and reasoning. I shall briefly argue that they need to be so assembled if the problem of relevance is to be solved through this type of analysis, but that it is unlikely this can be done.

The leading idea of the practice analysis is that some descriptive terms have been created for, and are correctly used only to describe behaviour occurring in, particular institutions. If these terms are used in a true statement, then the rules or principles which serve to define the institution in question are necessarily presupposed as binding for the evaluation of the behaviour being described. If it is a fact that Jones was thrown out attempting to steal second base, then the rules of baseball apply, and it follows that he ought to leave the field. But if, instead of that 'institutional fact' employing those terms, we had only stated the 'brute fact' that Jones ran between two bags staked to the ground and Smith caught a leather-covered ball thrown by Brown and tagged Jones with it, etc., then no such evaluative conclusion could be drawn.[8]

Rawls formulated this idea as part of an attempt to show Utilitarians how to defend themselves against the charge that their theory justifies punishing the innocent. But G. E. M. Anscombe soon pointed out that the distinction between brute facts and institutional facts has pervasive significance in moral discourse

---

of moral reflection and inter-personal reasoning. And in satisfying them, we do in fact limit the substantive principles we will be able to accept and use.

[8] Cf. John Rawls, 'Two Concepts of Rules', *Philosophical Rev.*, vol. 64 (1955), esp. Section III.

and other spheres of normative or evaluative reasoning.[9] It is often the case that the intuitive normative relevance of a certain statement of fact can be plausibly accounted for by spelling out the bit of standardized, rule-governed practice which the statement does presuppose in this way. To mention one of Anscombe's examples, when your grocer says you ought to pay him, it makes all the difference whether he 'delivered' the potatoes at your door or merely brought them and left them there, which he could very well do without delivering them. Delivery is part of commercial practice and presupposes that what is brought and left was 'purchased' or 'ordered'. Whether all morally relevant reasons can be so accounted for is doubtful since it isn't clear that all subjects of moral evaluation can be described in teims drawn from some definite practice or practices. But probably a great many intuitively relevant reasons can be accounted for in this way. The practice of promising and the principle that promises are to be kept have been usefully examined by many writers in this connection, and it is plausible to think that various other special rules of obligation might be exhibited as constitutive rules of practices. A description of behaviour in terms drawn from such practices might then have definite and necessary significance for the moral evaluation of the behaviour, because of such necessarily applicable rules. For example, being a *parent* in the relevant institutional sense (not merely the biological sense) will have certain moral consequences, such as being obligated to support children, being entitled to special consideration from then,[10] and so on, because there are rules of obligation and entitlement which serve to define the family and the role of parents.

Several things argue, nevertheless, that a true statement of institutional fact about some person or action will seldom (and maybe never) be a sufficient reason for a moral judgement of that person or action. Often, indeed, it will not even be a morally relevant reason. The most obvious point is that a given practice may itself be the subject of moral evaluation. Its very existence and the rules which define it may be morally objectionable.[11] Even a person who has 'entered' it and voluntarily incurred obli-

[9] 'On Brute Facts', *Analysis*, vol. 18 (1958).

[10] This example is used throughout A. I. Melden's *Rights and Right Conduct* (Oxford: Blackwell, 1959).

[11] Cf. R. S. Downie, 'Social Roles and Moral Responsibility', *Philosophy*, vol. 39 (1964).

gations under it may have moral standing to reject it and repudiate these obligations.[12] We criticize Eichmann morally for failing to do just that. And what is equally important, there may be sincere disagreement about whether a given practice is morally acceptable. Another obvious consideration is that practices 'intersect', often producing conflicts and moral dilemmas. I have promised to do *X*, and I am obligated as a parent (teacher, husband, son, citizen, partner, etc.) to do *Y*; but doing *Y* excludes doing *X*, and vice versa. Often enough it may seem obvious that one obligation is more important and 'overrides' the other as a 'clear exception' under the pertinent rules; but very often this will not be clear. There are seldom any quite general or absolute exceptions to moral rules, unlike some rules of games and statutory rules of law. There will usually be an element of judgement involved, even in many cases which we would nearly all judge in the same way. And, of course, there are many difficult cases about which we would disagree or would not be able to make up our minds. Still another consideration is that the moral significance of facts under a certain practice may have to be weighed against their contrary significance under no particular practice. What practice bids the Good Samaritan to break his date for golf?

If we bear these points in mind, it certainly *seems* as though the practice analysis could not enable us to determine the moral relevance of a set of facts in the sense of showing us what their total effect is for a particular moral question. At most it could help us understand why a given fact needs to be taken into account and given some 'weight' in favour of a certain moral conclusion. Even this point must be qualified by recalling that not all morally significant facts seem to be institutional facts, and that some institutional facts will presumably have no significance in moral reasoning because the practices in which they figure are morally abhorrent or trivial. If, in spite of these appearances, the practice analysis really is on the track of an adequate ethical method which will enable us to say just *how* various facts are relevant and precisely *what* their moral consequence is in particular cases, it must finally explain a number of things which seem to lie far beyond the reach of its leading idea summarized above. It must give us a systematic method of resolving conflicts of practices; it must enable us to explain when and how practices ought to be

[12] Cf. D. W. Hamlyn, 'The Obligation to Keep a Promise', *Proceedings of the Aristotelian Society*, vol. 62 (1961–2).

amended, when they ought to be abolished, when and how they ought to be created, when they ought to be ignored in moral evaluation, and so on. It is most unlikely that all this could be done unless we already had a *comprehensive* theory of *moral* practice; that is, unless we already knew what *the* point or fundamental standard of morality is, so that we would have a basis for justifiably correcting and systematizing all its various sub-practices and specialized rules. This refers us back to Mrs. Foot's project, which would have to be carried through before any successful development of the practice theory itself, or at least concurrently with it. We have already had reason to doubt that her project is feasible, and now we can appreciate even better how chancy the whole affair is. For, one reason why her project seemed unlikely to succeed was the very fact that justice and many special rules of obligation do not seem to be systematically tractable to considerations of welfare.

In spite of these criticisms, I think it must be allowed that the practice analysis has improved our understanding of the moral relevance of factual, non-moral statements. It tells us why the principle which gives us deductive passage from a non-evaluative statement to a moral conclusion cannot be accepted or rejected as we please once it has been shown that the institutional-fact premiss is true, provided we have somehow satisfied ourselves that the practice in question is morally significant and legitimate. This proviso is extremely important, of course; and we also have to choose what relative weight to assign to morally significant practices (if not generally, then in particular conflicts), and what relative significance to assign to other sorts of facts. But partly through its positive analysis and partly through the criticisms it provokes as a possible account of *moral* inference, the practice 'theory' does call attention to some important features of moral reasoning. In Section 2, I have tried to cover them at least briefly through the description of 'plausible' reasons and principles, and in my references to the weighing and discounting of principles.

R. W. Beardsmore, D. Z. Phillips, and H. O. Mounce have added another chapter to descriptivism.[13] Though sharply critical of Mrs. Foot, these three writers are as incredulous as she is that just any statement of fact can count as a moral reason. Their key

[13] In *Moral Reasoning* by Beardsmore, and *Moral Practices* by Phillips and Mounce (New York: Schoken Books; 1969 and 1970, respectively).

thought is that various descriptive concepts have moral import from their very origin in the moral practices and 'forms of life' in which we learn them, rather than being purely non-evaluative notions to which we later attach moral significance through the adoption of principles. *Lying*, for example, is such a concept for practically everyone, according to Beardsmore, who supports this with quotations from Piaget's *The Moral Judgement of the Child*, while *suicide* will be such a concept for many people (e.g. Roman Catholics) but not for everyone.[14] You cannot really decide to *adopt* such 'principles' as 'murder is wrong', 'honesty is good'. They are not general beliefs or policies one might question, disagree about, or test; they are the *presuppositions* of moral dispute; without them one cannot even understand a moral discussion.[15] Attention is repeatedly drawn to Wittgenstein's statement that 'If language is to be a means of communication there must be agreement not only in definitions but also (queer as this may sound) in judgements.'[16] Just as we wouldn't have words for the various colours and be able to communicate about the colour of objects unless people were widely agreed in their judgements of colour, these authors suggest that we also could not communicate in moral terms unless, having been reared in a common form of life (or in sufficiently similar forms), our moral attitudes and judgements were similar and we had learned to use the word 'wrong', for example, about much the same things. Thus we learn to disapprove of lying, hurting others, cheating, etc., and to use these as criteria for applying the word 'wrong'.

This still leaves the authors under discussion with a somewhat 'relativistic' account of moral judgement and reasoning, although they are reluctant to apply this term to their position.[17] They recognize that people from morally dissimilar societies will not share certain practices, so that some moral reasons for one group will not be moral reasons for the other, even if there must be *some* practices in common if there is to be any moral discussion between members of the two groups. Also, there will be groups of people within the same society who are in this condition relative

[14] Beardsmore, op. cit., p. 97.

[15] Ibid., Chap. 7.

[16] *Philosophical Investigations*, I: 242. Cf. Phillips & Mounce, op. cit., p. 62; Beardsmore, op. cit., p. 121.

[17] Phillips & Mounce, op. cit., section 7.

to each other. (Think of abortion, birth control, toleration of homosexuals, etc., along with suicide.) These authors also cover the familiar point that practices conflict, so that two people can very well disagree over which takes precedence and yields the *stronger* reason. And they observe that a person may be torn between two or more practices and be unable to resolve the dilemma even for himself. They rightly point out that our individual practices do not provide criteria for solving such problems; nor is there some larger system or method which will enable us to solve them. In this connection, they criticize Melden's suggestion that moral disagreements and dilemmas can be solved by preferring such reasons as will tend to strengthen or preserve the larger moral institution—e.g. the family, or the whole 'moral community'—of which the conflicting practices are a part.[18]

Beardsmore recognizes that one can 'learn from experience' to change one's moral views, so that even the descriptive-evaluative ties acquired in one's earlier 'form of life' are not exempt from criticism and change.[19] Here he argues plausibly that there cannot (logically) be a *complete* break, that even moral revolutionaries must retain something of the morality they are rebelling against. One cannot reject one's former principles or criteria *in toto* and then decide 'on the basis of pure facts' to adopt a new set; the pure facts would have no significance for such a decision. But even if this is so, I think it should also be pointed out that there is no *one* way in which a moral rebel or convert must reshape his former standards. And what facts will justify the change is logically open. Even if he must argue from *some* old principles, so that there is this much restriction on the kinds of facts that will be eligible as reasons for the change, the choice of principles can here be determined only 'psychologically', not logically, as an emotivist would say. The semantic rules holding good in the old 'form of life' could not control it.

In the main essay I have tried to explain how a choice of this kind—the adoption of moral principles—could nevertheless be justified. And I have also tried to explain how we can justify our answers to moral dilemmas for which the 'form of moral life' we are accustomed to live simply does not provide solutions.

[18] Ibid., section 8. criticizing Melden, op. cit., p. 84.
[19] Beardsmore, op. cit., pp. 87–91.

III. More of the Judicial Analogy

THE comparison of moral and judicial reasoning which was made in Section 4 and relied on in Section 5 can be developed in further detail in light of the analysis of moral argument offered in Section 6.

First I shall give an example of judicial reasoning which resembles the moral arguments considered in the latter section in several important respects. It has the same deductive structure, the way in which the evaluative premisses can be justified is also closely analogous; and the reason why the premisses can *safely* be said to be true in easy cases is also similar, although the basis of legal truth is conceptually unlike the basis of moral truth for reasons to be noted. We shall unpack a paradigmatically true legal conclusion much as we did this with true moral statements in Section 6.

Second, I shall illustrate the point made in Section 4 that many difficult legal cases lack true decisions for reasons closely similar to those we saw in connection with difficult moral problems. This will also help to support the main point of that section, namely, that good moral reasoning is indeed very similar to good judicial reasoning in legally open cases.

Third, I shall briefly comment on the notion of truth in law. There are some legal cases as to which it can be argued that a consentient basis of evaluative truth is also found in law. But this is somewhat doubtful, and such a basis certainly does not obtain generally in law. The reason why it does not should prove illuminating for my thesis that we do find it in morals in so far as it makes sense to speak of moral truth.

1.

In law as in morals, there are innumerable applications of rules which are entirely unproblematic. We can seldom decide the issues of litigated cases so easily, but we all do instantiate legal rules many times a day with no problem. We obey many traffic regulations; we make enforceable purchase contracts; we pay our bills; we use the correct form of order on our bank for a negotiable check; we do not assault people who provoke us; we abstain from theft; if we are lawyers routinely drawing a will, we use the correct number of witnesses, and so on. But in law as in morals, the application of rules in easy cases is always logically more complex than it may seem at first glance. Suppose Jones lies in wait for Smith, robs him, kills him to prevent being identified, and later confesses all in open court, offering nothing in mitigation of guilt. Let us suppose that he is advised by expert counsel, and is intelligent and psychologically normal according to court-appointed psychiatrists who have carefully examined him. That Jones is guilty of murder in the first degree follows automatically from these facts and the statute on homicides; there is nothing to ponder in applying the statute to him. But notice that in order that it be applied to him, it is logically necessary that his action be considered under a certain description and not others which would be equally true, i.e. as 'the deliberate, unprovoked killing of a human' rather than as 'causing the death of a large animal' or 'firing a gun'. In describing his action in the first way mentioned, we have the second premiss of our deduction, the first being supplied by the unquestionably valid statute which attaches certain legal consequences to the deliberate, unprovoked killing of humans, namely, that one is guilty of murder in the first degree.

Notice also that the effect of this statute *could* be changed by some other equally valid law. It makes Jones guilty of murder in the first degree *ceteris paribus,* i.e. in the absence of any other relevant provision of law which would suffice to cancel this effect in his case. Thus the legislature might have believed that people with bright red hair (like Jones) find it harder to control their evil impulses, and so might have provided in a separate statute that the guilt of such people shall be reduced by one degree in crimes having degrees. The judge in Jones's case will not think of this since he knows very well there is no such statute. But he may expect to be aware of any other, more plausible rules of law which might lessen or obviate Jones's guilt in the special circumstances of his case, or to be made aware of them by counsel. Hearing of none and being aware of none, he is entitled to assume that there are none, and therefore that other things *are* equal. So altogether, we have the following argument:

(1) Other things being equal, a person who deliberately and without provocation kills another person is guilty of murder in the first degree.

(2) Jones killed Smith deliberately and without provocation.

(3) Other things are equal; that is to say, there are no other facts in this case, and provisions of law, under which Jones is *not* guilty of murder in the first degree despite such action.

Therefore, Jones is guilty of murder in the first degree.

Of course it would be ridiculously pedantic for Jones's judge to spell this argument out or even rehearse it to himself. But this is because the case is so easy and not because its rational structure is any simpler than that. There is no need to explain why each of the premisses may be confidently asserted, or even to think of them separately, because we are sure to get the right result in such a case without doing so. But if the judge *were* to explain fully why it is the right result, he would have to say substantially what the above argument says, and he would have to justify his premisses substantially as I have done in the preceding paragraph. Let us spell that justification out in pedantic detail. (*a*) We need the *ceteris paribus* clause in the first premiss because it is always possible that the effect of one legal principle or statutory provision should be cancelled or limited by some other or others in the special circumstances of the case. (*b*) The validity of the first premiss is otherwise established by consulting the official statute book. (*c*) The second premiss is known to be true from the accused's confession in open court. (*d*) The judge, having carefully considered the case, being professionally competent himself, and having the assistance of expert counsel whose duty and interest it is to present any countervailing considerations, knows of no such considerations and is justified in concluding that there are none, i.e. that the third premiss is true.

This is a case calling for one and only one judgement, if there ever was one. And that is the structure of the reasoning which shows what the correct judgement is.

Yet, it is still possible that court and counsel have missed or forgotten some fact which *would* be legally relevant to reduce or cancel Jones's guilt. If they have, then it may still be false that Jones is guilty of murder in the first degree even though the judge is justified in finding him guilty after justifiably concluding that other things are equal. In the case described, this seems so unlikely that we would be justified in saying that we *know* Jones is guilty. Nevertheless, there would be a logical possibility (though an extremely high improbability) that Jones is innocent of murder in the first degree even if *every* disinterested lawyer would judge that he is guilty after carefully considering the case and, indeed, after being fully informed of all the *possibly* relevant facts. This logical possibility results simply from the fact that the statute on homicides, and any other rules of law providing conditions under which homicide is excused or mitigated, have their core of literal meaning independently of any such consensus. More on this later.

2.

Next I want to show how difficult legal cases may lack uniquely correct decisions for reasons very similar to those we saw in Section 6 when discussing difficult moral questions. I shall also point out how the structure of good judicial reasoning, whether in easy cases or difficult cases, is very similar to the structure of good moral reasoning which we illustrated in Section 6 with both easy and difficult moral questions.

Two valid principles can easily conflict in a particular case, giving opposite directions for disposing of it, with no well-recognized exception or clear priority to resolve the conflict. This occurs throughout the law, but perhaps its most familiar illustrations are found in the vague standards of the U.S. Constitution whose frequent conflicts give the Supreme Court even new opportunities for important policy making. Reasonable men may differ on how to resolve some conflicts between the contract clause and the 'police power' of the states,[1] between free speech and the war making power,[2] between the equal protection clause and the doctrine of political questions,[3] and so on, even in light of the

[1] As in the famous Dartmouth College and mortgage moratorium cases. *Dartmouth College* v. *Woodward* (1819), 4 Wheat. 518, 4 L.Ed. 629; *Home Building and Loan Assn.* v. *Blaisdell* (1934), 290 U.S. 398, 78 L.Ed. 413.

[2] As in *Schenck* v. *United States* (1919), 249 U.S. 47, 63 L.Ed. 470, in which the famous 'clear and present danger' test was first enunciated.

[3] As in the legislative reapportionment cases. *Baker* v. *Carr* (1962), 369 U.S. 186, 7 L.Ed. 2d 663; *Reynolds* v. *Sims* (1964), 377 U.S. 533, 12 L.Ed. 2d 506.

available precedents (often *because* of the great variety of the precedents). In many a case there simply is no *true* way to resolve the conflict. Whether this results logically from the fact that the experts would disagree, or only serves to explain their disagreement (the theoretical question which I postpone until the end of this Appendix), there can be little doubt that many such cases are legally open. Often there simply is no good reason to think that, despite appearances, the Constitution does somehow require but one outcome against all substantially contrary outcomes. Yet, even in such cases the judges attempt to justify their judgements and dissenting views; and their judgements and views often *are* justified in the way discussed in Section 4. That is, their written opinions often show that the judges are well informed about the legal and factual considerations which are salient for deciding the case, that they have weighed them in a disinterested spirit, and that they have constructed an argument expressing their sincere and reasonable view of the legally best way to dispose of the conflict.

Let us consider one famous case in some detail. In *Pennsylvania Coal Co.* v. *Mahon* (1922), 260 U.S. 393, 67 L.Ed. 322, the Supreme Court had to decide whether a statute requiring mining companies to leave or construct reinforcements under improved lands owned by others was a valid exercise of the police power, or whether it was a taking of property for public use without compensation, contrary to the due process clause of the Fourteenth Amendment. The most important consideration favouring the conclusion that it was such a taking was the fact that the 'surface owners' or their predecessors had not bargained or paid for such protection when buying land from the companies or selling mining rights to them. The statute now gave them such protection at the expense of the companies. But it is well settled that reasonable state regulations for the public 'health, safety, and morals' might lessen the value of land or other property without necessarily entitling the owners to compensation, even when an incidental effect is to confer special benefits on some other members of the public.

Mr. Justice Holmes, writing for the Court which held the statute unconstitutional, and Mr. Justice Brandeis in dissent both thought the issue turned on such questions as the value of the property interests involved, how much that value was diminished, whether the danger sought to be eliminated was a public nuisance, how extensive a public interest was being protected, whether the regulation was an appropriate means to its intended end, and whether it was required for the safety of persons. But in reviewing the factual background of the regulation and the various precedents cited by counsel, they gave very different answers to most of those questions, and their reasons display markedly different emphases of the several social and legal values quite obviously involved. Not that the two opinions are necessarily of equal persuasive force; rereading them after some years, it seems to me that Brandeis definitely has the better of the argument. The point is rather that, in 1922 and probably more recently, there surely would have been a substantial division of opinion about such a case among informed and disinterested lawyers who might have considered it. And whether or not this lack of a consensus is itself enough to show that the case could not have but one legally correct outcome, pretty obviously it could not. There is little reason to think that the facts plus the Constitution, precedents, contemporary political opinion, and whatever other factors may properly be considered to be part of 'existing Constitutional law' determined that the Pennsylvania statute definitely was constitutional, or that it definitely was not.

The Court's judgement was nevertheless justified, as its opinion sufficiently shows; and so was Brandeis justified in his view. It is no paradox that opposite judgements may be rationally justified even though they have identical bases (here, the same Constitution, precedents, and facts) where the subject is one which does not *admit* of a true judgement. Of course, the majority's judgement—the product of its act of judgement—*acquires* legal validity, or at least a very strong claim to it, from the mere fact that it is the majority's view.

Holmes' and Brandeis' major reasons and conclusions can be cast into the same deductive form that we have found in very easy legal cases and in both easy and doubtful moral cases. For Holmes, the argument goes approximately as follows.

(1) Other things being equal, a state may not take private property for public use without paying for it (per the due process clause).

(2) By this statute, Pennsylvania would take private property (by diminishing or destroying the value of certain interests in land) and would not pay for it.

(3) Other things are equal; that is, in the circumstances such taking without compensation is not simply an exercise of the state's police power, nor is there any other consideration which would validate the statute in spite of its infringement of the due process clause.

Therefore, the statute is unconstitutional.

In contrast, Brandeis's argument goes approximately as follows.

(1) Other things being equal, the state has the power to regulate the use of land in the interests of public health, safety, and morals without paying anything to the owners of land (per the established doctrine of the reserved police power of the states).

(2) Pennsylvania by its statute has made such a regulation.

(3) Other things are equal; that is, in the circumstances and in light of the precedents, the decrease in the value of interests in land resulting from such regulation is not a taking of property as contemplated by the due process clause, nor has any valid constitutional objection to the statute been raised.

Therefore, as far as has been shown, the statute is constitutional.

Here, as in moral arguments which are not completely one-sided, we have one principle figuring in premiss 1 and another figuring as the basis of countervailing considerations which, however, are denied to be sufficient in premiss 3. In the counter-argument, the positions and functions of these two principles are reversed, and different facts in the case are stated in premiss 2.

A most important point is that the reasoning on either side not only *can* be cast into this deductive form but must be understood to have this form if it claims to apply the law of the Constitution to the case at hand. To be sure, our deductive form itself does not show (and is not the form of) the reasoning which justifies giving one standard priority over another, i.e. which justifies *selecting* one arrangement of premisses, as shown in the above-stated deductive arguments, over the other. Also, this latter part of the reasoning, i.e. reasoning to justify such a selection, is more important than the deductive argument itself because it is more difficult and debatable. (That is, it demands more attention; there is nothing doubtful or debatable about the validity of simple deductive forms.) But the deduction is nevertheless an essential part of the reasoning. For it is only by *some* such argument that one's judgement can even claim to be required by the Constitution, that is, follow from the law of the Constitution in conjunction with the facts of the case. The legal conclusion on which one's judgement in the case rests is justified as a constitutional conclusion in so far as one's selection of premisses is justified whereby it *can* be deduced from that law.

In the past, this important and seemingly elementary point was obscured by much disparagement of 'logic', 'formal logic', 'deductive reasoning', and 'the syllogism' as models for judicial reasoning,[4] and it may still be useful to underscore the point in a slightly different way. It has been said that for a court to reason syllogistically—merely stating a principle of law plus facts of the case which together obviously entail such and such an outcome—'conceals a fatal weakness' because in most cases some other valid principle and some other facts might have been cited which entail an opposite conclusion.[5] This is very true, and we can make our point by saying that while good judicial reasoning is not basically syllogistic (since it is a minimum requirement that judges explain why they prefer one such syllogism to others which might plausibly be constructed for the case, rather than ignoring them) good judicial reasoning is nevertheless deductive in essential part. In that deductive part, the legal principle has to be accompanied by a *ceteris paribus* proviso, and this forces us to add a third premiss that 'other things are equal.'[6] This third premiss amounts to the explicit claim that no other principle of law *should* be allowed to control and dispose of the case, even if there are some others which apply to it in virtue of other facts which are considered less important than those recited in premiss 2. A

[4] See the references to well known authors collected by A. G. Guest in 'Logic in the Law' in *Oxford Essays in Jurisprudence*, 1st series, edited by Guest (Oxford: The Clarenden Pr., 1961).

[5] Jerome Frank, *Law and the Modern Mind* (New York: Brentano's, 1930; Doubleday-Anchor, 1963), p. 71 in Anchor.

[6] Many legal standards are commonly understood to be valid 'other things being equal' and not universally, so that any competent formulation of them might be expected to contain this reservation. For example, the 'rule' about how contractual obligations are created—offer, acceptance, consideration, etc.—has its well-known 'exceptions' covering fraud, duress, mistake, etc. But even a rule with an official, universal formulation (or with a closed list of absolute exceptions) such as one finds in many statutes, must still be so qualified. After all, some other statute (or judicial interpretation thereof) may have equal authority and may *force* an exception never mentioned or contemplated by the first statute.

good judge will make this claim and give his reasons for it. A judge who does not do so cannot show that his judgement is justified, i.e. that it is based on a careful consideration of facts and relevant legal materials—unless, indeed, the case is so simple that there are no competing principles worthy of consideration.

In the type of problematic case which we have just been discussing, two or more valid legal standards, coupled with appropriate statements of non-legal fact, compete for control of the case. The 'winning' combination takes over premisses 1 and 2, while the 'loser' or losers are banished to premiss 3 where they are denied sufficient weight or pertinence to control the result. Another type of problematic case is one where the legal validity of principles proposed by either side to control the case is itself in dispute. As noted in Section 4, this is analogous to moral disputes in which there is disagreement in principle. For example, the wording of a statute may not be debatable but its meaning and effect (the rule it requires for a case like the one before the court) often will be. Or, very often, the problem will be one of interpreting precedents—of determining what rule or rules various earlier decisions should be considered to stand for, especially in light of the facts of the case at bar which the rule, once identified, will control. A judge will be justified in settling the rule or rules required to dispose of the case if he has examined the problem in a thorough, disinterested, and professionally competent way, and has chosen the rule or rules he honestly thinks best for the case. 'Best' here means legally best, of course—the rule(s) which the law (in his judgement) can most plausibly be said to require or impose for such a case. 'The law' here means the pertinent precedents, especially those binding in his jurisdiction, relevant general policies and principles known in the judicial literature and reflected in statutes, and 'contemporary good sense' as it may tend to qualify or amend older notions about the proper grounds of legal liability.[7] Two or more judges may thus be justified in

[7] Here one may note a similarity in the substantive *grounds* of legal and moral decisions. When a judge has to decide a case that does not have but one correct outcome under existing doctrines and authorities, what he is doing is not only structurally similar to what one does in deciding a problematic moral 'case'. It may itself be a moral decision, in one sense. Deciding in a way that seems to be 'fair and reasonable' or to 'make good practical sense' is deciding morally. Yet, even here the professionally conscientious judge will cite widely held moral views for his decision, not his own views *as such*, and not his own views at all if they are very eccentric. Cf. L. L. Jaffe, *English*

producing contrary rules for the case before them if after proper reflection they sincerely disagree about what rule the law does demand. And whenever there would be a substantial division of informed and disinterested opinion, as there surely would be about many appealed cases, there probably is no 'true' rule for the case, except retrospectively by authority of the court's judgement.

These last remarks would no longer be thought controversial by most academic lawyers. But I need to add the point that the rule thus justifiably asserted will function, in effect, as premiss 1 in our form, and that the form will continue to be an essential aspect of judicial reasoning in this type of problematic case. To show this, let us examine one more famous decision.

In *MacPherson* v. *Buick Motor Co.* (1916), 217 N.Y. 382, 111 N.E. 1050, the New York Court of Appeals brought to a close the century-long development known as the rise and fall of the 'inherently dangerous' rule, or rather exception to a rule.[8] During the latter half of the nineteenth century, the common law rule that manufacturers are not responsible for personal injuries to remote purchasers of their products had been qualified with an exception covering articles which are dangerous by nature and without latent defects, such as explosives, poisons, and other implements of destruction. In adding this exception, the courts had relied on a number of earlier decisions going back to *Dixon* v. *Bell* (1816) 5 Maule & Selwyn 198. Subsequent decisions expanded the category of inherently dangerous articles until, in *MacPherson* and its British cousin *Donoghue* v. *Stevenson* (1932) A.C. 562, the exception finally 'swallowed up the rule' that manufacturers are not liable to consumers with whom they are not 'in privity of contract'. It was no longer necessary that a product be inherently dangerous in the sense just noted. It was enough if the thing by its nature were fairly certain to endanger life if negligently made, as where an undetected defect is extremely dangerous and probably would not be discovered by the 'middle

and American Judges as Lawmakers (Oxford: The Clarendon Pr., 1969), pp. 44–7. Jaffe thinks a judge whose personal moral view would not coincide with any opinion that is held fairly widely in the community should adopt the 'representative opinion which most satisfies his conscience or intelligence'.

[8] Often used to illustrate the 'nature of the judicial process' and 'growth of the law' (to use Cardozo's book titles), this development is traced in a concise and illuminating way by E. H. Levi in *An Introduction to Legal Reasoning* (Chicago: U. of Chicago Pr., 1948), pp. 8–27.

man' or by the ultimate purchaser or user until an accident occurred.

By far the most important part of Judge Cardozo's explicit reasoning in the MacPherson case is given to support this new statement of the law, showing how, in his opinion, the older and more recent cases may be said to require it when they are marshalled into a coherent doctrine. No doubt he also personally thought (but did not make it explicit in his opinion written for the court) that such a rule is more appropriate under modern conditions of mass production and mass distribution of products.[9] But once such a rule was adopted, the decision in the case could be legally extracted from it only through an inference which goes approximately as follows.

(1) Other things being equal, a manufacturer is liable in negligence for personal injuries to users of his product if the product by its nature is fairly certain to endanger life if negligently made.

(2) In this case, the plaintiff's injuries did result from the defendant manufacturer's negligence (in failing to inspect a defective wheel supplied to it by another company), and the defective product was fairly certain to endanger life (in case the wheel collapsed, as happened).

(3) Other things are equal.

Therefore, this defendant is liable to this plaintiff.

Such a conclusion obviously would follow from (1) and (2) without (3) if we eliminated the words 'other things being equal' from premiss (1). But while that would leave a logically valid argument, it would not be legally valid or 'good law'. That a certain true statement of facts brings a case under a certain valid rule of law is never a sufficient reason for deciding the case accordingly. It is also necessary that other facts of the case (and there always are other facts) and *other* valid rules should not override the facts and rule first mentioned, as we saw even in our open-and-shut case of first-degree murder. In *MacPherson*, for example, the plaintiff would probably not have been entitled to a favourable judgement if he had signed an agreement with the dealer and the manufacturer releasing them from liability as part of his pur-

[9] Cf. Chap. II and III of his *The Growth of the Law* (New Haven: Yale U. Pr., 1924).

chase, or limiting their liability to that of replacing defective parts.[10] And of course, various other imaginable facts would preclude, or arguably would preclude, such a judgement in the light of valid legal principles. The court is therefore justified in its conclusion only if it would be justified in holding that there are no such countervailing facts in the case, or at least none sufficient to defeat or prevent that conclusion.

The reader may have noticed that our two types of problematic cases overlap. Thus, the due process clause is unquestionably a 'valid standard', but its meaning and effect for a given case will often be subject to debate, and this debate will often proceed by an examination of precedents in which the clause has previously been applied. Further types of problematic cases could easily be formulated, and they also would overlap with the first two. For example, we have dealt with legal problems affecting the content of premisses 1 and 3 of our form; but 'mixed questions of law and fact' must often be answered in deciding on the proper content of premiss 2, a point which is reminiscent of our first moral illustration in Section 6, where we saw that the descriptive category 'causes severe harm' is partly evaluative. This is illustrated in *MacPherson* when the Buick Company is said in premiss 2 to have been 'negligent' in not inspecting a wheel received from another manufacturer.

Perhaps it will be unnecessary to give further illustrations to support the following observations and conclusions. Every judicial decision is supposed to be legally 'principled', i.e. to be the result of applying some 'legal norm' or 'law' to the individual case. And the legally valid application of any such law presupposes that there are no sufficient legal reasons not to apply it, as logically there always could be since no law can be guaranteed by its creators to be absolutely without exception, even though it be worded universally. Therefore, every legally justified decision requires a deductive inference of the form illustrated above; and it must also be the case that the judge(s) would be justified, in the way I have repeatedly explained, in asserting each one of the three premisses needed to deduce the judgement, i.e. the legal conclusion on which the court's official judgement or order will

[10] More recently, the law has been changing in this respect. Cf. *Henningsen v. Bloomfield Motors* (1960) 32 N.J. 358, 161 A.2d 69, where the court refused to enforce such an agreement. The case is discussed by R. M. Dworkin, 'Model of Rules', *U. of Chicago L. Rev.*, vol. 35 (1967–8).

be based. One need not insist that this reasoning be laid out in some pedantically obvious way. It will be obvious enough if the court explains why, in its opinion, a certain principle is valid law, is applicable to the case at hand, and properly controls that case despite contentions of counsel that such a case should rather be disposed of in some other way by invoking some other principle.

As I said a moment ago, it is that explanation and not the deductive form which is the heart of judicial reasoning. And it is the part which one needs professional training in law to produce or properly evaluate. Perhaps I should emphasize the point that we have said little or nothing about *its* nature or structures. We have not needed to go into it, whether by a juristic study of important legal concepts such as one finds in Hohfeld,[11] or by acquainting ourselves with hundreds of examples as every law student and practitioner must do. But no reader should be left with the impression that we have tried to present all the criteria of good judicial reasoning.

So much, then, for the essential claim in Sections 4 and 5 that good moral reasoning and good judicial reasoning in very difficult cases are closely similar in their major form, which consists of the three-premiss deduction and the criteria of reasonableness in settling the content of the premisses.

It may be helpful to add some further comments in defence of the claim that the most difficult cases lack uniquely correct decisions. In an article[12] more recent than those cited in Section 4, R. M. Dworkin makes a number of important points which indicate that cases of my fourth type may well be less common than I have suggested. But, as I shall briefly argue, these points do not show that type four is unnecessary, i.e. that there is practically always a uniquely correct decision to be reached in Anglo-American cases unless the court is specifically granted discretion by the law, as in sentencing offenders or devising remedies in equity.

On the basis of his 1964 article, I cited Dworkin in Section 4 as one who argues, in effect, that there is no objective standard (in my sense) for good judicial lawmaking. His later work is consistent with this. His suggestion now, as I understand it, is not that there is some all-governing objective which judicial lawmaking properly serves, but that in a lawmaking case a judge is

[11] W. N. Hohfeld, *Fundamental Legal Conceptions as Applied in Judicial Reasoning* (New Haven: Yale U. Pr., 1923; reprinted in part, 1964).

[12] 'Social Rules and Legal Theory', *Yale Law Journal,* vol. 81 (1972).

nevertheless bound to reach the ethically best decision, as this would be determined by the dominant moral assumptions and political traditions of his society. One thing favouring this view (as he notes) is that judges and practising lawyers—unlike most writers on jurisprudence—continue to treat every case, no matter how difficult, as though it does have a best decision which the judge is bound to give.

I think it can scarcely be denied that judicial duty is partly determined by principles of social and political morality. One could easily think of morally outrageous legal principles which it would be a clear violation of the judge's duty to attempt to introduce, even if no Constitutional or statutory language could be invoked against it. The practice of judging, in the Anglo-American tradition and no doubt in others, may safely be said to include restrictions of this kind, vague though they may be. And this shows that judges have less discretion than one would otherwise think, because it reminds us of further ways in which legal results and rationales may be eliminated as options for the judge to adopt. Perhaps it also explains how, in some difficult cases with an unavoidable lawmaking issue in them, only one decision will be correct because all the other possible decisions are ethically objectionable and 'clearly so', i.e. by a safe consensus.

These considerations do not eliminate my fourth type of case, however, because there is no reason to think that there would be a moral consensus on every important lawmaking issue that courts have to decide, or may properly decide. Principles and policies found in the contemporary moral climate and in the ongoing moral, political, and judicial traditions may simply not favour one result against another, even if they sometimes do so in their preponderant effect. For example, they may not tell us whether to follow the rule adopted in *Riggs* v. *Palmer*[13] or some

[13] 115 N.Y. 506, 22 N.E. 188 (1889). In this case, discussed by Dworkin in the article cited above, the court refused to award a bequest to an heir who had murdered the testator (his grandfather) to get it, even though he was entitled to it under the language of the statute on wills. The court cited the principle (i) that a man ought not to profit from his own wrongdoing, presumably feeling that this principle carries more weight (at least in the circumstances of this case) than the combined principles (ii) that courts ought not to add penalties to those fixed by criminal statute, (iii) that courts ought to respect the plain sense of statutes, (iv) that clear rules of property and titles thereunder should not be disturbed by courts but only by legislatures, and possibly other commonly recognized principles one could mention. Even if we didn't know that the American courts have split on the question, is there any reason

contrary rule. (I am told that in some American states it is not followed.) And certainly they will not tell us *when* to move, say, from the older doctrine of manufacturers' liability to the rule in *MacPherson* v. *Buick*, or when to enlarge that liability further, as in *Henningsen* v. *Bloomfield Motors*. Surely it would not have been an *error* for the New Jersey court *not* to take that next step in 1960; and surely it was not an error to take it then, rather than waiting until contemporary attitudes had become stronger as to the unfairness of such contractual limitations of liability as the defendants in that case had attempted to effect.

Another good illustration is suggested by H. L. A. Hart's comment on three widely discussed cases: *Mogul Steamship Co.* v. *Macgregor* (1892) A.C. 25, *Allen* v. *Flood* (1898) A.C. 1, and *Quinn* v. *Leathem* (1901) A.C. 495. In these cases, according to Hart, the courts were presented with the question 'whether an individual's liberty-rights to trade or employ labour or sell his labour are protected by a perimeter consisting only of duties corresponding to the specific torts of conspiracy, intimidation, and the inducement of breach of contract, or by a perimeter consisting also of a duty corresponding to the more general tort of interfering with the trade, business, or employment of a person without lawful justification or excuse'.[14] It will be obvious to anyone who studies these cases that the judges did not clearly see that this was the question they were struggling with, but I think an Hohfeldian analysis can show that it was.[15] And their several assertions that there is such a general tort, plus the holding in *Quinn* that the defendants had properly been found to have committed it, would amount to a choice of the second alternative in Hart's formulation. Now, did the standard of judicial duty

---

to think there would be a consensus that (i) does outweigh the rest, or that it does not?

[14] The effect of the latter duty would be that one who interferes with these economic affairs of another and is sued by the latter for damages will have the burden of justifying his behaviour even though it is not unlawful under one of the older and more specific torts. The quotation is from Hart's essay, 'Bentham on Legal Rights' in *Oxford Essays in Jurisprudence*, 2nd series, edited by A. W. B. Simpson (Oxford: The Clarendon Pr., 1973), p. 181. Here Hart has been using the idea of a protective perimeter while explaining the notion of a liberty-right (or privilege, in Hohfeld's terminology), and he cites these cases for illustration, along with *Rookes* v. *Barnard* (1964) A.C. 1129.

[15] See my article, 'A Paradigm of Philosophy: Hohfeld on Legal Rights', *Amer. Phil. Quart.*, vol. 13 (1976).

indicate in 1901 which principles and policies favouring and opposing the establishment of this new duty were to be taken into account by the judges, and which relative weights were to be assigned to them? And did these principles and weights dictate that it should be established then? Or did they perhaps dictate that it should not be established then? Perhaps it would not have been *correct* to establish it until 1964 when, as Hart notes, the House of Lords was still occupied with the question. Or perhaps it will only become *correct* at some future time to impose this new restriction on competitive economic behaviour. I think one has only to formulate these suggestions, while also remembering something of the ever-changing economic and statutory background affecting the right of collective bargaining,[16] to see how implausible it would be to insist that there is always an ethically best way for the courts to decide a question of legislative policy which is theirs to decide under the traditional practice. To be sure, one can always 'make a case', as Dworkin says, for the decision one thinks is ethically best, and one's case may indeed justify that decision if the theory of moral and legal reasoning presented in the main essay is sound. But by that same theory one cannot justify the claim that the decision is 'ethically best' if there would be no consensus of those qualified to judge. While it is very natural to say that the decision one favours is 'ethically the best' and so 'the only legally correct decision' even when there would not be a concensus—natural not only for advocates but for disinterested judges and scholars—it seems that such locutions in such cases can only express the sincerity of one's preferences, not evaluative truths.

3.

The notion of moral consensus and the notion of a consensus of disinterested professionals become prominent, as we have seen, when one thinks about difficult legal cases and how they are properly to be decided. This may suggest to some people that the truth of legal judgements is itself a matter of consensus after all. I wish to argue briefly that the very opposite is the case, and that the contrast between the authoritative basis of legal standards

[16] See the opening historical section of W. B. Gould's 'Taft-Hartley Comes to Britain', *Yale Law Journal*, vol. 81 (1972). For illustrations from various fields of law, see Chap. 32, 'Public Policy and Legal Evolution', in W. Friedmann, *Legal Theory*, 5th edn. (New York: Columbia U. Pr., 1967).

and the lack of any authoritative basis for the standards used by autonomous moral judges will underscore the need for a consensus theory of moral truth. I think it may also reinforce our claim that, at the deeper level of moral criticism, 'moral truth' and cognate expressions lose their literal significance while retaining important expressive uses.

A. It is a judge's *duty* to use various criteria for the validity and priority of legal rules, e.g. the idea of binding precedent in case law, or the fact that a rule has been enacted by the legislature or duly prescribed by an administrative agency pursuant to statute, or that it is to be found in the state or federal constitutional documents, or in authoritative interpretations thereof, and so on. Dworkin plausibly insists that this judicial duty cannot be understood merely by reference to the *practice* of judges in applying these criteria. After all, why ought they obey the Constitutional provisions regarding the jurisdiction and practices of the courts? Not, logically, because the Constitution says they ought; that would be circular. Nor can their own practice of recognizing such a duty make it their duty, although their traditional practices can help to determine the content of the duty. Rather, it is the larger moral and political tradition, the social and political morality of their society, which is the source of this duty. And it is their duty not only to apply the kinds of legal-validity criteria just mentioned, but to be guided by communal morality when formulating and applying broader 'principles' and 'policies' they may need to invoke in deciding problematic cases.[17]

B. This moral component of the judge's duty in determining what principles and rules to apply is not to be thought of as a

[17] Cf. Dworkin, op. cit., vol. 81. This account concedes nothing, by the way, to the idea that law is continuous with absolute ('Natural') morality. Dworkin does say that the standards of law and of socio-political (positive) morality are not ultimately distinguishable. But even this may be misleading if it is taken to be characteristic of all law. The statement might possibly be justified on the ground that *our* social morality and judicial tradition *require* that well-established criteria of legal validity be followed by the courts if they validate rules which are not *too* repugnant morally. Yet if the courts of a society began to reject *many* otherwise constitutional enactments because there was a severe conflict between the law-making regime and the moral consensus in the community on many issues, it might be less correct to say that these enactments were legally invalid than that the old legal system was breaking down, perhaps to be replaced by a tyrannical one using a purged judiciary.

direction to engage in autonomous moral reflection. To be sure, when he remains in doubt about how a case should be decided after using the criteria first mentioned above, and after considering the legal rules they yield, a judge must normally ask *himself* what rule for the case would be most desirable or practicable. This is because there is no official record or canon of the moral consensus for him to consult. Indeed, on a good many issues there would be no consensus in our society. And even in more homogeneous societies, we would hardly expect to find a consensus on many moral questions arising in technical legal contexts. They may be questions which simply do not arise in ordinary life.[18] Nevertheless, it is not part of our moral and political tradition that the judge is entitled to resolve legislative policy questions in a way that would be contrary to the dominant opinion of the community when this can be fairly estimated or is obvious. The observations of L. L. Jaffe cited on page 205 are again relevant here.

From the point of view of the individual judge or even of the whole judiciary, the validity of legal standards is therefore dependent on an external authority. It does not come from the consensus of the judges, or from some hypothetical consensus of disinterested legal experts.

Now it may be that legal experts will sometimes agree on the principles and priorities to apply when the more narrowly 'legal' rules do not yield an acceptable decision, or any decision, even though there would be no consensus in the community as to which principles are relevant and controlling. Perhaps we should say that such cases do have legally correct decisions, as we did in Section 4, because it might be more misleading to deny it. Here, perhaps, we do have a situation in which legal truth is a matter of consensus. But this is very much the exception and not the rule about how the notion of truth or evaluative correctness should be taken in law. For we have seen that there is a myriad of easy legal questions which must be answered in just one way according to some indisputably valid and controlling rule. It makes good sense to say they would still have these correct answers even if legal experts disagreed about them, although we would be astounded if

[18] The point is illustrated even by the relatively untechnical context of *Riggs* v. *Palmer*. There is no reason to think that people who are not professionally occupied with law would have *any* view on the proper weight or priority of the several principles listed in the note on pages 209–10.

that happened. It makes sense because the consensus of those who are professionally qualified to judge cases, or authorized to judge them officially, is not the source or authority for those valid rules, and is not required to give them their meaning, certainly not the core of their meaning. The theory that the law is whatever the courts say, or that rules of law are at most expert predictions of how the courts will decide various types of cases, is focused too narrowly on more difficult questions and on the situation of an attorney counselling his client.[19]

C. If we turn now to the account of moral truth offered in Sections 6 and 7, we may well ask what *other* authoritative source there could be for the rules or principles of morality *except* common agreement among those who are qualified to judge moral questions? From the viewpoint of the autonomous moral agent and judge, what other basis would there be for the 'validity' of moral standards? The consensus is of course not binding on the individual, but it will have great weight with him if he is properly reflective; it will have 'persuasive authority'. And by our definition of a moral consensus, practically all properly reflective people will in fact concur in it. Furthermore, in the easiest moral questions practically anyone, even if not reflective, will concur.

We have seen that an autonomous moral judge may remain in doubt after carefully reflecting, perhaps because anyone living the way of life he has learned to live would be in doubt, or because he is trying to live more than one way and needs to compose a coherent one. Where then is he to turn for the correct answer? Clearly, there is nowhere he can turn; there is no external authority, even in theory. He must make up his own mind as best he can.

For morally autonomous people in our culture, 'moral truth' can still refer to many principles which are shared by, and would no doubt be retained from, many ways of life, such as the principles that lying, cheating, wounding and killing people are

[19] That was the situation Mr. Justice Holmes was referring to most explicitly in the best known statement of his so-called prediction theory of law, i.e. 'The Path of the Law', *Harvard Law Rev.*, vol. 10 (1897). One would like to think that he intended it only as practical advice to future lawyers on how one is to *know* the *content* of the law as it would figure in doubtful cases, rather than as a theory of the nature of law. But it seems that he did become enamored of it as a paradoxical-but-true theory of the latter sort. Cf. *Holmes–Pollock Letters*, vol. 2 (Cambridge: Harvard U. Pr., 1941), p. 212.

wrong. But where there would be no consensus, 'moral truth' is a device of rhetoric, as we have said, and perhaps also a kind of Kantian Idea for those who continue to use it as though it did have sense apart from any consensus. It may be a logical myth and regulative fiction leading them to continue to seek agreement through moral reflection and discourse. For it claims to refer to principles which all people ought finally to accept and follow.

IV. A Note on Rawls's Ethical Theory

ALTHOUGH *A Theory of Justice* by John Rawls[1] is mainly concerned with the principles of social justice rather than with the theory of moral reasoning in general, it repeatedly discusses the latter topic in aid of its own programme.[2] Since it is easily the most widely read work of recent years in any branch of philosophy, we can further locate our own theory in contemporary discussions by briefly explaining its relationship to the account of moral reasoning found in Rawls.

As he tells us (xi, 46, 579), the ethical method employed in his book is similar in spirit to that presented in his early article, 'Outline of a Decision Procedure for Ethics',[3] which it will be helpful to describe. In that article, he laid down conditions to define a competent moral judge' and a 'considered moral judgement' somewhat as I have defined the conditions of moral reasonableness in Section 2. Moral principles were then to be obtained empirically by 'explicating' the class of intuitive judgements (judgements not invoking principles) made by competent judges in a considered way about not-especially-difficult moral questions arising in ordinary life. That is, we were to find an economical set of principles which would entail the great majority of such judgements when applied to the facts of such cases. The reasonableness of these principles was to be further tested by seeing whether competent moral judges would freely come to accept them and use them to decide more difficult questions, and to correct those intuitive judgements which had conflicted with them. This test is part of what Rawls later came to call 'reflective equilibrium' of principles and judgements. In reflective equilibrium, principles may also be

[1] Harvard and Oxford University Presses, 1971. All page references in the text are to this book.

[2] See pp. 17–22, 46–53, 108–17, 333 f., 342 f., 577–87.

[3] *Philosophical Rev.*, vol. 60 (1951). He now shortens this title to 'Outline of a Procedure for Ethics', presumably because the article does not present a decision procedure in the most familiar sense, that of formal logic.

modified in order to accommodate contrary judgements that we wish on further reflection to retain.

According to *A Theory of Justice*, most moral principles (including the principles of justice) are to be obtained not by such an explication but by considering what principles would be agreed to by a suitably described group of contracting parties. The characteristics of the contractors and the conditions under which they would seek agreement are again laid down in a way intended to guarantee reasonableness. Like the competent moral judges of 'Outline', they are to be intelligent and well informed about general matters of fact. While it is not specified that they are to attempt to be impartial and unbiased (as in the article), Rawls achieves a roughly similar effect by imposing a 'veil of ignorance' concerning their own special situations, natural capacities, and certain other facts, and by requiring that they agree to principles which will apply equally to everyone. Several other conditions are also imposed. Situated behind their special veil of ignorance, these rationally self-interested parties will perforce agree on principles which are unfair to no one. The bulk of Rawls's book is devoted to identifying, explaining, and defending the two principles or general criteria of just institutions which he thinks they would agree to. Much of his defence consists of arguments and illustrations purporting to show that these two principles will stand up better in reflective equilibrium than will certain leading candidates drawn from the utilitarian tradition of moral philosophy.

Rawls concedes that the conditions of reasonableness laid down for his imaginary contractors are not ethically neutral (579), so the question arises how *they* are to be justified. His answer to this question seems to have three parts. (1) We are not to claim self-evidence for these conditions or for any other moral principle, nor are we to try to establish their truth or validity by resorting to naturalistic definitions of moral terms. He says we lack an adequate theory of meaning even to attempt to justify such definitions; and although some moral principles may strike us as self-evident 'there are great obstacles to maintaining that they are necessarily true, or even to explaining what is meant by this' (578). But (2) certain 'philosophical considerations' may nevertheless persuade us to accept these conditions if we do not already accept them (21, 587). There are specific arguments for the reasonableness of the various conditions (582–3, cf. 130–50) and there is the general argument that the whole description of these conditions gains support from the reflective equilibrium of principles and considered judgements (cf. 20). That is, if our most mature judgements support Rawls's principles of justice against their utilitarian rivals, then they also confirm his described conditions of reasonableness against other conditions under which the contractors would agree to utilitarian principles: '... it seems best to regard these conditions simply as reasonable stipulations to be assessed eventually by the whole theory to which they belong' (578). And (3) Rawls thinks it is no damaging objection that his theory 'assumes not only an agreement among persons in their considered judgements, but also in what they regard as reasonable conditions to impose on the choice of first principles' (580). Justification is intended to 'reconcile by reason' after all, and if this is to be possible it must proceed from what the disagreeing parties hold in common. 'It is perfectly proper, then, that the argument for the principles of justice should proceed from some consensus' (581).

How our own theory stands in relation to Rawls's can be briefly indicated by commenting on those three points, taking them in reverse order.

(3) No doubt it is widely agreed that moral principles ought to be adopted or recognized in a reasonable way. And I certainly agree with Rawls that for purposes of ordinary moral debate there is no need to justify the second-order principle that people *ought* to be reasonable in choosing principles. But surely there is every need to do this when our purpose is to clarify the basis of moral reasoning, which presumably is Rawls's purpose when he deploys a general theory of moral reasoning to support his special argument for the principles of justice. The ethical sceptic or emotivist will say that the requirement of reasonableness is itself a moral principle which he may not care to embrace, and that we cannot prove to him that he must embrace it. If we point out to him that reasonableness fosters moral agreement (and Rawls does point this out for other purposes) the sceptic will answer that in *his* moral view agreement with others is of no special importance, and therefore that he need not accept those conditions or admit that the principles they lead people to adopt are justified. Now it seems to me that we cannot hope to understand how moral reasoning is basically coherent until we explain quite clearly why this argument is incoherent. As usual in philosophy, we need not take the sceptic's *conclusion* very seriously, but we will not have fully clarified the form of discourse whose logical obscurity his *argument* exploits until we have explained what is wrong with that argument.

(2) I think the considerations that Rawls refers to here *are* persuasive. But it is no good trying to *persuade* the sceptic. His logical point, if it is a good one, will stand up just as well even if he should happen to be persuaded to be reasonable. We must give a convincing explanation that he is talking nonsense when he reserves the logical right to be morally unreasonable (as other people would describe it) when he purports to carry on moral discourse with us.

(1) In the main essay, we agreed with Rawls in rejecting naturalistic definitions of moral terms, although only at the more deeply critical level of moral discourse. We also sketched in Part II a 'theory of meaning' and an account of discursive practice according to which they *cannot* be justified there. We also agreed with him in rejecting claims of self-evidence for substantive moral principles entertained at that level. And even as to the basic procedural principle of reasonableness, we began by actually detailing those 'great obstacles to maintaining that [it is] necessarily true, or even to explaining what is meant by this'. But then, in an argument extending through the remainder of Part I, we did our best to overcome those obstacles and give such an explanation. We tried to show that the commonly recognized requirements of moral reasonableness cannot be coherently challenged or rejected by anyone if he is to engage in moral reasoning at all.

In thus attempting to do something which Rawls apparently thinks it impossible to do, we can nevertheless draw a measure of support from his theory. For he also gives great prominence to two important aspects of moral thought on which we have crucially relied. His contractors not only *seek agreement* but are fully *autonomous* as to the substantive principles they may choose to adopt. We have tried to show how the fact that reasonableness does foster agreement between autonomous persons can validate the ordinary criteria of reasonableness as a binding standard for moral reasoning by and between such persons.

There are other major differences between Rawls's ethical theory and that of the present book. To mention the most important of them, we have *not* assumed that people who *are* morally reasonable will always agree either in their considered judgements or in the principles they are willing to accept on mature reflection. Indeed, it seems highly unlikely that they will always or nearly always agree in either of these things. We have tried to give an account of moral reasoning which is sufficiently complex to allow for this important fact.

Bibliography

A. WORKS CITED

ANSCOMBE, G. E. M. 'On Brute Facts', *Analysis*, vol. 18 (1958)

AYER, A. J. *Language, Truth and Logic*. London: Victor Gollancz, 1948

BEARDSMORE, R. W. *Moral Reasoning*. New York: Schoken Books, 1969

BRANDT, R. B. *Ethical Theory*. Englewood Cliffs, N.J.: Prentice-Hall, 1959

—— Review of Hare's *Freedom and Reason* in *The Journal of Philosophy*, vol. 61 (1964)

CARDOZO, B. N. *The Growth of the Law*. New Haven: Yale University Press, 1924

CORCORAN, John. 'Conceptual Structure of Classical Logic', *Philosophy and Phenomenological Research*, vol. 33 (1971–2)

DOORBAR, ROGER. 'Meaning, Rules, and Behaviour', *Mind*, vol. 80 (1971)

DOWNIE, R. S. 'Social Rules and Moral Responsibility', *Philosophy*, vol. 39 (1964)

DWORKIN, R. M. Review of Wasserstrom's *The Judicial Decision* in *Ethics*, vol. 75 (1964–5); reprinted with minor changes in *Yale Law Journal*, vol. 76 (1965)

—— 'The Model of Rules', *University of Chicago Law Review*, vol. 35 (1967–8); reprinted in *Essays in Legal Philosophy*, ed. R. S. Summers. Berkeley and Los Angeles: The University of California Press, 1968

—— 'Social Rules and Legal Theory', *Yale Law Journal*, vol. 81 (1972)

FOOT, PHILIPPA. 'Goodness and Choice', *Proceedings of the Aristotelian Society*, supp. vol. 35 (1961)

—— 'Moral Arguments', *Mind*, vol. 67 (1958)

—— 'Moral Beliefs', *Proceedings of the Aristotelian Society*, vol. 59 (1958–9)

FRANK, JEROME. *Law and the Modern Mind*. New York: Brentano's, 1930, and Doubleday-Anchor, 1963

FRIEDMANN, WOLFGANG. *Legal Theory*, 5th edn. New York: Columbia University Press, 1967

GOULD, W. B. 'Taft-Hartley Comes to Britain', *Yale Law Journal*, vol. 81 (1972)

GUEST, A. G. 'Logic in the Law', in *Oxford Essays in Jurisprudence* (1st series), ed. A. C. Guest. Oxford: The Clarendon Press, 1961

HAMLYN, D. W. 'The Obligation to Keep a Promise', *Proceedings of the Aristotelian Society*, vol. 62 (1961–2)

HARE, R. M. *The Language of Morals*. Oxford: The Clarendon Press, 1952

—— *Freedom and Reason*. Oxford: The Clarendon Press, 1963

—— Review of Toulmin's *An Examination of the Place of Reason in Ethics* in *Philosophical Quarterly*, vol. 1 (1950–1)

HARRISON, JONATHAN. *Our Knowledge of Right and Wrong*. London: Allen & Unwin, 1971

HART, H. L. A. *The Concept of Law*. Oxford: The Clarendon Press, 1961

—— 'Bentham on Legal Rights', in *Oxford Essays in Jurisprudence* (2nd series), ed. A. W. B. Simpson. Oxford: The Clarendon Press, 1973

HOHFELD, W. N. *Fundamental Legal Conceptions as Applied in Judicial Reasoning*. New Haven: Yale University Press, 1923; reprinted in part, 1964

HOLMES, O. W. 'The Path of the Law', *Harvard Law Review*, vol. 10 (1897)

—— and POLLOCK, FREDERICK. *Holmes–Pollock Letters*, ed. M. D. Howe. Cambridge, Mass.: Harvard University Press, 1941

JAFFE, L. L. *English and American Judges as Lawmakers*. Oxford: The Clarendon Press, 1969

KOVESI, JULIUS. *Moral Notions*. New York: Humanities Press, 1967

LEVI, E. H. *An Introduction to Legal Reasoning*. Chicago: University of Chicago Press, 1948

—— 'The Nature of Judicial Reasoning', in *Law and Philosophy*, ed. S. Hook. New York: New York University Press, 1964

LYONS, DAVID. *Forms and Limits of Utilitarianism*. Oxford: The Clarendon Press, 1965

MACNIVEN, C. D. 'Strong and Weak Descriptivism', *Mind*, vol. 81 (1972)

MELDEN, A. I. *Rights and Right Conduct*. Oxford: Blackwell, 1959

MILL, J. S. *Utilitarianism*. 1861

MOORE, G. E. *Principia Ethica*. Cambridge: Cambridge University Press, 1903

MOUNCE, H. O. See Phillips, D. Z.

PERRY, T. D. 'Moral Autonomy and Reasonableness', *The Journal of Philosophy*, vol. 65 (1968)

—— Review of Warnock's *The Object of Morality* in *Ethics*, vol. 83 (1973)

—— 'A Paradigm of Philosophy: Hohfeld on Legal Rights', *American Philosophical Quarterly*, vol. 13 (1976)

PHILLIPS, D. Z. and MOUNCE, H. O. 'On Morality's Having a Point', *Philosophy*, vol. 40 (1965)

—— *Moral Practices*. New York: Schoken Books, 1970

PRICHARD, H. A. 'Does Moral Philosophy Rest on a Mistake', *Mind*, vol. 21 (1912); reprinted in his *Moral Obligation*, Oxford: The Clarendon Press, 1949, and in various anthologies

RAWLS, JOHN. 'Outline of a Procedure for Ethics', *Philosophical Review*, vol. 60 (1951)

—— 'Two Concepts of Rules', *Philosophical Review*, vol. 64 (1955)

—— *A Theory of Justice*. Cambridge, Mass: Harvard University Press, 1971, and Oxford: The Clarendon Press, 1971

ROSS, W. D. *The Right and the Good*. Oxford: The Clarendon Press, 1930

—— *Foundations of Ethics*. Oxford: The Clarendon Press, 1939

SILVERSTEIN, H. S. 'A Note on Imagining Oneself in the Place of Another', *Mind*, vol. 81 (1972)

STEVENSON, C. L. *Ethics and Language*. New Haven: Yale University Press, 1944

—— 'The Nature of Ethical Disagreement', in *Readings in Philosophical Analysis*, ed. H. Feigl and W. Sellars. New York: Appleton-Century-Crofts, 1949

—— 'Relativism and Nonrelativism in the Theory of Value', in his *Facts and Values*. New Haven: Yale University Press, 1963

TAYLOR, C. C. W. Review of Hare's *Freedom and Reason* in *Mind*, vol. 74 (1965)

TOULMIN, S. E. *An Examination of the Place of Reason in Ethics*. Cambridge: Cambridge University Press, 1950

WELLMAN, CARL. 'Emotivism and Ethical Subjectivity', *American Philosophical Quarterly*, vol. 5 (1968)

WARNOCK, G. J. *Contemporary Moral Philosophy*. London: Macmillan, 1967

—— *The Object of Morality*. London: Methuen, 1971

WITTGENSTEIN, LUDWIG. *Philosophical Investigations*, 2nd edn., trans. G. E. M. Anscombe. Oxford: Blackwell, 1958

B. SOME MODERN ANTHOLOGIES AND TEXTBOOKS ON ETHICAL THEORY

BRANDT, R. B. *Ethical Theory*. Englewood Cliffs, N.J.: Prentice-Hall, 1959

FOOT, PHILIPPA (ed.) *Theories of Ethics*. Oxford: Oxford University Press, 1967

FRANKENA, W. K. *Ethics*. Englewood Cliffs, N.J.: Prentice-Hall, 1963; 2nd edn., 1973

HUDSON, W. D. *Modern Moral Philosophy*. New York: Doubleday-Anchor, 1970

HUDSON, W. D. (ed.) *The Is–Ought Question*. London: Macmillan, 1969. With this see T. D. Perry, 'A Refutation of Searle's Amended "Is–ought" Argument', *Analysis*, vol. 34 (1974)

HOSPERS, JOHN. *Human Conduct: Problems of Ethics*. New York: Harcourt, 1961; shorter edn., 1972

KERNER, G. C., *The Revolution in Ethical Theory*. Oxford: The Clarendon Press, 1966

MELDEN, A. I. (ed.) *Essays in Moral Philosophy*. Seattle: University of Washington Press, 1958

PAHEL, K. and SCHILLER, M. (eds.) *Readings in Contemporary Ethical Theory*. Englewood Cliffs, N.J.: Prentice-Hall, 1970

SELLARS, W. and HOSPERS, J. (eds.) *Readings in Ethical Theory*, 2nd edn. Englewood Cliffs, N.J.: Prentice-Hall, 1970

WARNOCK, MARY. *Ethics Since 1900*. London and New York: Oxford University Press, 1966

Index